Revision

Maths

Hilary Koll and Steve Mills

Age 11–14
Years 7–9
Key Stage 3

Hachette UK's policy is to use papers that are natural, renewable and recyclable products and made from wood grown in sustainable forests. The logging and manufacturing processes are expected to conform to the environmental regulations of the country of origin.

Orders: please contact Bookpoint Ltd, 130 Milton Park, Abingdon, Oxon OX14 4SB. Telephone: (44) 01235 827720. Fax: (44) 01235 400454. Lines are open 9.00a.m.–5.00p.m., Monday to Saturday, with a 24-hour message answering service. Visit our website at www.hoddereducation.co.uk.

© Hilary Koll and Steve Mills 2013
First published in 2013 exclusively for WHSmith by
Hodder Education
An Hachette UK Company
338 Euston Road
London NW1 3BH

Impression number   10 9 8 7 6 5
Year   2018 2017 2016 2015 2014

This edition has been updated, 2014, to reflect National Curriculum changes.

Cover illustration by Oxford Designers and Illustrators Ltd
All other illustrations by Fakenham Prepress Solutions, Fakenham, Norfolk NR21 8NN
Typeset in 10pt Helvetica Neue by Fakenham Prepress Solutions, Fakenham, Norfolk NR21 8NN
Printed in Spain

A catalogue record for this title is available from the British Library.

ISBN: 978 1444 189 322

Contents

1 Whole numbers and decimals (1) 6
2 Place Value 8
3 Whole numbers and decimals (2) 10
4 Fractions (1) 12
5 Fractions (2) 14
6 Fractions (3) 16
7 Percentages (1) 18
8 Percentages (2) 20
9 Percentages (3) 22
10 Proportion (1) 24
11 Proportion (2) 26
12 Direct Proportion (1) 28
13 Direct Proportion (2) 30
14 Ratio (1) 32
15 Ratio (2) 34
16 Ratio (3) 36
17 Integers 38
18 Factors and multiples 40
19 Prime numbers (1) 42
20 Prime numbers (2) 44
21 Powers and roots 46
22 Index notation 48
23 Test (1) 50
24 Test (2) 52
25 Calculation Strategies (1) 54
26 Calculation Strategies (2) 56
27 Calculations and problems 58
28 Written calculations 60
29 Using a calculator 62
30 Simplifying expressions (1) 64
31 Simplifying expressions (2) 66
32 Simplifying expressions (3) 68
33 Equations (1) 70
34 Equations (2) 72
35 Formulae and substituting (1) 74
36 Formulae and substituting (2) 76
37 Formulae and substituting (3) 78
38 Trial and improvement 80
39 Functions (1) 82
40 Functions (2) 84
41 Sequences (1) 86
42 Sequences (2) 88
43 Straight line graphs (1) 90
44 Straight line graphs (2) 92
45 Straight line graphs (3) 94
46 Distance-time graphs 96
47 Test (3) 98
48 Test (4) 100
49 Measurement (1) 102
50 Measurement (2) 104
51 Measurement (3) 106
52 Measurement (4) 108
53 Perimeter and area 110
54 Area 112
55 Volume and surface area (1) 114
56 Volume and surface area (2) 116
57 Angles (1) 118
58 Angles (2) 120
59 Angles (3) 122
60 Angles (4) 124
61 Bearings (1) 126
62 Bearings (2) 128
63 Construction 130
64 Loci 132
65 Co-ordinates (1) 134
66 Co-ordinates (2) 136
67 Transformations (1) 138
68 Transformations (2) 140
69 2-D shape (1) 142
70 2-D shape (2) 144
71 Circles 146
72 3-D shape (1) 148
73 3-D shape (2) 150
74 Statistics (1) 152
75 Statistics (2) 154
76 Collecting data (1) 156
77 Collecting data (2) 158
78 Graphs and charts (1) 160
79 Graphs and charts (2) 162
80 Graphs and charts (3) 164
81 Probability (1) 166
82 Probability (2) 168
83 Test (5) 170
84 Test (6) 172
Answers 174

How to use this book

What this book will do for you and your child

The *Maths Revision* series is designed to help children, aged 11–14, to revise all the Maths topics in the curriculum at Key Stage 3.

The book is designed to be used by children for on-going revision throughout the year. Each double-page spread provides clear information about the nature of the topic and the key aspects that children are expected to master, and provides opportunities for them to practise and test their own understanding.

The Maths curriculum at KS3

The Key Stage 3 National Curriculum provides a framework for teaching Mathematics in Years 7, 8 and 9, identifying the aspects of Maths to be taught and the expectations for pupils. The main strands of learning at Key Stage 3 are:

- Using and applying Mathematics to solve problems
- Numbers and the number system
- Calculations
- Algebra
- Shape, space and measures
- Handling data.

Children may be given tests by their school at the end of Key Stage 3. The results are used by the school to assess each child's level of knowledge and progress in Maths, English and Science. They also provide guidance for the child's next teacher when he or she is planning the coming year.

Maths Revision provides opportunities for children to prepare for these tests. **The children who succeed in Maths are those who evaluate their own understanding of each topic as they encounter it and take steps to improve areas of difficulty by further study.** This book provides all the necessary information and guidance to assist children in this.

Levels of attainment

Teachers gain information about your child's progress through testing and on-going teacher assessment and you will be informed each year of your child's level of achievement. For the new National Curriculum, schools are able to develop their own systems of levels. Each level is a measure that teachers use to check how much your child knows, understands and can do. National expectations are that by the end of Key Stage 1 pupils achieve at least level 2, by the end of Key Stage 2 level 4 and above, by the end of Key Stage 3 level 5 and above.

These levels are no longer a part of the National Curriculum. We present them here, for now, as we know that they are a familiar reference point for teachers, parents and students.

Stage	Age	Year	National expectations (previous regulations)
Foundation	3–4 4–5		
Key Stage 1	5–6 6–7	Year 1 Year 2	Level 2 and above
Key Stage 2	7–8 8–9 9–10 10–11	Year 3 Year 4 Year 5 Year 6	Level 4 and above
Key Stage 3	11–12 12–13 13–14	Year 7 Year 8 Year 9	Level 5 and above
Key Stage 4	14–15 15–16	Year 10 Year 11	Grade C and above

How to use this book

Encourage your child to use and reuse this book alongside his or her school work. Your child should know which Maths topic he or she is covering in school and so can use this book to reinforce and develop his or her understanding of the topic. It is not necessary to work through the topics in the order that they are given. Each double-page spread clearly states the facts, skills or concepts that your child should learn.

Throughout the book are revision tips which can guide your child towards developing good working practices. These give suggestions for ways to make revision more effective and the learning more long-lasting.

What can parents do to help?

Learning, and especially revision, is best if active. If your child just reads information he or she is unlikely to retain it all. He or she needs to work, memorise and practise on his or her own. This book can help your child do this effectively. Once a child thinks he or she has mastered a topic it can help if you offer to be the pupil! Can he or she teach it to you? If your child can teach you something, he or she really knows and understands it! Explaining something to someone else is one of the best ways of consolidating learning. This approach also shows that you are interested in the topics your child is learning and are acknowledging and celebrating his or her progress.

What next?

Once children are confident with all the topics, they can prepare for the National Tests using the *WHS National Tests Practice Papers* books. These contain practice tests to be taken under exam conditions and can help you to assess the level at which your child is working.

In this unit you will revise:

▶ how to round numbers to the nearest 10, 100 or 1000

▶ how to round decimals to the nearest whole number or to one decimal place.

> When revising, take regular breaks. If you can, get some fresh air outside. It will help to clear your head and you will come back to your revision feeling more alert.

What you should know

Multiples of 10 end in a zero, such as 30, 50, 470, 600 and 23 750.

Multiples of 100 end in two zeros, such as 500, 8000, 6700, 400 and 42 600.

Multiples of 1000 end in three zeros, such as 20 000, 9000, 25 000 and 6000.

It is important to know the value of each digit in a number.

Millions	Hundred thousands	Ten thousands	Thousands	Hundreds	Tens	Units
2	5	4	6	3	8	1

The number **2 546 381** has seven digits. The digit 2 is worth 2 million, the digit 5 is worth 5 hundred thousand and the digit 3 is worth 3 hundred and so on. It can be partitioned (split) like this:

2 000 000 + 500 000 + 40 000 + 6000 + 300 + 80 + 1

Two million, five hundred and forty-six thousand, three hundred and eighty-one

The decimal **375.289** has six digits, three of them after the **decimal point**.

Hundreds	Tens	Units	.	tenths	hundredths	thousandths
3	7	5	.	2	8	9

300 + 70 + 5 + 0.2 + 0.08 + 0.009

Three hundred and seventy-five point two, eight, nine

Get started

When rounding a number to the nearest 10 write down the multiples of ten that lie either side of the number.

*Round **287** to the nearest 10*   The answer will be either 280 or 290.

If the **units** digit is below 5, you need to round down to the previous multiple of 10.

If the **units** digit is 5 or greater, you need to round up to the next multiple of 10. **287 → 290**

When rounding to the nearest 100 write the multiples of a hundred that lie either side of the number.

*Round **4563** to the nearest 100*   The answer will be either 4500 or 4600.

If the **tens** digit is below 5, you need to round down to the previous multiple of 100.

If the **tens** digit is 5 or greater, you need to round up to the next multiple of 100. **4563 → 4600**

When rounding to the nearest 1000 write the multiples of a thousand that lie either side.

*Round **5236** to the nearest 1000*   The answer will be either 5000 or 6000.

If the **hundreds** digit is below 5, you need to round down to the previous multiple of 1000. 5236 → **5000**

If the **hundreds** digit is 5 or greater, you need to round up to the next multiple of 1000.

1
> Round:
>
> a) 146 to the nearest 10 ___150___ ✓
>
> b) 739 to the nearest 100 ___700___ ✓
>
> c) 4254 to the nearest 1000 ___4000___ ✓
>
> d) 265 to the nearest 10 ___270___ ✓
>
> e) 4390 to the nearest 100 ___4400___ ✓
>
> f) 16 861 to the nearest 1000 ___17000___ ✓

When rounding a decimal to the nearest tenth (to one decimal place) write the tenths that lie either side of it.

*Round **3.427** to the nearest tenth*   The answer will be either 3.4 or 3.5.

If the **hundredths** digit is below 5, you need to round down to the previous tenth.   **3.427 → 3.4**

If the **hundredths** digit is 5 or greater, you need to round up to the next tenth.

When rounding a decimal to the nearest whole number write the whole numbers that lie either side.

*Round **24.601** to the nearest whole number*   The answer will be either 24 or 25.

If the **tenths** digit is below 5, you need to round down to the previous whole number.

If the **tenths** digit is 5 or greater, you need to round up to the next whole number.   **24.601 → 25**

❷ Round these decimals:

a) 0.487 to the nearest tenth __0·5__ ✓

b) 3.629 to the nearest tenth __3·6__ ✓

c) 3.45 to the nearest whole number __4__ ✓

d) 9.711 to the nearest whole number __10__ ✓

Practice

❶ Round each number to the nearest 10, 100 and 1000 and complete this table:

Number	To the nearest 10	To the nearest 100	To the nearest 1000
5541	5540 ✓	5500 ✓	6000 ✓
2943	2940 ✓	2900 ✓	3000 ✓
8467	8470 ✓	8500 ✓	9000 ✗ 8000
12 489	12490 ✓	12500 ✓	13000 ✗ 12000
31 555	31560 ✓	31600	32000
6004	6000 ✓	6000 ✓	6000 ✓
2985	2990 ✓	3000 ✓	3000 ✓

❷ Round each number to the nearest 1000 and join it with a line to the answer. One has been done for you.

(98 529) (97 489) (99 501) (99 499) (97 517) (100 741)

97 000 / 98 000 / 99 000 / 100 000 / 101 000   ✓

(96 699) (98 480) (96 500) (97 541) (100 388) (99 801)

❸ These questions might be asked in a mental Maths test.

a) Round thirty point six four to the nearest tenth. __30·6__ ✓
   30.64

b) Write the number fifty-eight point one five to one decimal place. __58·2__ ✓
   58·15

c) Write the number sixteen point seven one to the nearest whole number. __17__ ✓
   16·71

d) Round twenty-two point four nine to the nearest whole number. __23__ ✗ 22
   22·④9

How did I do?

I can round numbers to the nearest 10, 100 or 1000.   ☑ ✓

I can round decimals to the nearest whole number or to one decimal place.   ☑

2: Place value

In this unit you will revise:

▶ integer (whole number) powers of 10

▶ how to multiply and divide by any integer power of 10

▶ the effects of multiplying and dividing by numbers between 0 and 1.

It can help to make your own revision notes. When you finish this page, write a few lines to help you remember what you have learnt. Keep them somewhere safe to look at again.

What you should know

Our number system is based on groups of 10. In this table you will see what happens when you keep dividing by 10, starting with the number one billion. Notice how the numbers can be written with powers, such as 10^4 or 10^{-1}.

B	HM	TM	M	HTh	TTh	Th	H	T	U	.	t	h	th		
1	0	0	0	0	0	0	0	0	0	.				one billion	10^9
	1	0	0	0	0	0	0	0	0	.				one hundred million	10^8
		1	0	0	0	0	0	0	0	.				ten million	10^7
			1	0	0	0	0	0	0	.				one million	10^6
				1	0	0	0	0	0	.				one hundred thousand	10^5
					1	0	0	0	0	.				ten thousand	10^4
						1	0	0	0	.				one thousand	10^3
							1	0	0	.				one hundred	10^2
								1	0	.				ten	10^1
									1	.				one	10^0
									0	.	1			one tenth	10^{-1}
									0	.	0	1		one hundredth	10^{-2}
									0	.	0	0	1	one thousandth	10^{-3}

Get started

Negative powers of 10 stand for numbers less than 1.

● 10^{-1} stands for one tenth which can also be written as $\frac{1}{10}$.

● 10^{-2} stands for one hundredth which can also be written as $\frac{1}{10^2}$.

● 10^{-3} stands for one thousandth which can also be written as $\frac{1}{10^3}$.

Notice also that $10^0 = 1$.

❶ Sort these into three groups, so that everything in a group is equivalent (worth the same):

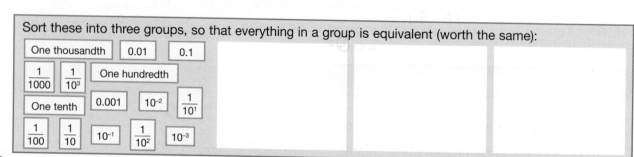

One thousandth   0.01   0.1

$\frac{1}{1000}$ $\frac{1}{10^3}$ One hundredth

One tenth   0.001 10^{-2} $\frac{1}{10^1}$

$\frac{1}{100}$ $\frac{1}{10}$ 10^{-1} $\frac{1}{10^2}$ 10^{-3}

Sometimes two different calculations produce the same result:

Multiplying by 0.1 is the same as dividing by 10
Multiplying by 0.01 is the same as dividing by 100
Multiplying by 0.001 is the same as dividing by 1000

Dividing by 0.1 is the same as multiplying by 10
Dividing by 0.01 is the same as multiplying by 100
Dividing by 0.001 is the same as multiplying by 1000

Notice that:

● Multiplying by a number between 0 and 1 produces a smaller result
● Dividing by a number between 0 and 1 produces a larger result.

❷ Answer these questions without a calculator:

a) $6.24 \times 1000 =$ _____

b) $42.5 \times 10^2 =$ _____

c) $27.5 \times 10^3 =$ _____

d) $9 \times 0.1 =$ _____

e) $7.6 \times 0.01 =$ _____

f) $3.2 \times 0.001 =$ _____

g) $427 \div 10^3 =$ _____

h) $126 \div 10^2 =$ _____

i) $6532 \div 10^1 =$ _____

j) $20 \div 0.1 =$ _____

k) $2.64 \div 0.001 =$ _____

l) $92 \div 0.01 =$ _____

Practice

❶ Write these numbers using powers of ten:

a) 1000 _____

b) one hundredth _____

c) 100 _____

d) 10 000 000 _____

e) 0.001 _____

f) one million _____

g) one tenth _____

h) 100 000 _____

i) 1 _____

j) 0.01 _____

k) 10 _____

l) $\frac{1}{10}$ _____

❷ Answer these questions without a calculator:

a) $83.86 \times 10 =$ _____

b) $49.03 \times 10^2 =$ _____

c) $9.2 \times 10^3 =$ _____

d) $4.75 \times 10^{-1} =$ _____

e) $8.34 \times 10^{-3} =$ _____

f) $19.42 \times 10^{-2} =$ _____

g) $83.86 \div 10^1 =$ _____

h) $19.7 \div 10^2 =$ _____

i) $954.5 \div 10^3 =$ _____

j) $6 \div 10^{-1} =$ _____

k) $7 \div 10^{-2} =$ _____

l) $15 \div 10^{-3} =$ _____

❸ Which of these statements are true and which are false?

a) Multiplying by 0.01 makes a number smaller.   True ☐ False ☐
b) Dividing always makes a number smaller.   True ☐ False ☐
c) Dividing by one tenth makes a number larger.   True ☐ False ☐
d) Dividing by 0.1 gives the same answer as multiplying by 10.   True ☐ False ☐
e) When you multiply by a number between 0 and 1 the answer is always larger.   True ☐ False ☐
f) When you divide by a number between 0 and 1 the answer is always larger.   True ☐ False ☐

How did I do?

I can write powers of 10 in different ways.

I can multiply integers and decimals by powers of 10.

I know the effects of multiplying and dividing by numbers between 0 and 1.

3: Whole numbers and decimals (2

In this unit you will revise:
- ▶ how to round decimals to the nearest whole number
- ▶ how to round decimals to 1, 2 or 3 decimal places
- ▶ how to use rounding to make estimates.

It can help to make your own revision notes. When you finish this page, write a few lines to help you remember what you have learnt. Keep them somewhere safe to look at again.

What you should know

When rounding a decimal to the nearest whole number think of the whole numbers either side.

*Round **29.601** to the nearest whole number.*   *The answer will be either 29 or 30.*

If the **tenths** digit is below 5, you need to round down to the previous whole number.

If the **tenths** digit is 5 or greater, you need to round up to the next whole number.   **29.601 → 30**

Get started

When rounding a decimal to 1 decimal place (1 d.p.) think of the tenths either side of the number.

*Round **3.927** to 1 d.p.*   *The answer will be either 3.9 or 4.0*

If the **hundredths** digit is below 5, you need to round down to the previous tenth.   **3.927 → 3.9**

If the **hundredths** digit is 5 or greater, you need to round up to the next tenth.

When rounding a decimal to 2 decimal places (2 d.p.) think of the hundredths either side.

*Round **24.3125** to 2 d.p.*   *The answer will be either 24.31 or 24.32*

If the **thousandths** digit is below 5, you need to round down to the previous tenth.   **24.3125 → 24.31**

If the **thousandths** digit is 5 or greater, you need to round up to the next tenth.

When rounding a decimal to 3 decimal places (3 d.p.) think of the thousandths either side.

*Round **34.4996** to 3 d.p.*   *The answer will be either 34.499 or 34.500*

If the **ten thousandths** digit is below 5, you need to round down to the previous tenth.

If the **ten thousandths** digit is 5 or greater, you need to round up to the next tenth.   **34.4996 → 34.500**

1 Round each number to the nearest whole number, 1 d.p., 2 d.p. and 3 d.p. and complete this table:

Number	To the nearest whole number	To 1 d.p.	To 2 d.p.	To 3 d.p.
32.1522				
86.8379				
39.6045				
9.989				
7.4993				

To estimate the size of an answer to a calculation, make an approximation. Round each number in the question and then do the calculation with the rounded numbers. You can choose how the numbers are rounded yourself. Look at these approximations:

$322 \times 9.7 \approx 300 \times 10 = 3000$

$704 \div 6.9 \approx 700 \div 7 = 100$

$\sqrt{(48.37 - 11.912)} \approx \sqrt{(48 - 12)} = \sqrt{36} = \pm 6$

$(1094 \div 212) \times 3987 \approx (1000 \div 200) \times 4000 = 20\,000$

② Round these numbers and make suitable approximations.

a) 3291×46 _____

b) $492 \div 8.1$ _____

c) $5.75 \times (3.46 - 0.48)$ _____

d) $6.34 \times (3.08 + 2.78)$ _____

e) $(5895 \div 1967) \times 207$ _____

f) $\sqrt{(8.1 \times 1.98)} + 15.89$ _____

g) $(0.031 \times 19.6)^2$ _____

Practice

① Use a calculator to work out the answers to these questions. Round your answers each time.

a) $5.4 \div 1.6 =$ _____ (to 1 d.p.)   b) $12 \div 9 =$ _____ (to 3 d.p.)

c) $7 \div 11 =$ _____ (to 2 d.p.)   d) $8 \div 7 =$ _____ (to 1 d.p.)

e) $3.8 \div 2.6 =$ _____ (to 1 d.p.)   f) $64 \div 11 =$ _____ (to 2 d.p.)

g) $13 \div 6 =$ _____ (to 3 d.p.)   h) $200 \div 3 =$ _____ (to 3 d.p.)

② Round these numbers and make suitable approximations.

a) $(4.5 \div 2.38) \times 9.8 \approx$ _____

b) $(17.87 \div 2.69) + 17.48 \approx$ _____

c) $7.88 \times (4.58 \times 4.51) \approx$ _____

d) $\dfrac{(5.91 \times 4.09)}{\sqrt{(0.25)}} \approx$ _____

e) $\dfrac{(0.41 \times 0.49)}{(0.1)^2} \approx$ _____

How did I do?

✔

I can round decimals to the nearest whole number. ☐

I can round decimals to 1, 2 or 3 decimal places. ☐

I can use rounding to make estimates. ☐

4: Fractions (1)

It can help to make your own revision notes. When you finish this page, write a few lines to help you remember what you have learnt. Keep them somewhere safe to look at again.

In this unit you will revise:

▶ how to order fractions by writing them with a common denominator
▶ how to use division to convert a fraction to a decimal
▶ how to order fractions by converting them to decimals.

What you should know

A **fraction** is part of something that has been split into equal parts.

The bottom number, or **denominator**, shows how many equal parts the whole has been split into.

The top number, or **numerator**, shows how many of those equal parts are being described.

$\frac{3}{5}$ means that a whole has been split into 5 equal parts and that 3 of these parts are being described.

To change a fraction to an equivalent one, multiply or divide the numerator and denominator by the same number, like this:

Fractions, decimals and **percentages** are ways of describing parts of a whole. A decimal such as 0.354 is equivalent to (has the same value as) the fraction $\frac{354}{1000}$ or $\frac{177}{500}$.

Get started

One way to compare and order fractions is to change them so that every fraction has the same denominator.

When comparing $\frac{5}{7}$ and $\frac{3}{4}$, change them to **equivalent fractions** with a common denominator, like this:

Then it is easy to see that $\frac{21}{28}$ is larger than $\frac{20}{28}$, so $\frac{3}{4}$ is larger than $\frac{5}{7}$.

❶ Compare the fractions in each pair, by changing them to equivalent fractions with a common denominator. Tick the larger fraction each time.

a) $\frac{2}{3}$ and $\frac{5}{8}$ b) $\frac{3}{5}$ and $\frac{3}{4}$ c) $\frac{5}{6}$ and $\frac{7}{8}$ d) $\frac{7}{9}$ and $\frac{8}{10}$ e) $\frac{4}{7}$ and $\frac{3}{5}$

_____   _____   _____   _____   _____

❷ Put these fractions in order from smallest to largest. Change each so that it has the denominator 24.

$\frac{3}{4}$ $\frac{5}{6}$ $\frac{5}{8}$ $\frac{5}{12}$ $\frac{2}{3}$ _____

There is another way of comparing fractions that can be quicker if you have a calculator:

Change all the fractions into equivalent decimals and compare the decimals.

To change a fraction to a decimal, divide the numerator by the denominator. $\frac{5}{8}$ = 5 ÷ 8 = 0.625.

Order these fractions: $\frac{2}{3}$ $\frac{3}{8}$ $\frac{4}{5}$ $\frac{7}{10}$ $\frac{3}{4}$

Key in   2 ÷ 3   3 ÷ 8   4 ÷ 5   7 ÷ 10   3 ÷ 4

                          0.6666...   **0.375**   **0.8**   **0.7**   **0.75**

When comparing decimals, work from left to right starting at the left-hand digit.

The order from smallest to largest is: 0.375   0.666...   0.7   0.75   0.8

                                              $\frac{3}{8}$ $\frac{2}{3}$ $\frac{7}{10}$ $\frac{3}{4}$ $\frac{4}{5}$

❸ Put these fractions in order from smallest to largest. Use a calculator to change the fractions to decimals.

a) $\frac{1}{4}$ $\frac{3}{5}$ $\frac{5}{8}$ $\frac{2}{9}$ $\frac{3}{10}$ _____

b) $\frac{4}{9}$ $\frac{5}{6}$ $\frac{2}{5}$ $\frac{7}{8}$ $\frac{2}{3}$ _____

If you don't have a calculator you can still use this method, by dividing on paper like this:

$\frac{3}{4}$ 3 ÷ 4   0 . 7 5
                                          4) 3 .^{3}0 ^{2}0

Practice

❶ Put these fractions in order from smallest to largest. Change each to have a common denominator.

a) $\frac{1}{4}$ $\frac{2}{5}$ $\frac{3}{10}$ $\frac{7}{20}$ _____

b) $\frac{5}{6}$ $\frac{7}{12}$ $\frac{3}{4}$ $\frac{5}{8}$ $\frac{2}{3}$ _____

c) $\frac{5}{9}$ $\frac{5}{6}$ $\frac{3}{4}$ $\frac{11}{18}$ $\frac{4}{9}$ _____

❷ Order these fractions and decimals, using a calculator:

a) $\frac{3}{4}$ 0.85 $\frac{3}{5}$ 0.7 $\frac{5}{8}$ _____

b) $\frac{8}{15}$ 0.48 0.6 $\frac{2}{3}$ $\frac{7}{10}$ _____

c) 0.1666... $\frac{5}{12}$ 0.25 $\frac{3}{8}$ $\frac{1}{3}$ _____

❸ Change each fraction to a decimal by dividing on paper:

a) $\frac{1}{5}$ b) $\frac{7}{8}$ c) $\frac{5}{9}$

How did I do?

I can order fractions by writing them with a common denominator.

I can use division to convert a fraction to a decimal.

I can order fractions by converting them to decimals.

✔
☐
☐
☐

13

5: Fractions (2)

In this unit you will revise:
- ▶ how to calculate fractions of quantities (fraction answers)
- ▶ how to multiply an integer by a fraction
- ▶ how to add and subtract simple fractions by writing them with a common denominator.

> When you are revising, if you don't understand something immediately, don't panic. Read it through several times and ask someone for help. Perhaps a teacher or an older brother or sister can help you.

What you should know

A **fraction** is part of something that has been split into equal parts.

The bottom number, or **denominator**, shows how many equal parts the whole has been split into.

The top number, or **numerator**, shows how many of those equal parts are being described.

$\frac{3}{5}$ means that a whole has been split into 5 equal parts and that 3 of these parts are being described.

Some fractions are **equivalent** which means they are worth the same amount, like $\frac{3}{6}$ and $\frac{1}{2}$.

Get started

There are two possible ways to find a fraction of a number or amount:

Divide by the denominator   or   **Multiply by the numerator**
and multiply by the numerator   **and put the answer over the denominator**

$\frac{3}{10}$ of 11 $\frac{3}{10}$ of 11

11 ÷ **10** × 3   11 × 3 **over 10**

1.1 × **3** = 3.3   33 **over 10** = $\frac{33}{10}$

Try to use the first method, but if the division by the denominator isn't easy, use the second method, like this:

$\frac{3}{7}$ of 10 $\frac{3}{7}$ of 10

10 ÷ **7** × 3 (10 ÷ 7 is not easy) →   10 × 3 **over 7**

                                                       30 **over 7** = $\frac{30}{7}$

Remember that questions like these can be written in different ways:

$\frac{3}{5} \times 40$ and $40 \times \frac{3}{5}$ and $\frac{3}{5}$ of 40 are the same.

❶ Answer these questions, giving your answers as fractions where necessary:

a) $\frac{3}{4}$ of 60 = _____

b) $\frac{2}{5}$ of 40 = _____

c) $\frac{4}{7}$ of 10 = _____

d) $\frac{5}{9}$ of 11 = _____

e) $\frac{2}{3} \times 27$ kg = _____

f) $\frac{3}{10} \times 9$ km = _____

g) $\frac{6}{7} \times 35$ m = _____

h) $\frac{8}{9} \times 10$ cm = _____

i) $30 \times \frac{9}{10}$ = _____

j) $7 \times \frac{2}{8}$ = _____

k) $21 \times \frac{3}{10}$ = _____

l) $9 \times \frac{7}{11}$ = _____

If two fractions have the **same denominator** it is easy to add or subtract them. Remember these rules:

● **Add or subtract the numerators**

$$\frac{5}{9} + \frac{8}{9} = \frac{13}{9} \text{ or } 1\frac{4}{9}$$

● **Leave denominators the same**

$$\frac{6}{7} - \frac{4}{7} = \frac{2}{7}$$

❷ Answer these questions. The fractions in each pair have the same denominator. Write fractions in their simplest form.

a) $\frac{3}{7} + \frac{2}{3} = $ _____

b) $\frac{3}{11} + \frac{5}{11} = $ _____

c) $\frac{7}{15} + \frac{8}{15} = $ _____

d) $\frac{9}{20} + \frac{7}{20} = $ _____

e) $\frac{8}{9} - \frac{4}{9} = $ _____

f) $\frac{7}{12} - \frac{5}{12} = $ _____

g) $\frac{5}{6} - \frac{4}{6} = $ _____

h) $\frac{23}{24} - \frac{15}{24} = $ _____

If two fractions do NOT have the **same denominator** you must change them to **equivalent fractions** that DO have the same denominator, like this:

$$\boxed{\frac{1}{5}} + \boxed{\frac{3}{4}} = ?$$

To do this, look at both denominators and ask yourself: *What is the lowest number that both 5 and 4 divide into exactly?* The answer is 20.

So change both fractions to **equivalent** ones with the denominator **20**.

Now the question is: $\boxed{\frac{4}{20}} + \boxed{\frac{15}{20}} = \boxed{\frac{19}{20}}$

❸ Answer these questions. The fractions in each pair do NOT have the same denominator. Write fractions in their simplest form.

a) $\frac{3}{10} + \frac{2}{3} = $ _____

b) $\frac{3}{8} + \frac{1}{6} = $ _____

c) $\frac{3}{8} + \frac{3}{7} = $ _____

d) $\frac{1}{3} + \frac{3}{5} = $ _____

e) $\frac{7}{8} - \frac{5}{6} = $ _____

f) $\frac{3}{4} - \frac{1}{10} = $ _____

g) $\frac{7}{10} - \frac{3}{8} = $ _____

h) $\frac{4}{5} - \frac{3}{7} = $ _____

Practice

❶ Answer these questions, giving your answers as fractions where necessary:

a) $\frac{6}{10}$ of 11 = _____

b) $\frac{5}{8}$ of 9 = _____

c) $\frac{7}{12}$ of 5 = _____

d) $\frac{2}{6} \times 8 = $ _____

e) $\frac{6}{7} \times 10 = $ _____

f) $\frac{3}{10} \times 21 = $ _____

g) $11 \times \frac{3}{5} = $ _____

h) $6 \times \frac{2}{7} = $ _____

❷ Answer these questions:

a) $\frac{1}{5} + \frac{1}{8} = $ _____

b) $\frac{1}{7} + \frac{1}{5} = $ _____

c) $\frac{3}{4} + \frac{2}{5} = $ _____

d) $\frac{3}{10} + \frac{3}{4} = $ _____

e) $\frac{4}{5} - \frac{4}{9} = $ _____

f) $\frac{1}{3} - \frac{1}{10} = $ _____

g) $\frac{11}{12} - \frac{1}{6} = $ _____

h) $\frac{3}{4} - \frac{1}{5} = $ _____

How did I do?

I can calculate simple fractions of quantities (fraction answers). ☐

I can multiply an integer by a fraction. ☐

I can add and subtract fractions by writing them with a common denominator. ☐

✔

6: Fractions (3)

In this unit you will revise:
- how to add and subtract fractions
- how to multiply and divide fractions.

⚠ Revise in small bursts. Don't spend more than 30–45 minutes working without a break.

What you should know

A **fraction** is part of something that has been split into equal parts.

The bottom number, or **denominator**, shows how many equal parts the whole has been split into.

The top number, or **numerator**, shows how many of those equal parts are being described.

$\frac{3}{5}$ means that a whole has been split into 5 equal parts and that 3 of these parts are being described.

To change a fraction to an equivalent one, multiply or divide the numerator and denominator by the same number, like this:

Get started

If fractions have the **same denominator** it is easy to add or subtract them.

- **Add or subtract the numerators.** $\frac{5}{9} + \frac{3}{9} + \frac{8}{9} = \frac{16}{9}$ or $1\frac{7}{9}$

- **Leave denominators the same.** $\frac{6}{7} - \frac{4}{7} = \frac{2}{7}$

If the fractions do NOT have the **same denominator** you must change them to **equivalent fractions** that DO have the same denominator.

$$\boxed{\frac{3}{5}} + \boxed{\frac{3}{4}} + \boxed{\frac{1}{2}} = ?$$

To do this, look at the denominators and ask yourself: *What is the lowest number that 5, 4 and 2 divide exactly into?* The answer is 20.

So change the fractions to **equivalent** ones with the denominator **20**.

$$\boxed{\frac{12}{20}} + \boxed{\frac{15}{20}} + \boxed{\frac{10}{20}} = \boxed{\frac{37}{20}} \text{ or } \boxed{1\frac{17}{20}}$$

❶
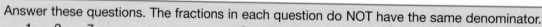

Answer these questions. The fractions in each question do NOT have the same denominator.

a) $\frac{1}{3} + \frac{2}{5} + \frac{7}{10} =$ _____

b) $\frac{2}{3} + \frac{5}{6} + \frac{1}{8} =$ _____

c) $\frac{4}{5} + \frac{1}{3} + \frac{3}{4} =$ _____

d) $\frac{1}{4} + \frac{4}{9} + \frac{5}{6} =$ _____

e) $\frac{5}{8} - \frac{1}{4} =$ _____

f) $\frac{7}{9} - \frac{3}{5} =$ _____

g) $\frac{5}{9} - \frac{3}{8} =$ _____

h) $\frac{6}{7} - \frac{2}{9} =$ _____

Multiplying fractions is easy:

● **Multiply the numerators.**

● **Multiply the denominators.**

$$\frac{5}{9} \times \frac{3}{4} = \frac{15}{36} \qquad \text{This can be simplified to } \frac{5}{12}$$

To make the multiplication easier, change each fraction to its simplest form and try to cancel diagonally (by dividing the numerator of one fraction and the denominator of the other by a common **factor**), like this:

$$\frac{\overset{1}{5}}{\underset{7}{49}} \times \frac{\overset{2}{14}}{\underset{3}{15}} = \frac{2}{21}$$

Dividing fractions can be done using multiplication. This makes it much easier. Turn the second fraction in the question upside down and multiply them. You get the same answer!

● Turn the second fraction upside down

● **Multiply the numerators.**

● **Multiply the denominators.**

$$\frac{4}{5} \div \frac{3}{4} = \frac{4}{5} \times \frac{4}{3} \qquad \frac{4}{5} \times \frac{4}{3} = \frac{16}{15} \text{ or } 1\frac{1}{15}$$

Practice

1 Answer these questions. Give each fractional answer in its simplest form.

a) $\frac{15}{16} \times \frac{20}{35} = $ _____

b) $\frac{5}{34} \times \frac{17}{11} = $ _____

c) $\frac{35}{64} \times \frac{8}{25} = $ _____

d) $\frac{5}{9} \times \frac{18}{55} = $ _____

e) $\frac{15}{24} \times \frac{16}{40} = $ _____

f) $\frac{21}{30} \times \frac{5}{28} = $ _____

2 Tick which of these are true statements:

a) $\frac{10}{16} \div \frac{25}{20} = \frac{10}{16} \times \frac{20}{25}$

b) $\frac{5}{36} \div \frac{11}{18} = \frac{5}{36} \times \frac{18}{11}$

c) $\frac{35}{72} \div \frac{8}{25} = \frac{35}{72} \times \frac{8}{25}$

d) $\frac{3}{12} \div \frac{75}{18} = \frac{3}{12} \times \frac{18}{75}$

3 Answer these questions. Give each fractional answer in its simplest form.

a) $\frac{15}{16} \div \frac{20}{24} = $ _____

b) $\frac{3}{25} \div \frac{9}{15} = $ _____

c) $\frac{35}{72} \div \frac{25}{8} = $ _____

d) $\frac{45}{32} \div \frac{60}{8} = $ _____

e) $\frac{5}{36} \div \frac{11}{18} = $ _____

f) $\frac{7}{12} \div \frac{35}{18} = $ _____

How did I do?

I can add and subtract fractions.   ☐

I can multiply and divide fractions.   ☐

7: Percentages (1)

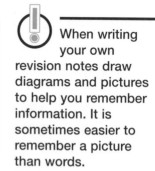

In this unit you will revise:

▶ how to calculate percentages of numbers and quantities mentally

▶ how to write one number as a percentage of another without a calculator

▶ how to write one number as a percentage of another with a calculator.

When writing your own revision notes draw diagrams and pictures to help you remember information. It is sometimes easier to remember a picture than words.

What you should know

Percentages can be used to show parts of a whole. A percentage is a fraction with a denominator of 100, but written in a different way.

36% means $\frac{36}{100}$.

Per cent means out of a hundred. So 36% is read as 'thirty-six per cent' or 'thirty six out of a hundred'.

Here are some ways to calculate percentages mentally:

To find **50%**:	halve the number	To find **10%**:	just divide the number by 10
To find **25%**:	halve the number and halve the answer (or you can just divide by 4)	To find **75%**:	halve the number and halve the answer then add your two answers together
To find **20%**:	divide by 10 and multiply by 2 (double)	To find **30%**:	divide by 10 and multiply by 3
To find **40%**:	divide by 10 and multiply by 4	To find **60%**:	divide by 10 and multiply by 6
To find **70%**:	divide by 10 and multiply by 7	To find **80%**:	divide by 10 and multiply by 8
To find **90%**:	divide by 10 and multiply by 9	To find **5%**:	divide by 10 and then halve the answer
To find **1%**:	just divide the number by 100		

Get started

Many percentages of amounts can be calculated in your head, using some of the strategies listed above.

For example, if you need to find 15% of a number, first find 10% and 5% and add the two answers together. The example below shows how to find 61% of a number:

Find 61% of 120.

To find 60%: divide by 10 and multiply by 6 $120 \div 10 \times 6 = 12 \times 6 = 72$

To find 1%: just divide the number by 100 $120 \div 100 = 1.2$

$72 + 1.2 = \mathbf{73.2}$

1 Answer these percentage questions **without** a calculator:

a) 11% of £110 _____

b) 15% of 48 m _____

c) 35% of £60 _____

d) 21% of 300 g _____

e) 51% of 210 cm _____

f) 26% of 80 m _____

g) 76% of 40 cm _____

h) 95% of 120 kg _____

To write a number, such as a test score, as a percentage of another, make a fraction and then change the fraction to a percentage. Remember that a percentage is a fraction with a denominator of 100.

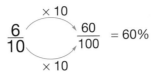

I scored 42 out of 50.

$\times 2$

$\dfrac{42}{50}$ $\dfrac{84}{100}$ = 84%

$\times 2$

I scored 6 out of 10.

$\times 10$

$\dfrac{6}{10}$ $\dfrac{60}{100}$ = 60%

$\times 10$

I scored 425 out of 500.

$\div 5$

$\dfrac{425}{500}$ $\dfrac{85}{100}$ = 85%

$\div 5$

2 Write each score as a percentage:

a) 13 out of 20 _____

b) 8 out of 25 _____

c) 4 out of 5 _____

d) 6 out of 10 _____

e) 14 out of 50 _____

f) 225 out of 500 _____

g) 18 out of 25 _____

h) 180 out of 200 _____

If the denominator of the fraction cannot be multiplied or divided easily to make 100, divide the numerator by the denominator on a calculator and multiply by 100.

I scored 42 out of 47.   → 42 ÷ 47 × 100 = 89.3617   Round the answer → 89.4%

Practice

1 Fill in the missing amounts in this diagram, finding different percentages of £240. Do **not** use a calculator. One has been done for you.

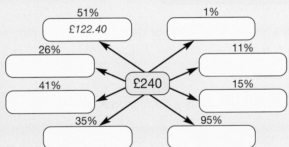

51%
£122.40

1%

26%

11%

41%

£240

15%

35%

95%

2 Andy, Mandy and Sandy took different Maths tests.

Andy scored 8 out of 10,   Mandy scored 21 out of 25,   Sandy scored 210 out of 300.

Write these scores as percentages (without a calculator) and tick the person with the highest percentage:

Andy _____%   Mandy _____%   Sandy _____%

3 On a mountain, the wind speed was recorded as gale force on 292 days out of 365 last year. What percentage is this? You may use a calculator.

_____%

4 In a phone-in vote, approximately 13 million out of 19 million voted for the winner. About what percentage is this? You may use a calculator.

_____%

How did I do?

✔

I can calculate percentages of numbers and quantities mentally. ☐

I can write one number as a percentage of another without a calculator. ☐

I can write one number as a percentage of another with a calculator. ☐

8: Percentages (2)

In this unit you will revise:

▶ how to calculate simple percentages using a calculator

▶ how to find the outcome of a given percentage increase or decrease.

Revision shouldn't just happen when you get close to exams. Students who do well in exams are usually those who have worked hard throughout the year. They know which topics they are good at and those which they need more work on. Do you?

What you should know

Fractions, decimals and percentages are all used to describe parts of a whole.

A percentage is a fraction with a denominator of 100, but written in a different way. **Per cent** means out of a hundred. 36% means $\frac{36}{100}$ and is read as 'thirty-six per cent' or 'thirty-six out of a hundred'.

This diagram shows how to change a percentage into a fraction and into a decimal:

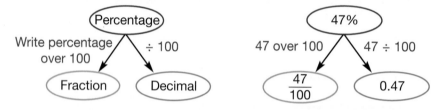

Get started

Because a percentage can be written as a fraction or decimal, there are different ways of calculating percentages on a calculator.

1. The fraction way

Remember that a percentage can be written as a fraction 'out of 100' or 'divided by 100'.

32% of £146

$\frac{32}{100} \times £146$ Key into the calculator 32 ÷ 100 and then × 146   **£46.72**

2. The decimal way

Another way is to write each percentage as a decimal.

32% of £146

0.32 × £146   Key into the calculator 0.32 × 146   **£46.72**

Choose which way you like best and remember to use the multiplication sign in place of the word 'of'.

---

❶

Answer these percentage questions using a calculator:

a) 38% of £40 = _____

b) 45% of £22 = _____

c) 82% of £58 = _____

d) 21% of 26 kg = _____

e) 6% of 39 kg = _____

f) 56% of 144 kg = _____

g) 19% of 53 ml = _____

h) 87% of 125 ml = _____

i) 99% of 305 ml = _____

To **increase** an amount by a percentage:

● first find the percentage of the amount
● then **add** this on to the original amount.

    Increase £350 by 84%.

● Find **84% of £350**
● Then finally **add** this to the original amount →

      Key in 84 ÷ 100 × 350 or 0.84 × 350 = **£294**
                       £350 + £294 = **£644**

❷ **Increase** each price by the percentage shown.

a) Increase £80 by 24% _____

b) Increase £25 by 64% _____

c) Increase £48 by 82% _____

d) Increase £93 by 13% _____

e) Increase £134 by 47% _____

f) Increase £228 by 73% _____

To **decrease** an amount by a percentage:

● first find the percentage of the amount
● then **subtract** this from the original amount.

    Decrease £350 by 84%.

● Find **84% of £350**
● Then finally **subtract** this from the original amount →

      Key in 84 ÷ 100 × 350 or 0.84 × 350 = **£294**
                       £350 − £294 = **£56**

❸ **Decrease** each price by the percentage shown.

a) Decrease £80 by 24% _____

b) Decrease £25 by 64% _____

c) Decrease £48 by 82% _____

d) Decrease £93 by 13% _____

e) Decrease £134 by 47% _____

f) Decrease £228 by 73% _____

Practice

❶ Answer these percentage change questions using a calculator:

a) Increase £90 by 63% _____

b) Increase £67 by 34% _____

c) Increase £48 by 7% _____

d) Decrease £93 by 1% _____

e) Decrease £137 by 27% _____

f) Decrease £180 by 99% _____

❷ Answer these percentage change questions using a calculator:

a) A car drives at 60 m.p.h. It **increases** its speed by 15% of that. How fast is the car travelling now?

_____

b) A man's weight **decreases** by 22%. His original weight was 84 kg. How much does he weigh now?

_____

c) A restaurant increases all its prices by 8%. A sirloin steak used to cost £12.50. What is the new price?

_____

How did I do?

I can calculate percentages using a calculator. ☐

I can find the outcome of a given percentage increase or decrease. ☐

9: Percentages (3)

In this unit you will revise:

▶ how to find the outcome of a given percentage increase or decrease
▶ how to solve problems involving percentage changes.

Percentages is quite a difficult topic but a very important one. When you finish this page, write some notes to remind you what you have done and try question 6 on page 20.

What you should know

Percentages can be used to show parts of a whole. A percentage is a fraction with a denominator of 100, but written in a different way. 36% means $\frac{36}{100}$. **Per cent** means out of a hundred. So 36% is read as 'thirty-six per cent' or 'thirty-six out of a hundred'.

There are different ways of calculating a percentage of an amount using a calculator. Choose whichever method you prefer.

1. The fraction way
A percentage can be written as a fraction 'out of 100' or 'divided by 100'.

32% of £146

$\frac{32}{100} \times £146$ 　　Key into the calculator 32 ÷ 100 and then × 146 　　**£46.72**

2. The decimal way
Each percentage can be written as a decimal.

32% of £146

$0.32 \times £146$ 　　Key into the calculator 0.32 × 146 　　**£46.72**

3. The unitary way
Find 1% of the number by dividing by 100 first, then multiply.

32% of £146

£146 ÷ 100 × 32 　　Key into the calculator 146 ÷ 100 and then × 32 　　**£46.72**

Get started

To **increase** an amount by a percentage:
● first find the percentage of the amount
● then **add** this on to the original amount

Increase £350 by 84%.

Using a calculator **84% of £350 = £294**

£350 + £294 = **£644**

To **decrease** an amount by a percentage:
● first find the percentage of the amount
● then **subtract** this from the original amount

Decrease £350 by 84%.

Using a calculator **84% of £350 = £294**

£350 – £294 = **£56**

① Answer these percentage change questions, using a calculator:

a) Increase £49 by 24% _____
b) Increase £74 000 by 66% _____
c) Increase £26.50 by 8% _____
d) Decrease £94 by 73% _____
e) Decrease £13 400 by 52% _____
f) Decrease £45.80 by 6% _____

Other types of percentage change problems can be solved if you know the new amount as a percentage of the original amount.

● If a price has been **increased** by 15% the new price will be 115% of the original price.
● If a price has been **decreased** by 15% the new price will be 85% of the original price.

② Complete this percentage change table:

Original price	Percentage change	New price	New price as percentage of original price
£37	17% increase	£43.29	100% + 17% = 117%
£85	8% decrease		100% – 8% =
£143	63% increase		
£12 400	36% decrease		

If a question gives the **new** price of something after a percentage change, you can find the **original** price, like this:

In a sale, prices are reduced by 28%. A jacket costs £42.84 in the sale. What was its original price?

Original price	Percentage change	New price	New price as percentage of original price
?	28% **decrease**	£42.84	72%

● Write the new price and new percentage

● Divide the new price to find 1%

● Multiply by 100 to find 100% (the original price)

£42.84 = **72%**

£42.84 ÷ 72 = 0.595 = **1%**

0.595 × 100 = 59.50 = **100%**

Original price **£59.50**

Practice

① Answer these percentage change questions, using a calculator.

a) In a sale, prices are reduced by 55%.
A jumper costs £19.08 in the sale. What was its original price? _____

b) In the New Year, prices **rise** by 5%.
A coat costs £36.75 after the rise. What was its original price? _____

c) In the New Year, prices **rise** by 12%.
A hat costs £14.28 after the rise. What was its original price? _____

d) A car is driving along a road. It **decreases** its speed by 20% to reach a
speed of 36 m.p.h. At what speed was it travelling before it slowed down? _____

e) A man's weight goes up by 22% to 83.57 kg. How much did he weigh before the increase? _____

How did I do?

I can find the outcome of a given percentage increase or decrease. ☐

I can solve problems involving percentage changes. ☐

In this unit you will revise:
- the equivalence of percentages, fractions and decimals
- how to use fractions, decimals and percentages to compare proportions.

When you are revising, take regular breaks. Doing some exercises can help you to feel more alert and will help you to concentrate better.

What you should know

Proportion has several meanings in Maths. Someone can ask 'What proportion of these sweets are red?' Proportion, here, means 'part of the whole set' and could be answered using a **fraction**, a **decimal** or a **percentage**. The answer could be 'A quarter ($\frac{1}{4}$) of them are red' or '0.25 are red' or '25% are red'.

Fractions, decimals and percentages are all used to describe parts of a whole.

It is important to know fractions, decimals and percentages with the same values. This number line shows how some of them are related.

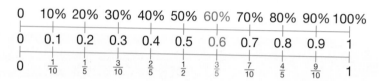

Get started

This diagram shows how to find equivalent fractions, percentages and decimals. Move clockwise around the diagram, changing from a percentage to a fraction to a decimal and so on. Use a calculator.

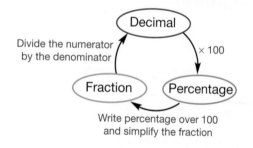

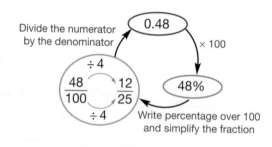

1 Write the fraction, decimal and percentage equivalents to complete these tables. Give fractions in their simplest form.

a)

F	D	P
$\frac{1}{10}$		
$\frac{3}{4}$		
$\frac{27}{100}$		

b)

D	P	F
0.01		
0.4		
0.81		

c)

P	F	D
27%		
5%		
20%		

This clothing label shows proportions of material that add up to 1 whole or 100%:

- To find the **percentage** of the material that is cotton, change all the proportions to percentages, find their total and subtract it from 100%.

- To find the **fraction** of the material that is cotton, change all the proportions to fractions with the same denominator (such as 100), find the total and subtract it from 1.

> 20% nylon
> $\frac{1}{10}$ lycra
> $\frac{2}{5}$ wool
> 10% polyester
> _____ cotton

20% nylon	$\frac{2}{10}$ nylon
10% lycra	$\frac{1}{10}$ lycra
40% wool	$\frac{4}{10}$ wool
10% polyester	$\frac{1}{10}$ polyester
$\overline{80\%}$ $100 - 80 = 20$	$\frac{8}{10}$ $1 - \frac{8}{10} = \frac{2}{10} = \frac{1}{5}$
20% cotton	$\frac{1}{5}$ cotton

Practice

1

a) What fraction is silk?

> 35% nylon
> $\frac{1}{100}$ lycra
> $\frac{8}{50}$ viscose
> 9% nylon
> ? silk

_____ silk

b) What percentage is viscose?

> $\frac{3}{10}$ polyester
> 12% nylon
> $\frac{2}{5}$ lycra
> $\frac{1}{10}$ silk
> ? viscose

_____ viscose

c) What fraction is elastane?

> $\frac{1}{25}$ lycra
> 8% nylon
> $\frac{7}{50}$ polyester
> $\frac{1}{10}$ cotton
> ? elastane

_____ elastane

d) What percentage is wool?

> 12% elastane
> $\frac{1}{10}$ polyester
> $\frac{7}{20}$ lycra
> $\frac{3}{25}$ silk
> ? wool

_____ wool

2 What proportion of each shape is shaded? Give each answer as a fraction in its simplest form, as a decimal, and as a percentage.

a) 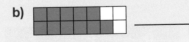 _____

b) _____ _____

c)  _____

_____ _____   _____ _____   _____ _____

3 At a concert the proportion of the whole crowd that is male is 17%. What proportion of the crowd is female? Give your answer as a decimal, as a percentage and as a fraction.

_____ _____ _____

How did I do?

I understand that percentages, fractions and decimals can be equivalent. ☐

I can change between fractions, decimals and percentages. ☐

I can use fractions, decimals and percentages to compare proportions. ☐

11: Proportion (2)

In this unit you will revise:

▶ the equivalence of percentages, fractions and decimals
▶ when fractions or percentages are needed to compare proportions
▶ how to use proportional reasoning to solve problems.

What you should know

Proportion has several meanings in Maths. Someone can ask 'What proportion of these sweets is red?' Proportion, here, means 'part of the whole set' and could be answered using a **fraction**, a **decimal** or a **percentage**. The answer could be 'A quarter ($\frac{1}{4}$) of them are red' or '0.25 are red' or '25% are red'.

Fractions, decimals and percentages are all used to describe parts of a whole.

Get started

This diagram shows how to find equivalent fractions, percentages and decimals. Move clockwise around the diagram, changing from a percentage to a fraction to a decimal and so on.

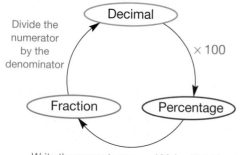

Divide the numerator by the denominator

× 100

Write the percentage over 100 (multiply the numerator and denominator by a power of 10 if necessary) and simplify the fraction

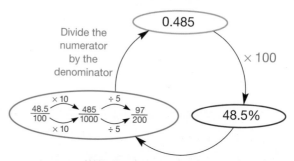

Divide the numerator by the denominator

× 100

Write the percentage over 100 (multiply the numerator and denominator by 10 to remove the decimal point) and simplify the fraction

1 Write the fraction, decimal and percentage equivalents to complete these tables. Use a calculator where necessary. Give fractions in their simplest form. Round decimals to 3 **decimal places** and percentages to 1 decimal place.

a)

F	D	P
$\frac{3}{7}$		
$\frac{5}{9}$		
$\frac{37}{235}$		

b)

D	P	F
0.24		
0.635		
0.805		

c)

P	F	D
9%		
41%		
17.5%		

Converting fractions to percentages is often very useful when solving problems, as it is easier to compare percentages.

Three different factories manufacture paperclips. A proportion of the paperclips they make are rejected.

● *The number rejected in Factory A was* **1636** *out of a total of* **55 000** *paperclips.*

● *The number rejected in Factory B was* **37 631** *out of a total of* **1 000 000** *paperclips.*

● *The number rejected in Factory C was* **88** *out of a total of* **3000** *paperclips.*

Which factory has the lowest rejection rate?

Factory A	Factory B	Factory C
$\dfrac{1636}{55\,000}$	$\dfrac{37\,631}{1\,000\,000}$	$\dfrac{88}{3000}$

Fractions are not easy to compare, so use a calculator to convert them to percentages.
Round the percentages to 2 decimal places.

$1636 \div 55\,000 \times 100$	$37\,631 \div 1\,000\,000 \times 100$	$88 \div 3000 \times 100$
$= 2.97\%$	$= 3.76\%$	$= 2.93\%$

Now it is easy to see that Factory C has the lowest rejection rate and Factory B has the highest.

❷ Which of these countries has the highest Muslim population as a percentage of the total population?

In the UK (population 60 million), about 600 000 people are Muslim.

In India (population 1030 million), about 124 million people are Muslim.

In Bangladesh (population 144 million), about 120 million people are Muslim.

_____

Practice

❶ Which of these euro coins has the highest proportion of copper?

The 1 cent coin has a total mass of 2.3 g of which 0.138 g is copper. ☐

The 2 cent coin has a total mass of 3.06 g of which 0.1683 g is copper. ☐

The 5 cent coin has a total mass of 3.92 g of which 0.196 g is copper. ☐

❷ Which of these euro coins has the highest proportion of steel?

The 1 cent coin has a total mass of 2.3 g of which 2.162 g is steel. ☐

The 2 cent coin has a total mass of 3.06 g of which 2.8917 g is steel. ☐

The 5 cent coin has a total mass of 3.92 g of which 3.724 g is steel. ☐

❸ Which of these euro coins has the highest proportion of zinc?

The 50 cent coin has a total mass of 7.8 g of which 0.39 g is zinc. ☐

The €1 coin has a total mass of 7.5 g of which 0.758 g is zinc. ☐

The €2 coin has a total mass of 8.5 g of which 0.82 g is zinc. ☐

How did I do?

I know how to convert between fractions, decimals and percentages. ☐

I can use proportional reasoning to solve problems. ☐

12: Direct proportion (1)

In this unit you will revise:
- ▶ how to recognise when two things are in direct proportion
- ▶ how to use direct proportion to solve simple problems.

It can help to make your own revision notes. When you finish this page, write a few lines to help you remember what you have learnt. Keep them somewhere safe to look at again.

What you should know

For working on ideas of **proportion**, you need to be confident in multiplying and dividing numbers mentally and on paper. The better you know your multiplication tables facts and the related division facts, the easier you will find this work. Do you know these facts?

| $6 \times 6 = 36$ | $6 \times 7 = 42$ | $6 \times 8 = 48$ | $7 \times 7 = 49$ | $7 \times 8 = 56$ | $8 \times 8 = 64$ |

Remember that division facts are the inverse (or opposite) of these:

| $36 \div 6 = 6$ | $42 \div 6 = 7$ | $48 \div 6 = 8$ | $49 \div 7 = 7$ | $56 \div 7 = 8$ | $64 \div 8 = 8$ |
| | or $42 \div 7 = 6$ | or $48 \div 8 = 6$ | | or $56 \div 8 = 7$ | |

Get started

When a quantity gets larger or smaller, it is said to change.

Sometimes a change in one quantity causes a change, or is linked to a change, in another quantity.

If these changes happen in the same **ratio**, then the quantities are said to be in **direct proportion**.

In the table on the right, as the number of pizzas grows so does the price.

To be certain whether two things are in direct proportion, divide one quantity by the other for each pair of values. You should always get the same answer.

Price ÷ number of pizzas

$£5 \div 1 = 5$ $£10 \div 2 = 5$ $£40 \div 8 = 5$ $£500 \div 100 = 5$

If the answer to every division is the same, then the two quantities are said to be in **direct proportion**.

Number of pizzas	Price
1	£5
2	£10
8	£40
100	£500

Tick which sets of numbers are in direct proportion by dividing one quantity by the other for each pair of values. You should always get the same answer if these are in direct proportion.

a)

1	8
2	16
5	40
30	240

b)

4	8
5	20
6	30
7	70

c)

5	10
10	20
15	30
50	100

Problems can be solved using these ideas:

If all pizzas cost the same and three pizzas cost £18, how much will 5 pizzas cost?

Because the pizzas are all the same price we know that the number of pizzas and the price are in **direct proportion**. **Divide** to find how much 1 pizza costs, then **multiply** to find how much 5 cost.

$£18 \div 3 = £6$, so 1 pizza costs £6

Now multiply £6 by 5 = £30

So 5 pizzas will cost £30.

Remember, **divide** to find how much one costs and **multiply** to find how much several cost.

Number of pizzas	Price
3	£18
1	?
5	?

2 Answer these direct proportion questions:

a) Three kebabs cost £21. How much will 5 cost? _____

b) Four chicken kormas cost £20. How much will 7 cost? _____

c) Two spring rolls cost £12. How much will 5 cost? _____

d) Three pies cost £12. How much will 4 cost? _____

Practice

1 Tick which sets of numbers are in direct proportion.

a)

1	6
2	12
5	30
40	240

b)

5	15
10	30
20	50
40	100

c)

7	14
14	28
21	42
50	100

2 Answer these direct proportion questions:

a) Seven portions of chips cost £14. How much will 3 cost?

b) Four pasties cost £12. How much will 7 cost?

c) Six onion bhajis cost £18. How much will 5 cost?

d) Two prawn kormas cost £14. How much will 5 cost?

e) Eight ribs cost £16. How much will 3 cost?

f) Four cheese slices cost £12. How much will 3 cost?

3 The numbers in each table are in proportion. Fill in the missing numbers:

a)

1	6
3	18
5	30
6	

b)

4	8
5	10
6	12
9	

c)

3	15
8	40
10	50
12	

4 Rewrite the recipe so that the amounts are suitable for two people.

Spinach parcels for 5 people	Spinach parcels for 2 people
205 g flour	_____ g flour
5 eggs	_____ eggs
150 ml water	_____ ml water
195 g spinach	_____ g spinach

How did I do?

I know how to recognise when two things are in direct proportion. ☐

I can solve simple direct proportion problems. ☐

13: Direct proportion (2)

In this unit you will revise:

- using conversion graphs to solve direct proportion problems
- how to use the unitary method to solve problems involving direct proportion.

It can help to make your own revision notes. When you finish this page, write a few lines to help you remember what you have learnt. Keep them somewhere safe to look at again.

What you should know

When a quantity gets larger or smaller, it is said to change.

Sometimes a change in one quantity causes a change, or is linked to a change, in another quantity.

If these changes happen in the same **ratio**, then the quantities are said to be in **direct proportion**.

In this table below, as the number of pizzas grows so does the price.

Number of pizzas	Price
1	£5
2	£10
8	£40
100	£500

To be certain whether two things are in direct proportion, divide one quantity by the other for each pair of values. You should always get the same answer.

Price ÷ number of pizzas:

£5 ÷ 1 = 5   £10 ÷ 2 = 5   £40 ÷ 8 = 5   £500 ÷ 100 = 5

If the answer to every division is the same, then the two quantities are said to be in **direct proportion**.

Get started

Conversion graphs can be used to show amounts in direct proportion.

This conversion graph shows the relationship between centimetres and inches.

To find the number of centimetres that is approximately equal to 3 inches, read across to the line and then down, giving your answer as accurately as possible:

3 inches ≈ 7.6 cm

To find the number of inches that is approximately equal to 11 cm, read up to the line and then across:

11 cm ≈ 4.3 inches

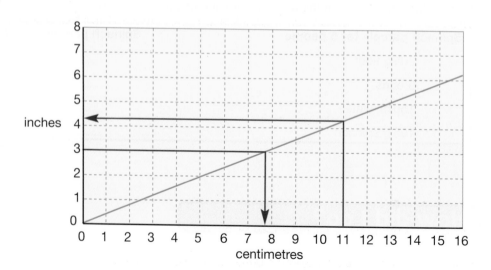

1 Use the graph to answer these questions. Be as accurate as you can.

a) 1 inch = _____ cm

b) 2 inches = _____ cm

c) 4 inches = _____ cm

d) 1.5 inches = _____ cm

e) 5.5 inches = _____ cm

f) 6 inches = _____ cm

g) _____ inches = 5 cm

h) _____ inches = 14 cm

i) _____ inches = 6.5 cm

j) _____ inches = 4 cm

k) _____ inches = 12 cm

l) _____ inches = 7 cm

To solve problems involving **direct proportion** use this method (sometimes called the unitary method):

● Divide to find 'one'

● then multiply to find 'many'.

Here are two examples:

5 pizzas cost £16. What will 7 pizzas cost?

● Divide £16 by 5 to find how much 'one' will cost

● then multiply £3.20 by 7 to find how much 7 will cost

£16 ÷ 5 = £3.20

£3.20 × 7 = **£22.40**

£11 is worth the same as 17.38 Euros. How many Euros is £48?

● Divide 17.38 by 11 to find how many Euros is the same as 'one' pound

● then multiply 1.58 by 48 to find how much £48 is in Euros

17.38 ÷ 11 = 1.58

1.58 × 48 = **75.84 Euros**

2 Answer these direct proportion questions. You may use a calculator:

a) If £5 is worth 916.9 Japenese yen, how many yen will I get for £23? _____

b) 4 chicken kormas cost £22, how much will 7 kormas cost? _____

Practice

1 Answer these direct proportion questions, using a calculator:

a) 6 pies cost £8.28, how much will 5 pies cost? _____

b) If £2 is worth 2.92 US dollars, how many dollars will I get for £38? _____

c) 5 miles is approximately equal to 8 km. How many kilometres are approximately equal to 7 miles?

_____

2 This recipe is written in ounces. 7 ounces is about 200 grams. Rewrite the recipe in grams to the nearest whole number:

11 ounces flour	_____ g flour
8 ounces margarine	_____ g margarine
5 ounces sugar	_____ g sugar
2 ounces cocoa	_____ g cocoa

How did I do?

I can use conversion graphs to solve direct proportion problems. ✔ ☐

I can use the unitary method to solve problems involving direct proportion. ☐

14: Ratio (1)

In this unit you will revise:

▶ the relationship between ratio and proportion
▶ how to solve simple problems about ratio using informal strategies
▶ how to divide a quantity into two parts in a given ratio.

What you should know

Ratio is the relationship between two or more numbers or quantities. It compares 'part with part'.

Look at this rod: ▉▉▉☐☐ **Ratio 3 : 2**

If we compare *the red parts with the white parts* we can say '3 red squares for every 2 white squares' so the **ratio** of red to white is 3 to 2 written **3 : 2**.

Proportion compares the part with the whole.

▉▉▉☐☐ **Proportion** $\frac{3}{5}$

Altogether there are 5 parts, so the **proportion** that is red is 3 out of 5, or $\frac{3}{5}$.

We can also describe a proportion as a decimal or percentage, like 0.6 or 60%.

Get started

When solving ratio problems it is useful to write the ratio under headings and to set it out like this:

At a party the ratio of males to females is 3 : 4. There are 15 males. How many females are there?

To solve the problem find out what 3 has been multiplied by to get 15.
15 ÷ 3 = 5.

Males : Females
$\times ?$ $\overset{3 : 4}{\underset{15 : \underline{\quad}}{}}$

If one number in a ratio has been multiplied by 5, then the other number must also be multiplied by 5 to get the answer.

4 × 5 = 20, so there are 20 females at the party.

Males : Females
$\times 5$ $\overset{3 : 4}{\underset{15 : 20}{}}$ $\times 5$

---

1 Answer these ratio questions, using the diagram to help you:

a) At a party the ratio of males to females is 2 : 5. There are 12 males.
   How many females are there?

Males : Females
$\times ?$ $\overset{2 : 5}{\underset{12 : \underline{\quad}}{}}$

b) At a party the ratio of males to females is 3 : 7. There are 14 females.
   How many males are there?

Males : Females
$\overset{3 : 7}{\underset{\underline{\quad} : 14}{}}$ $\times ?$

2 Change each ratio to the form 1 : *n*, by dividing the second number in the ratio by the first. Use a calculator.

a) 2 : 7   b) 4 : 9   c) 5 : 17   d) 8 : 11

_____   _____   _____   _____

e) 16 : 25   f) 10 : 7   g) 20 : 13   h) 14 : 42

_____   _____   _____   _____

Practice

1 Four T-shirts are made from polyester (P) and cotton (C). Change each ratio to the form 1 : *n*.

a)   T-shirt 1   b)   T-shirt 2   c)   T-shirt 3   d)   T-shirt 4

     P : C   P : C   P : C   P : C

     2 : 5   5 : 6   3 : 2   4 : 7

_____   _____   _____   _____

Which T-Shirt has the highest proportion of cotton? _____

2 This table shows the attendance for evening classes at the local college.

Subject	Number of males	Number of females
Geology	16	10
Greek (beginners)	10	28
Art	8	28
Yoga	15	27
Woodwork	24	21

a) For each course, write the ratio of males to females in its simplest form and then in the form 1 : *n*.

Geology   _____   _____

Greek (beginners)   _____   _____

Art   _____   _____

Yoga   _____   _____

Woodwork   _____   _____

b) Which course had the **highest** ratio of females to males?   _____

c) Which course had the **lowest** ratio of females to males?   _____

How did I do?

I can write a ratio in its simplest whole number form.   ☐

I can compare ratios by converting them to the form 1 : *n*.   ☐

16: Ratio (3)

In this unit you will revise:

▶ how to use the unitary method to solve ratio problems

▶ how to use scales on maps to solve problems.

In an exam, read questions carefully. For ratio questions see whether you are given the whole to split into a ratio or whether you are given just one part of the ratio.

What you should know

Ratio is the relationship between two or more numbers or quantities. It compares 'part with part'.

Get started

To solve problems involving **ratio** the following method, called the unitary method, can be used.

● **Divide** to find what 'one' part is worth

● then **multiply** to find 'many' parts.

Mrs Collyer gives her three daughters, Lucy, Emily and Alice, some money in the ratio 4 : 3 : 2. How much will they each get if she gives them a total of £72?

● **Divide** £72 by the total number of parts (4 + 3 + 2) to find 'one' part   £72 ÷ 9 = £8

● then **multiply** £8 by 4 parts to find Lucy's amount   Lucy £8 × 4 = **£32**

      £8 by 3 parts to find Emily's amount   Emily £8 × 3 = **£24**

   and £8 by 2 parts to find Alice's amount   Alice £8 × 2 = **£16**

   Check that the total is £72.   £32 + £24 + £16 = £72 ✔

1 Answer these ratio questions:

a) At a party of 64 people the ratio of males to females is 7 : 1. How many males and females are there?

   Males _____   Females _____

b) Ali and Baz share £99 in the ratio 7 : 4. How much does each get?

   Ali _____   Baz _____

c) Pete, Christine and Louis split £96 in the ratio 4 : 7 : 1. How much does each get?

   Pete _____   Christine _____   Louis _____

d) Three angles meet at a point (they have a total of 360°) and are in the ratio 14 : 3 : 1. What are their sizes?

   _____°   _____°   _____°

e) In a recipe Claire uses 3 parts flour to 2 parts sugar to 4 parts butter. If she makes 720 g of this mix, how much of each ingredient will she need?

   flour _____ g   sugar _____ g   butter _____ g

Maps use ratios to show the scale. A scale of **1 : 25 000** means that each centimetre on a map represents 25 000 centimetres in real life. Make sure you know how many centimetres are equal to one metre and one kilometre:

100 cm = 1 metre   100 000 cm = 1 km

The scale 1 : 25 000 means that 1 cm on the map equals 250 m or 0.25 km.

❷ A map has a scale of 1 : 25 000. What distances in real life do these lengths on the map represent? Give your answers in km.

a) 4 cm _____   b) 22 cm _____   c) 48 cm _____

❸ The map has a scale of 1 : 25 000. What lengths on the map will represent these distances in real life?

a) 3 km _____   b) 8 km _____   c) 4.2 km _____

Practice

❶ Answer these ratio questions:

a) Three interior angles of a triangle (they have a total of 180°) are in the ratio 3 : 1 : 5. What are their sizes?

_____ °   _____ °   _____ °

b) In a recipe Molly uses 3 parts flour to 2 parts sugar to 5 parts butter. If she makes 820 g of this mix, how much of each ingredient will she need?

flour _____ g   sugar _____ g   butter _____ g

❷ A map has a scale of 1 : 50 000. What distances in real life do these lengths on the map represent? Give your answers in km.

a) 2 cm _____   b) 3.5 cm _____   c) 4.2 cm _____

❸ A map has a scale of 1 : 50 000. What lengths on the map will represent these distances in real life?

a) 2 km _____   b) 5 km _____   c) 12 km _____

❹ A map has a scale of 1 : 125 000. What distances in real life do these lengths on the map represent? Give your answers in km.

a) 3.2 cm _____   b) 4.1 cm _____   c) 1.5 cm _____

❺ A map has a scale of 1 : 125 000. What lengths on the map will represent these distances in real life?

a) 3 km _____   b) 8 km _____   c) 42 km _____

How did I do?

I can use the unitary method to solve ratio problems. ☐

I can use scales on maps to solve problems. ☐

17: Integers

In this unit you will revise:
- adding and subtracting integers
- multiplying and dividing integers.

What you should know

Integers are the set of numbers made up of **positive** and **negative** whole **numbers** and zero. These are all integers: 5, 125, 4, –6, 0, –27, 36, –100.

Here some are shown on a number line.

-20 –18 –16 –14 –12 –10 –8 –6 –4 –2 0 2 4 6 8 10 12 14 16 18 20

On this line, the numbers get smaller as you move to the left and get larger as you move to the right.

Get started

When **adding** numbers, count along the number line, moving towards the **right**.

$$-16 + 22 \ =$$ (answer is 6)

Point to –16 on the line   move to the right   22 places

It can help to think about zero. If you move 16 of the 22 places to the right first you will reach zero, so now you only have 6 more to go. Also, with addition, remember that you can reorder the numbers so that the question is 22 + –16 or 22 – 16. This is sometimes easier to work out.

When **subtracting** numbers, count along the number line, moving towards the **left**.

$$-5 - 12 \ =$$ (answer is –17)

Point to –5 on the line   move to the left   12 places

Sometimes, when you are adding and subtracting, two signs appear next to each other, like these:

$$11 - -16 \ =$$

subtraction sign   the number –16

$$-12 + -7 \ =$$

addition sign   the number –7

If this happens, there are some rules you can follow to make it easier:

So you can rewrite the questions to make them easier, like this:

$$11 - -16 \ =$$
$$11 + 16 = 27$$

$$-12 + -7 \ =$$
$$-12 - 7 = -19$$

– – think of as a +
+ – think of as a –

❶ Answer these questions, moving along the number line:

a) –8 + 14 = _____

b) –15 + 20 = _____

c) –13 + 9 = _____

d) –16 + 13 = _____

e) –11 + 22 = _____

f) –10 – 7 = _____

g) 15 – 25 = _____

h) –13 – 6 = _____

i) 19 – 30 = _____

j) –11 – 7 = _____

2 Change each question to make it easier to answer and then answer it. One has been done for you.

a) 15 – –5 = **15 + 5 = 20**

b) –17 – –14 = _____

c) –19 + –1 = _____

d) 20 + –32 = _____

e) 8 – –15 = _____

f) –16 + –4 = _____

When multiplying and dividing integers, treat them as if they are positive numbers first and write down the answer. Then look at whether the numbers in the question are both positive or both negative or one of each. Use the information below to help you decide what sign the answer should have:

positive × positive = positive	7 × 8 = 56	positive ÷ positive = positive	56 ÷ 8 = 7
positive × negative = negative	7 × –8 = –56	positive ÷ negative = negative	56 ÷ –8 = –7
negative × positive = negative	–7 × 8 = –56	negative ÷ positive = negative	–56 ÷ 8 = –7
negative × negative = positive	–7 × –8 = 56	negative ÷ negative = positive	–56 ÷ –8 = 7

Because two negatives make a positive when a negative number is squared the answer is positive:

$$7^2 = 7 \times 7 = 49 \qquad\qquad (-7)^2 = -7 \times -7 = 49$$

This means that there are two solutions to $\sqrt{49}$. One answer is 7 and the other is –7. To show both solutions the ± sign is used. $\sqrt{49} = \pm7$

Practice

1 Answer these addition and subtraction questions:

a) –15 – 3 = _____

b) –20 – –31 = _____

c) 10 + –29 = _____

d) –17 + 28 = _____

e) –13 + 30 = _____

f) 11 – –11 = _____

g) –13 + –7 = _____

h) –16 – –35 = _____

2 Answer these multiplication and division questions:

a) –9 × –8 = _____

b) –11 × 9 = _____

c) –42 ÷ 6 = _____

d) –49 ÷ –7 = _____

e) 8 × –4 = _____

f) –6 × –8 = _____

g) –28 ÷ –4 = _____

h) 64 ÷ –8 = _____

i) –6 × –9 = _____

j) 7 × –5 = _____

k) –72 ÷ –9 = _____

l) –36 ÷ 6 = _____

3 Find the **square root** of each of these numbers. Write your answers with the ± sign.

a) $\sqrt{36}$ = _____

b) $\sqrt{64}$ = _____

c) $\sqrt{81}$ = _____

d) $\sqrt{100}$ = _____

e) $\sqrt{9}$ = _____

f) $\sqrt{49}$ = _____

g) $\sqrt{25}$ = _____

h) $\sqrt{144}$ = _____

How did I do?

I can add and subtract integers. ☐

I can multiply and divide integers. ☐

18: Factors and multiples

In this unit you will revise:

▶ what factors and multiples are and how to find factors and multiples of numbers

▶ how to find common factors and to find the highest common factor

▶ how to find common multiples and to find the lowest common multiple.

What you should know

Factors are whole numbers that divide exactly into another number without a remainder. Every whole number has the factor 1 and itself. The factors of 12 are **1, 2, 3, 4, 6** and **12** as they are the only whole numbers that divide exactly into 12 without a remainder.

Learn these simple tests to see what factors a number has:

● If a number is even, it has the factor **2**.

● If the digits add up to a multiple of 3, it has the factor **3**.

● If, when halved, the answer is even, it has the factor **4**.

● If a number ends in 0 or 5, it has the factor **5**.

● If it's even and if the digits add up to a multiple of 3, it has the factor **6**.

● If, when halved and halved again, the answer is even, it has the factor **8**.

● If the digits add up to a multiple of 9, it has the factor **9**.

● If a number ends in 0, it has the factor **10**.

To see whether 7 is a factor, use a calculator to divide the number by 7. If the answer is a whole number then 7 is a factor.

A **multiple** is a number that is in a times table or beyond. Multiples of 5 are 5, 10, 15, 20, 25, 30, ... and carry on, such as 85, 115, 500. The answer to a multiplication question is a multiple of both the numbers multiplied, for example, $6 \times 7 = 42$, so 42 is a **multiple** of 6 and 7.

Get started

A number is a **common factor** if it divides into more than one number.

The factors of **24** are **1, 2, 3, 4, 6, 8, 12** and **24**. The factors of **18** are **1, 2, 3, 6, 9** and **18**.

So the **common factors** of **24** and **18** are **1, 2, 3** and **6** (the factors in both lists).

Notice that the **highest common factor** of 24 and 18 is the factor **6**.

❶ Find the factors of the two numbers given and write down the common factors:

a) 12 and 24 _____   b) 45 and 27 _____

c) 28 and 32 _____   d) 18 and 30 _____

e) 24 and 40 _____   f) 30 and 36 _____

❷ For each pair above write the highest common factor.

a) _____   b) _____   c) _____   d) _____

e) _____   f) _____

A number is a **common multiple** if it is a multiple of more than one number.

Some multiples of 3:

3	6	9	12	15	18	21	24	27	30

Some multiples of 4:

4	8	12	16	20	24	28	32

As 12 and 24 appear in both lists, **12** and **24** are **common multiples** of **3** and **4**.

Notice that **12** is the **lowest common multiple** of **3** and **4** as it is the lowest number that appears in both lists.

❸ Find some multiples of the two numbers given and write down three common multiples:

a) 3 and 5 _____ _____ _____   b) 4 and 6 _____ _____ _____

c) 7 and 4 _____ _____ _____   d) 9 and 3 _____ _____ _____

e) 5 and 7 _____ _____ _____   f) 6 and 8 _____ _____ _____

❹ For each pair above write the lowest common multiple.

a) _____   b) _____

c) _____   d) _____

e) _____   f) _____

Practice

❶ James picks two number cards and finds the highest common factor of the two numbers.

72	35	42	80	54

Which two numbers has he chosen if the highest common factor is:

a) 8? _____ _____

b) 6 (there are 2 possible answers)? _____ _____

c) 7? _____ _____

d) 5? _____ _____

e) 2 (there are 2 possible answers)? _____ _____

f) 18? _____ _____

❷ Find the **lowest common multiple** of:

a) 11 and 6 _____   b) 10 and 8 _____   c) 12 and 4 _____

d) 5 and 12 _____   e) 15 and 4 _____

How did I do?

✔

I know what a factor is and can find factors of numbers. ☐

I know what a multiple is and can find multiples of numbers. ☐

I can find common factors and say which is the highest common factor. ☐

I can find common multiples and say which is the lowest common multiple. ☐

19: Prime numbers (1)

In this unit you will revise:

▸ prime numbers and how to check whether a number is prime
▸ how to find the prime factor decomposition of a number.

What you should know

Factors are whole numbers that divide exactly into another number without a remainder.

The factors of 12 are **1, 2, 3, 4, 6** and **12** as they are the only whole numbers that divide exactly into 12 without a remainder.

| The factors of 2 are **1 and 2**. | The factors of 10 are **1, 2, 5** and **10**. | The factors of 13 are **1** and **13**. |

To find the factors of a number, use these simple tests to see what factors a number has:

- If a number is even, it has the factor **2**.
- If the digits add up to a multiple of 3, it has the factor **3**.
- If, when halved, the answer is even, it has the factor **4**.
- If a number ends in 0 or 5, it has the factor **5**.
- If it's even and if the digits add up to a multiple of 3, it has the factor **6**.
- If, when halved and halved again is even, it has the factor **8**.
- If the digits add up to a multiple of 9, it has the factor **9**.
- If a number ends in 0, it has the factor **10**.
- To see whether 7 is a factor, use a calculator to divide the number by 7. If the answer is a whole number then 7 is a factor.

Get started

Prime numbers are whole numbers that have only **two** factors, the number itself and 1, for example:

2, 3, 5, 7, 11, 13, 17, 19, 23, 29, ...

Notice that the number 1 is not prime because it doesn't have two factors, its only factor is 1.

To find whether a number is a prime number, see how many factors it has. If it has exactly two factors then it is prime. Test for factors up to 10.

Is 103 prime?　　Tick the factors → 1 ☐　2 ☐　3 ☐　4 ☐　5 ☐　6 ☐　7 ☐　8 ☐　9 ☐　10 ☐

103 ☐　　　　　　　　　　　　　　　　　　　**103 is prime**

1

> Test for factors up to 10 to see if each number is prime or not.
>
> **a)** Is 51 prime?　Tick the factors → 1 ☐　2 ☐　3 ☐　4 ☐　5 ☐　6 ☐　7 ☐　8 ☐　9 ☐　10 ☐
>
> 51 ☐
>
> _____
>
> **b)** Is 79 prime?　Tick the factors → 1 ☐　2 ☐　3 ☐　4 ☐　5 ☐　6 ☐　7 ☐　8 ☐　9 ☐　10 ☐
>
> 79 ☐
>
> _____
>
> **c)** Is 91 prime?　Tick the factors → 1 ☐　2 ☐　3 ☐　4 ☐　5 ☐　6 ☐　7 ☐　8 ☐　9 ☐　10 ☐
>
> 91 ☐
>
> _____

Factor trees help you to find all the prime factors of a number.

Start with the number in a circle: →

Divide by the lowest prime factor that you can, like 2, 3 or 5:

Continue dividing until you are left with a prime number:

This is called finding the **prime factor decomposition** of a number.

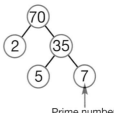

Prime number $70 = 2 \times 5 \times 7$

---

2 Use these factor trees to find the **prime factor decomposition** of these numbers:

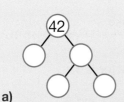

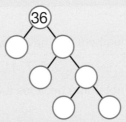

a) 42 = _____

b) 45 = _____

c) 36 = _____

d) 60 = _____

If a prime factor is repeated the multiplication can be written using powers:

$360 = 2 \times 2 \times 2 \times 3 \times 3 \times 5 = 2^3 \times 3^2 \times 5$

Practice

1 Circle the five prime numbers in this list:

49   51   53   54   57   59   61   63   67   69   73

2 Write these prime factor decompositions using powers:

a) $18 = 2 \times 3 \times 3 =$ _____   b) $100 = 2 \times 2 \times 5 \times 5 =$ _____

c) $28 = 2 \times 2 \times 7 =$ _____   d) $96 = 2 \times 2 \times 2 \times 2 \times 2 \times 3 =$ _____

3 Draw your own factor trees and find the prime factor decomposition for each of these numbers:

a) 140 = _____   b) 84 = _____

c) 88 = _____   d) 72 = _____

e) 54 = _____   f) 120 = _____

How did I do?

I know what a prime is and can check whether a number is prime.   ☐

I can find the prime factor decomposition of a number.   ☐

20: Prime numbers (2)

In this unit you will revise:
- ▶ how to find the prime factor decomposition of a number
- ▶ how to use the prime factor decomposition to find the highest common factor
- ▶ how to use the prime factor decomposition to find the lowest common multiple.

What you should know

Prime numbers are whole numbers that have **two** factors, the number itself and 1, like:

$$2, 3, 5, 7, 11, 13, 17, 19, 23, 29, \dots$$

Notice that the number 1 is not prime because it doesn't have two factors, its only factor is 1.

Prime factors are the factors of a number that are prime. The **prime factors** of 12 are **2** and **3**.

Get started

Factor trees help you to write a number as the product of its prime factors.

Start with the number in a circle.

Divide by the lowest prime factor that you can, like 2, 3 or 5.

Continue dividing until you are left with a prime number.

This is called finding the **prime factor decomposition** of a number.

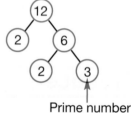

Prime number

$$12 = 2 \times 2 \times 3$$

If a prime factor is repeated the multiplication can be written using powers: $12 = 2 \times 2 \times 3 = 2^2 \times 3$

---

❶ Use these factor trees to find the **prime factor decomposition** of these numbers. Write each prime factor decomposition using powers.

a)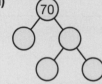

b)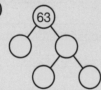

c)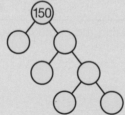

d)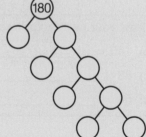

70 = _____   63 = _____   150 = _____   180 = _____

The prime decompositions of two numbers can be used to find their highest common factor (HCF) and their lowest common multiple (LCM).

$96 = 2 \times 2 \times 2 \times 2 \times 2 \times 3$ $60 = 2 \times 2 \times 3 \times 5$

The **highest common factor** (HCF) of two numbers is found using the prime factors that appear in the prime decompositions of **both** numbers.

HCF of 96 and 60 → $2 \times 2 \times 3 = 12$ 12 is the highest factor that divides into both 96 and 60.

The **lowest common multiple** (LCM) of two numbers is the set of factors that includes both decompositions.

LCM of 96 and 60 → $2 \times 2 \times 2 \times 2 \times 2 \times 3 \times 5 = 480$ 480 is the lowest multiple of both 96 and 60.

Practice

1 Draw your own factor trees and find the prime factor decomposition for each of these numbers. Write each prime factor decomposition using powers.

a) 120 = _____ b) 64 = _____

c) 48 = _____ d) 135 = _____

e) 98 = _____ f) 210 = _____

2 The prime decompositions of 45 and 300 are shown.

$45 = 3 \times 3 \times 5$

$300 = 2 \times 2 \times 3 \times 5 \times 5$

a) Find the highest common factor (HCF) of 45 and 300. _____

b) Find the lowest common multiple (LCM) of 45 and 300. _____

3 Use your answers to question 1 to answer these questions:

a) Find the highest common factor (HCF) of 120 and 48. _____

b) Find the lowest common multiple (LCM) of 120 and 48. _____

c) Find the highest common factor (HCF) of 135 and 210. _____

d) Find the lowest common multiple (LCM) of 135 and 210. _____

How did I do?

I can find the prime factor decomposition of a number. ☐

I can use the prime factor decomposition to find the highest common factor. ☐

I can use the prime factor decomposition to find the lowest common multiple. ☐

21: Powers and roots

In this unit you will revise:
- ▶ squares and cubes including how to write them using powers
- ▶ square roots and cube roots.

Revise in small bursts. Don't spend more than 30–45 minutes working without a break.

What you should know

These numbers are called **square numbers**:

1 4 9 16 25 36 49 64 81 100 121 144 ...

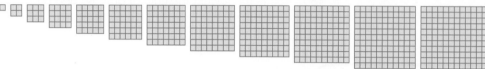

If we multiply a whole number by itself the answer is a square number.

Square numbers are created by '**squaring**' a number:

1^2 (1 squared) = 1×1 = **1**

2^2 (2 squared) = 2×2 = **4**

3^2 (3 squared) = 3×3 = **9**

4^2 (4 squared) = 4×4 = **16**

Finding the **square root** is the opposite of squaring. The number being multiplied by itself is found. Square roots are written using the $\sqrt{}$ sign. $\sqrt{16}$ means 'What number is multiplied by itself to make 16?'. The answer is 4, because $4 \times 4 = 16$.

$\sqrt{1}$ (the square root of 1) = 1

$\sqrt{4}$ (the square root of 4) = 2

$\sqrt{9}$ (the square root of 9) = 3

$\sqrt{16}$ (the square root of 16) = 4

Get started

Both positive and negative numbers can be squared. Watch what happens when a positive or negative number is squared (multiplied by itself):

$4^2 = 4 \times 4 = 16$

$(-4)^2 = -4 \times -4 = 16$

> When two **negative numbers** are multiplied the answer is positive (see page 17).

When *any* negative number is squared the answer will be positive. Notice also that you get the same answer for both questions above. This means that there are two answers to the question 'What is the square root of 16?'. There are two different numbers that can be multiplied by themselves to make 16: 4 and –4. To show the two answers the ± sign is used:

$\sqrt{16} = \pm 4$

1

Write the value, remembering to use the ± sign for square root questions.

a) $(-7)^2$ _____

b) $\sqrt{25}$ _____

c) $(-9)^2$ _____

d) $\sqrt{49}$ _____

e) 10^2 _____

f) $(-5)^2$ _____

g) $\sqrt{4}$ _____

h) 6^2 _____

i) $\sqrt{9}$ _____

j) $(-12)^2$ _____

Here are the first five cubic numbers:

1   8   27   64   125 ...

If we multiply three numbers that are the same together the answer is a cubic number.

Cubic numbers are created by '**cubing**' a number:

1^3 (1 cubed) = 1 × 1 × 1 = **1**
2^3 (2 cubed) = 2 × 2 × 2 = **8**
3^3 (3 cubed) = 3 × 3 × 3 = **27**
4^3 (4 cubed) = 4 × 4 × 4 = **64**

Finding the **cube root** is the opposite of cubing. Cube roots are written using the $\sqrt[3]{}$ sign.

$\sqrt[3]{27}$ = 3, because 3 × 3 × 3 = 27.

$\sqrt[3]{1}$ (the cube root of 1) = 1
$\sqrt[3]{8}$ (the cube root of 8) = 2
$\sqrt[3]{27}$ (the cube root of 27) = 3
$\sqrt[3]{64}$ (the cube root of 64) = 4

2 Write the value of:

a) 5^3 _____   b) $\sqrt[3]{64}$ _____   c) $\sqrt[3]{8}$ _____   d) 10^3 _____   e) $\sqrt[3]{1}$ _____

Practice

1 Use a calculator to find the value of:

a) $(-32)^2$ _____   b) $\sqrt{2916}$ _____   c) 48^2 _____   d) $\sqrt{8464}$ _____

e) $(-13)^2$ _____   f) 7^3 _____   g) $\sqrt[3]{512}$ _____   h) $\sqrt[3]{216}$ _____

i) 9^3 _____   j) 11^3 _____

2 Use your calculator to help you mark Sandeep's work. If there is a mistake, correct it.

a) $\sqrt{324}$ = 18 _____   b) 45^2 = 2225 _____   c) $\sqrt[3]{4913}$ = 17 _____

d) 64^3 = 4 _____   e) $(0.1)^2$ = 0.1 _____   f) $\sqrt{71\,824}$ = 268 _____

g) $\sqrt[3]{300.763}$ = 6.7 _____   h) 65^3 = 274 625 _____   i) $(13.7)^3$ = 2571.353 _____

3 Answer these mental Maths test questions:

a) Write the value of seven squared. _____   b) What is the square root of sixteen? _____

c) What is the difference in value between eight squared and four cubed? _____

d) Look at these **expressions**. Tick which is equivalent to n times n.

n^3 $\sqrt{n}$ n^2 $\sqrt[3]{n}$

e) Tick which of these is the best estimate of the square root of 47.

6.1   8.2   6.9   5.5   23.5

How did I do?

I know how to write squares and cubes using powers. ☐

I can find squares and cubes of numbers with and without a calculator. ✔ ☐

I can find square roots and cube roots of numbers. ☐

22: Index notation

In this unit you will revise:

 ▶ the index law for multiplication of positive integer powers
 ▶ the index law for division of positive integer powers
 ▶ the meaning of negative powers.

What you should know

The index, or power, of a number shows how many times the number is to be multiplied by itself.

$$3^2 \text{ (three squared)} = 3 \times 3 = 9$$

$$2^3 \text{ (two cubed)} = 2 \times 2 \times 2 = 8$$

$$5^4 \text{ (five to the power four)} = 5 \times 5 \times 5 \times 5 = 625$$

Here 3^2, 2^3, and 5^4 are all written in **index notation.**

Any number to the power 1 is the number itself $n^1 = n$

Any number to the power zero is 1 $n^0 = 1$

Get started

When **multiplying** numbers or letters written in index notation you can **add** the powers, but only if the numbers or letters are the same. This is known as the **index law of multiplication.**

$7^2 \times 7^4 = (7 \times 7) \times (7 \times 7 \times 7 \times 7) = 7 \times 7 \times 7 \times 7 \times 7 \times 7 = 7^6$ $7^2 \times 7^4 = 7^{(2+4)} = 7^6$

$8^3 \times 8^2 = (8 \times 8 \times 8) \times (8 \times 8) = 8 \times 8 \times 8 \times 8 \times 8 = 8^5$ $8^3 \times 8^2 = 8^{(3+2)} = 8^5$

$a^3 \times b^4$ cannot be simplified in this way but $a^3 \times \mathbf{a}^4 = a^7$

$4^2 \times 3^5$ cannot be simplified in this way but $4^2 \times \mathbf{4}^5 = 4^7$

1
Write the answers in index notation.

a) $4^3 \times 4^2 =$ _____

b) $3^7 \times 3^5 =$ _____

c) $2^2 \times 2^3 =$ _____

d) $10^9 \times 10^2 =$ _____

e) $f^6 \times f^3 =$ _____

f) $g^4 \times g^1 =$ _____

g) $d^7 \times d^4 =$ _____

h) $n^3 \times n^3 =$ _____

When **dividing** numbers or letters written in index notation you can **subtract** the powers, but only if the numbers or letters are the same. This is known as the **index law of division.**

$7^5 \div 7^2 = \dfrac{7 \times 7 \times 7 \times 7 \times 7}{7 \times 7} = 7^3$ $7^5 \div 7^2 = 7^{(5-2)} = 7^3$

$8^3 \div 8^2 = \dfrac{8 \times 8 \times 8}{8 \times 8} = 8^1 = 8$ $8^3 \div 8^2 = 8^{(3-2)} = 8^1 = 8$

Remember also that divisions can be written in two ways:

$\dfrac{7^3}{7^2}$ or $7^3 \div 7^2$

2 Write the answer in index notation.

a) $7^9 \div 7^5 =$ _____

b) $4^5 \div 4^5 =$ _____

c) $2^8 \div 2^2 =$ _____

d) $\dfrac{a^5}{a^2} =$ _____

e) $\dfrac{9^{11}}{9^5} =$ _____

f) $\dfrac{y^6}{y^5} =$ _____

Sometimes when subtracting powers the index is a negative number, like this:

$$7^2 \div 7^5 = \dfrac{7 \times 7}{7 \times 7 \times 7 \times 7 \times 7} = 7^{-3} \qquad\qquad 7^2 \div 7^5 = 7^{(2-5)} = 7^{-3}$$

The negative sign in a power tells you that it is a fraction with the numerator 1, like these:

$$7^{-3} = \dfrac{1}{7^3} \qquad\qquad 4^{-2} = \dfrac{1}{4^2} \qquad\qquad 3^{-5} = \dfrac{1}{3^5} \qquad\qquad 2^{-1} = \dfrac{1}{2}$$

3 Write the answer to each of these calculations in two different ways. The first has been done for you.

a) $7^3 \div 7^7 = 7^{-4} = \dfrac{1}{7^4}$

b) $4^3 \div 4^5 =$ _____

c) $2^3 \div 2^4 =$ _____

d) $a^4 \div a^8 =$ _____

e) $\dfrac{9^2}{9^9} =$ _____

f) $\dfrac{y^6}{y^{10}} =$ _____

Practice

1 Write the answers in index notation

a) $8^3 \times 8^2 =$ _____

b) $4^5 \times 4^5 =$ _____

c) $a^4 \times a^1 =$ _____

d) $6^6 \div 6^3 =$ _____

e) $y^2 \div y^5 =$ _____

f) $2^5 \div 2^6 =$ _____

g) $\dfrac{3^5}{3^9} =$ _____

h) $\dfrac{m^6}{m^6} =$ _____

i) $\dfrac{y^6}{y^5} =$ _____

2 Lisa has made a mistake in each of these questions. Can you see why?
Rewrite each one to make it correct.

a) $3^2 \times 3^5 = 3^{10}$ _____

b) $7^3 \times 7^5 = 7^{15}$ _____

c) $2^3 \times 2^3 = 4^6$ _____

d) $4^2 \div 4^5 = 4^3$ _____

e) $y^1 \times y^7 = y^7$ _____

f) $a^6 \div a^6 = a^1$ _____

g) $4^2 \div 4^3 = 4^1$ _____

h) $m^3 \div m^5 = m^2$ _____

i) $n^2 \div n^3 = n^5$ _____

How did I do?

I can use the index law for multiplication of positive integer powers.

I can use the index law for division of positive integer powers.

I know the meaning of negative powers.

23: Test (1)

1 Answer these questions without a calculator:

a) $3.81 \times 10^3 =$ _____

b) $18.6 \times 10^2 =$ _____

c) $26.4 \times 10^4 =$ _____

d) $7.12 \times 10^{-1} =$ _____

e) $5.37 \times 10^{-3} =$ _____

f) $23.48 \times 10^{-2} =$ _____

g) $512 \div 10^3 =$ _____

h) $134 \div 10^2 =$ _____

i) $2846 \div 10^1 =$ _____

j) $8 \div 10^{-1} =$ _____

k) $4 \div 10^{-2} =$ _____

l) $16 \div 10^{-3} =$ _____

2 Write these numbers using powers of ten:

a) 100 _____

b) one thousandth _____

c) 1000 _____

d) 10 000 _____

e) 0.01 _____

f) 10 000 000 _____

g) one tenth _____

h) 10 _____

i) 1 _____

j) 0.001 _____

k) 100 000 _____

l) $\dfrac{1}{10}$ _____

3 Answer these questions. The fractions in each pair do NOT have the same denominator.

a) $\dfrac{3}{8} + \dfrac{2}{5} + \dfrac{3}{4} =$ _____

b) $\dfrac{7}{8} + \dfrac{5}{7} + \dfrac{1}{4} =$ _____

c) $\dfrac{3}{4} + \dfrac{6}{11} + \dfrac{1}{8} =$ _____

d) $\dfrac{1}{3} + \dfrac{2}{5} + \dfrac{1}{6} =$ _____

e) $\dfrac{7}{8} - \dfrac{3}{7} =$ _____

f) $\dfrac{3}{8} - \dfrac{3}{10} =$ _____

g) $\dfrac{7}{10} - \dfrac{3}{5} =$ _____

h) $\dfrac{4}{7} - \dfrac{1}{5} =$ _____

4 Answer these questions:

a) $\dfrac{3}{12} \times \dfrac{10}{21} =$ _____

b) $\dfrac{7}{38} \times \dfrac{19}{15} =$ _____

c) $\dfrac{15}{63} \times \dfrac{9}{25} =$ _____

d) $\dfrac{9}{12} \times \dfrac{18}{72} =$ _____

5 Answer these percentage change questions using a calculator:

a) Increase £1396 by 22.5% _____

b) Decrease £52 000 by 12.5% _____

c) Increase £6400 by 9% _____

d) Reduce £140 by 85.5% _____

e) Decrease £126 by 24% _____

f) Increase £7430 by 30.5% _____

6 Write the fraction, decimal and percentage equivalents to complete these tables. Use a calculator where necessary. Give fractions in their simplest form. Round decimals to 3 decimal places and percentages to 1 decimal place.

a)

F	D	P
$\frac{1}{7}$		
$\frac{8}{9}$		
$\frac{26}{234}$		

b)

D	P	F
0.42		
0.586		
0.904		

c)

P	F	D
7%		
36%		
37.5%		

7 This table shows the attendance for evening classes at the local college.

Subject	Number of males	Number of females
French	18	12
Greek (advanced)	8	34
Art	9	30
Yoga	3	18
Photography	16	21

a) For each course, write the ratio of males to females in its simplest form and then in the form $1:n$.

French   _____   _____

Greek (advanced)   _____   _____

Art   _____   _____

Yoga   _____   _____

Photography   _____   _____

b) Which course had the **highest** ratio of females to males? _____

c) Which course had the **lowest** ratio of females to males? _____

8 Answer these questions without a calculator.

a) $-12 - 3 =$ _____

b) $-8 - -11 =$ _____

c) $6 + -19 =$ _____

d) $-12 + 24 =$ _____

e) $-1 + 20 =$ _____

f) $14 - -12 =$ _____

g) $-11 + -7 =$ _____

h) $-23 - -15 =$ _____

i) $-7 \times -8 =$ _____

j) $-6 \times 9 =$ _____

k) $-36 \div 6 =$ _____

l) $-63 \div -7 =$ _____

m) $8 \times -5 =$ _____

n) $-8 \times -8 =$ _____

o) $-24 \div -4 =$ _____

p) $49 \div -7 =$ _____

9 Find the square root of each of these numbers. Write your answers with the $\pm$ sign.

a) $\sqrt{49} =$ _____

b) $\sqrt{81} =$ _____

c) $\sqrt{121} =$ _____

d) $\sqrt{144} =$ _____

10 Write the answer in index notation.

a) $6^9 \times 6^5 =$ _____

b) $4^5 \times 4^3 =$ _____

c) $7^5 \times 7^2 =$ _____

d) $a^5 \div a^4 =$ _____

e) $b^9 \div b^5 =$ _____

f) $n^8 \div n^6 =$ _____

g) $\dfrac{a^6}{a^3} =$ _____

h) $\dfrac{9^9}{9^4} =$ _____

i) $\dfrac{c^8}{c^5} =$ _____

24: Test (2)

1 Use a calculator to work out the answers to these questions. Round your answers each time.

a) $7.4 \div 3.6 =$ _____ (to 1 d.p.)

b) $15 \div 7 =$ _____ (to 3 d.p.)

c) $12 \div 11 =$ _____ (to 2 d.p.)

d) $8 \div 9 =$ _____ (to 1 d.p.)

e) $3.2 \div 2.1 =$ _____ (to 3 d.p.)

f) $51 \div 11 =$ _____ (to 2 d.p.)

2 Round these numbers and make suitable approximations:

a) $(4.9 \div 2.46) \times 10.8 \approx$ _____

b) $(19.57 \div 3.96) + 6.18 \approx$ _____

c) $7.16 + (4.23 \times 8.71) \approx$ _____

d) $\dfrac{\sqrt{(6.11 \times 5.92)}}{0.5} \approx$ _____

3 Answer these questions. Give each fractional answer in its simplest form.

a) $\dfrac{12}{16} \times \dfrac{20}{36} =$ _____

b) $\dfrac{5}{18} \times \dfrac{9}{11} =$ _____

c) $\dfrac{16}{64} \times \dfrac{8}{48} =$ _____

d) $\dfrac{5}{8} \times \dfrac{12}{55} =$ _____

4 Tick which of these are true statements.

a) $\dfrac{8}{9} \div \dfrac{25}{20} = \dfrac{8}{9} \times \dfrac{20}{25}$

b) $\dfrac{5}{36} \div \dfrac{6}{11} = \dfrac{5}{36} \times \dfrac{11}{6}$

c) $\dfrac{35}{72} \div \dfrac{8}{15} = \dfrac{35}{72} \times \dfrac{8}{15}$

d) $\dfrac{3}{12} \div \dfrac{35}{16} = \dfrac{3}{12} \times \dfrac{16}{35}$

5 Answer these questions. Give each fractional answer in its simplest form.

a) $\dfrac{7}{8} \div \dfrac{20}{24} =$ _____

b) $\dfrac{3}{25} \div \dfrac{12}{20} =$ _____

c) $\dfrac{35}{63} \div \dfrac{25}{9} =$ _____

d) $\dfrac{15}{32} \div \dfrac{40}{8} =$ _____

6 Answer these percentage change questions, using a calculator. Round your answers to the nearest penny.

a) In a sale, prices are reduced by 25%. A jumper costs £16.80 in the sale. What was its original price?

_____

b) In the New Year, prices **rise** by 5%. A coat costs £32.04 after the rise. What was its original price?

_____

c) In the New Year, prices **rise** by 18%. A hat costs £21.56 after the rise. What was its original price?

_____

7 This recipe is written in ounces. 7 ounces is about 200 grams. Rewrite the recipe in grams to the nearest whole number:

8 ounces flour	_____ g flour
3 ounces margarine	_____ g margarine
9 ounces sugar	_____ g sugar
4 ounces cocoa	_____ g cocoa

8 Each table shows quantities in direct proportion. Complete each table and then write an equation showing the relationship between the quantities.

a)

Number of magazines (n)	Cost (c)
7	£17.50
9	
15	
24	

_____

b)

Number of spring rolls (n)	Cost (c)
2	£4.30
3	
7	
20	

_____

c)

Number of pasties (n)	Cost (c)
5	£10.50
9	
11	
100	

_____

9 Answer these ratio questions:

a) Three interior angles of a triangle (they have a total of 180°) are in the ratio 4 : 2 : 3. What are their sizes?

_____°   _____°   _____°

b) In a recipe Jack uses 3 parts flour to 2 parts sugar to 5 parts butter. If he makes 640 g of this mix, how much of each ingredient will he need?

flour _____ g   sugar _____ g   butter _____ g

10 A map has a scale of 1 : 50 000. What distances in real life do these lengths on the map represent? Give your answers in km.

a) 4 cm _____   b) 5.5 cm _____   c) 6.2 cm _____

11 A map has a scale of 1 : 50 000. What lengths on the map will represent these distances in real life?

a) 4 km _____   b) 7 km _____   c) 15 km _____

12 Draw your own factor trees and find the prime factor decomposition for each of these numbers. Write each prime factor decomposition using powers.

a) 96 = _____   b) 36 = _____

c) 64 = _____   d) 110 = _____

13 Use your answers to question 13 to answer these questions:

a) Find the highest common factor (HCF) of 96 and 36. _____

b) Find the lowest common multiple (LCM) of 96 and 64. _____

c) Find the highest common factor (HCF) of 110 and 96. _____

25: Calculation strategies (1)

In this unit you will revise:
- the order of precedence (BODMAS)
- using mental methods to evaluate (find the value of) expressions.

> ! In a written test, always show your working as, even if you make a mistake, you can sometimes get marks for your working out.

What you should know

The letters of the word **BODMAS** can help us to remember the order of the operations (sometimes called the order of precedence). Mathematicians have agreed on an order that you must do calculations, otherwise everyone would get different answers, like this:

$4 + 3 \times 5 - 1 =$	If working from left to right, you would get the answer 34.
$4 + 3 \times 5 - 1 =$	If doing the multiplication part first, the answer would be 18.
$4 + 3 \times 5 - 1 =$	If doing the subtraction and addition parts first, the answer would be 28.

To make sure no one gets confused, this is the order that has been agreed:

Do anything in **brackets** first	**Brackets**
Next do **other** things such as squares, roots and powers	**Other**
Then **divide** and **multiply** next	**Divide**
	Multiply
Finally **add** and **subtract**	**Add**
	Subtract

So the correct answer to **$4 + 3 \times 5 - 1$** is **18**, because the multiplying must be done before the adding and subtracting.

Sometimes people use the word **BIDMAS** where the letter I stands for Index or Indices, which are powers.

Get started

When a calculation has a division line, write brackets around what is above and below the line. Work them out before you divide.

Like this: $\dfrac{4 + 8^2}{8 - 2^2} = \dfrac{(4 + 8^2)}{(8 - 2^2)} = \dfrac{(4 + 64)}{(8 - 4)} = \dfrac{68}{4} = 17$

The **O** in **BODMAS** stands for **Other** operations such as using powers and roots.

When a calculation involves indices or roots, remember to work them out before division, multiplication, addition and subtraction.

If y is 5, then the value of $2y^2$ is found by first **squaring** 5 and then multiplying by 2, not the other way around.

$2y^2 = 2 \times 25 = 50.$

1 Work out the correct answers for these questions.

a) $36 \div (3 + 9) - 7 + 3 \times (8 \div 4)^3$ _____

b) $(21 - 17) \div (3 - 1)^2 + 3^2 + 5 \times 4$ _____

c) $\dfrac{\sqrt{144} + 10^2}{(2 \times -2)^2}$ _____

d) $\dfrac{5^2 \times 2}{10 \div \sqrt{4}}$ _____

There is a difference between -4^2 and $(-4)^2$. Brackets are worked out before powers, and powers are worked out before subtraction. This means that -4^2 is found by squaring 4 and then making the answer negative, whereas $(-4)^2$ means that -4 is squared.

$$-4^2 = -16 \qquad\qquad (-4)^2 = -4 \times -4 = 16$$

2 Write the value of each expression.

a) $-3^2 =$ _____

b) $(-3)^2 =$ _____

c) $-10^2 + 2 =$ _____

d) $-5^2 + (-5)^2 =$ _____

e) $-3^2 \times (-2)^2 =$ _____

f) $-6^2 \div (-3)^2 =$ _____

g) $(-6)^2 \div (-3)^2 =$ _____

h) $-8^2 \div (-4)^2 =$ _____

i) $(-8)^2 \div (-4)^2 =$ _____

When two brackets are written side by side, this means that you multiply them.

$$(4 \times 3^2)(11 - 3^2) = (4 \times 9)(11 - 9) = 36 \times 2 = 72$$

$$(\sqrt{16} + 1)^2(7 - \sqrt{25}) = (4 + 1)^2(7 - 5) = 5^2 \times 2 = 25 \times 2 = 50$$

Practice

1 Work out the answers to these questions:

a) $\dfrac{(5 - 3)^2(7 - \sqrt{25})}{(7 - 5)^2} =$ _____

b) $\dfrac{(6 - 1)^2(8 - \sqrt{16})}{(8 + 2)^2} =$ _____

c) $6 + 2 \times (13 - 7)^2 - 5 \times \sqrt{100} =$ _____

d) $(4 + 3)^2 - 4^3 \div 2 + (5 - 4)^3 =$ _____

2 Write the value of each **expression** if $a = 2$.

a) $3a^2 - 9 =$ _____

b) $3(a^2 - 9) =$ _____

c) $(3a)^2 - 9 =$ _____

3 In each pair of **equations, one is correct** and **one is incorrect**.

Find the incorrect answer in each pair and correct it.

If **a is 3** then:

a) $-a^2 + 4 = 13$ $(-a)^2 + 4 = 13$ _____

b) $3(a^2 + 1) = 30$ $3a^2 + 1 = 30$ _____

c) $\sqrt{(16 \times a + 1)} = 7$ $\sqrt{16} \times a + 1 = 7$ _____

d) $-5a^2 - 2 = -47$ $-5(a^2 - 2) = -47$ _____

How did I do?

I know the order of precedence (BODMAS). ☐

I can use mental methods to evaluate (find the value of) expressions. ☐

26: Calculation strategies (2)

In this unit you will revise:

▶ the commutative law for addition and multiplication
▶ the associative law for addition and multiplication
▶ the distributive law for multiplication.

Revision shouldn't just happen when you get close to exams. Students who do well in exams are usually those who have worked hard throughout the year. They know which topics they are good at and those which they need more work on. Do you?

What you should know

These statements are <u>true</u>:

Numbers can be **added** in any order. The answer is the same. ✓
46 + 32 = 78   32 + 46 = 78

Numbers can be **multiplied** in any order. The answer is the same. ✓
9 × 6 = 54   6 × 9 = 54

These statements are <u>false</u>:

Numbers can be **subtracted** in any order. The answer is the same. ✗
16 − 2 = 14   2 − 16 = −14

Numbers can be **divided** in any order. The answer is the same. ✗
10 ÷ 2 = 5   2 ÷ 10 = 0.2

Only addition and multiplication will produce the same answers if the order is reversed. This is known as the **commutative law**.

Get started

These statements are <u>true</u>:

When **adding** more than two numbers, they can be grouped in any way. The answer is the same. ✓

54 + 22 + 15   (54 + 22) + 15 = 76 + 15 = 91   54 + (22 + 15) = 54 + 37 = 91

When **multiplying** more than two numbers, they can be grouped in any way. The answer is the same. ✓

2.5 × 2 × 1.5   (2.5 × 2) × 1.5 = 5 × 1.5 = 7.5   2.5 × (2 × 1.5) = 2.5 × 3 = 7.5

This is not true for subtraction and division. Notice how the answers are different when this division is grouped in different ways:

64 ÷ 4 ÷ 2   (64 ÷ 4) ÷ 2 = 16 ÷ 2 = 8   64 ÷ (4 ÷ 2) = 64 ÷ 2 = 32

Only addition and multiplication will produce the same answers if the numbers are grouped in different ways. This is known as the **associative law**.

1

Use the commutative and/or associative laws to help you answer these questions using mental methods. Group or reorder the numbers whichever way you think is easiest.

a) 16 + 28 + 64 = _____   b) 3.9 + 4.2 + 5.8 = _____

c) 127 + 456 + 73 = _____   d) 5.5 + 3.8 + 2.7 = _____

e) 0.82 + 0.65 + 0.13 = _____   f) 189 + 634 + 286 = _____

g) 4 × 9 × 75 = _____   h) 26 × 8 × 4 = _____

i) 60 × 35 × 2 = _____

This statement is also <u>true</u>:

When **multiplying** you can split either number into parts and multiply each part separately. Then add them to get the answer.

This is known as the **distributive law**.

It doesn't matter which number you choose to split. For the question 24 × 1.3:

the 1.3 could be split into 1 and 0.3

$$24 \times 1.3 = (24 \times 1) + (24 \times 0.3)$$
$$= 24 + 7.2 = 31.2$$

or the 24 could be split into 20 and 4

$$24 \times 1.3 = (20 \times 1.3) + (4 \times 1.3)$$
$$= 26 + 5.2 = 31.2$$

or you can even split both numbers

$$24 \times 1.3 = (20 \times 1) + (20 \times 0.3) + (4 \times 1) + (4 \times 0.3)$$
$$= \quad 20 \quad + \quad 6 \quad + \quad 4 \quad + \quad 1.2$$
$$= 31.2$$

2 Use the distributive law to help you answer these questions:

a) 48 × 1.2 = _____

b) 2.5 × 14 = _____

c) 3.7 × 11 = _____

d) 4.2 × 15 = _____

e) 4.6 × 2.4 = _____

f) 3.8 × 1.6 = _____

Practice

1 Use the commutative and/or associative laws to help you answer these addition questions using mental methods. Group or reorder the numbers whichever way you think is easiest.

a) 3.6 + 34.8 + 5.4 = _____

b) 8.9 + 7.2 + 3.8 = _____

c) 12.9 + 75.6 + 7.1 = _____

d) 0.45 + 0.38 + 0.27 = _____

e) 389 + 187 + 813 = _____

f) 4.24 + 6.36 + 2.89 = _____

2 Use the commutative and/or associative laws to help you answer these multiplication questions using mental methods. Group or reorder the numbers whichever way you think is easiest.

a) 4.5 × 0.8 × 2 = _____

b) 25 × 33 × 8 = _____

c) 7.5 × 4 × 8 = _____

d) 12 × 7.5 × 4 = _____

e) 2.8 × 0.2 × 5 = _____

f) 24 × 4 × 0.5 = _____

g) 11 × 7.5 × 8 = _____

h) 4 × 4.5 × 4.5 = _____

i) 3.5 × 8 × 2 = _____

3 Use the distributive law to help you answer these questions:

a) 5.6 × 12 = _____

b) 32 × 1.5 = _____

c) 0.8 × 1.7 = _____

d) 5.1 × 1.3 = _____

How did I do?

✔

I know and can use the commutative law for addition and multiplication. ☐

I know and can use the associative law for addition and multiplication. ☐

I know and can use the distributive law for multiplication. ☐

27: Calculations and problems

In this unit you will revise:
- how to use written methods of calculation for decimals
- how to solve word problems involving decimals.

> When solving a problem, always circle or underline the key numbers. Before calculating, make an approximation by rounding the numbers. Show your working and always remember to check your final answer.

What you should know

There are many different ways to add, subtract, multiply and divide on paper. Do you use any of these methods?

```
  H T U
    6 6 5
  + 2 3 8
   ,9,0 3
```

```
  H T U
    2 3 4
  ×   2 6
  1 4 0 4    (234 × 6)
  4 6 8 0    (234 × 20)
  6 0 8 4
```

```
      H T U
        7 ³4 ¹3
      – 0 2 8
        7 1 5
```

	200	30	4	
20	4000	600	80	4680
6	1200	180	24	1404
				6084

```
        1 7 3
  4)6 ²9 ¹2
```

```
  4)6 9 2
  – 6 0 0    (4 × 150)
      9 2    (4 ×  23)
    – 9 2
        0        173
```

> Always show all your working when using a written method.

Get started

Adding, subtracting, multiplying and dividing decimals on paper is similar to calculating with whole numbers. When adding and subtracting decimals on paper, always make sure that you line up the decimal points. Then just add or subtract in the normal way:

```
  T U . t
  6 6 . 5
+ 2 3 . 8
 ,9,0 . 3
```

```
  U . t h
  7 . ³4 ¹3
– 0 . 2 8
  7 . 1 5
```

```
  T U . t h
  1 6 . 5
+    2 . 3 8
  1 8 . 8 8
```

1 | Use a written method to answer these questions (use a separate sheet of paper if necessary):

a) 36.3 + 67.9 _____   b) 5.19 + 6.48 _____   c) 0.876 + 3.5 _____

d) 6.594 + 4.069 _____   e) 57.2 – 38.9 _____   f) 18.53 – 5.74 _____

g) 9.374 – 2.98 _____   h) 15.7 – 3.91 _____

When multiplying and dividing decimals on paper, make an approximation first and write it down. Then just multiply or divide the numbers as if they were whole numbers. Finally, put the decimal point into the answer so that the answer is close to your approximation.

2.34 × 2.6 → approximation 2 × 3 = 6

```
    2 3 4
  ×   2 6
  1 4 0 4    (234 × 6)
  4 6 8 0    (234 × 20)
  6 0 8 4  → So the answer must be 6.084
```

49.2 ÷ 4 → approximation 48 ÷ 4 = 12

```
        1 2 3
  4)4 9 ¹2
```
→ So the answer must be **12.3**

❷ Use a written method to answer these questions (use a separate sheet of paper if necessary):

a) 26.4 × 1.6 _____

b) 5.6 × 20.4 _____

c) 2.65 × 3.2 _____

d) 7.34 × 5.1 _____

e) 8.52 ÷ 4 _____

f) 10.35 ÷ 5 _____

g) 18.48 ÷ 3 _____

h) 21.9 ÷ 6 _____

When solving a word problem, always read it carefully and underline or circle any key numbers. Decide which operations you will use. Make an approximation first to get an idea of roughly what the answer might be. Then do the calculation. Remember to check your answer and see if it is close to your approximation.

A sofa is 1.68 m long. A shop wants to display six sofas in a line. How much space will it need?

● Circle any key numbers.

● Decide which operations you will use → 1.68 × 6

● Make an approximation by rounding the numbers → 2 × 6 = 12

● Now do the calculations

```
      1 6 8
  ×         6
   1 0 0 8        → So the answer must be 10.08 m.
```

❸ Follow the steps above to solve these problems (use a separate sheet of paper if necessary):

a) Seven houses are joined as a terrace. Each house is 3.87 m wide. Find the width of the terrace.

_____

b) Four suitcases weigh a total of 78.84 kg. If all the cases weigh the same, how heavy is each of them?

_____

Practice

❶ Use a written method to answer these questions (use a separate sheet of paper if necessary):

a) 53.6 + 48.7 = _____

b) 3.52 + 4.28 = _____

c) 0.848 + 4.7 = _____

d) 6.374 + 5.052 = _____

e) 67.3 − 49.3 = _____

f) 46.33 − 5.74 = _____

g) 7.374 − 1.68 = _____

h) 17.3 − 4.91 = _____

i) 64.6 × 1.2 = _____

j) 7.5 × 18.4 = _____

k) 3.55 × 3.3 = _____

l) 49.3 × 5.1 = _____

m) 16.52 ÷ 4 = _____

n) 25.35 ÷ 5 = _____

o) 24.48 ÷ 3 = _____

p) 27.9 ÷ 6 = _____

❷ Solve these problems:

a) Two planks are laid end to end. One is 5.35 m long and the other is 0.79 m long. What is their total length? _____

b) A length of string is 5.6 m long. A 3.74 m piece is cut from it and taken away. How much string remains? _____

How did I do?

I can add, subtract, multiply and divide decimals on paper. ☐

I can solve word problems involving decimals. ☐

28: Written calculations

When solving a problem, always circle or underline the key numbers. Before calculating, make an approximation by rounding the numbers. Show your working and always remember to check your final answer.

What you should know

Adding, subtracting, multiplying and dividing decimals on paper is similar to calculating with whole numbers. When adding and subtracting decimals using a written method, always make sure that you line up the **decimal points**. Then just add or subtract in the normal way:

```
  T U . t h th            U .  t h             H T U . t h
  6 6 . 5                 8 . ³4 ¹0              1 9 6 . 4
+ 2 3 . 8 5 3           − 0 . 2 8            +     3 2 . 3 8
 ₁9 ₁0 . 3 5 3            8 . 1 2              ₁2 2 8 . 7 8
```

When multiplying and dividing decimals on paper, make an approximation first and write it down. Then just multiply or divide the numbers as if they were whole numbers. Finally, put the decimal point into the answer so that the answer is close to your approximation.

2.34 × 2.6 → approximation 2 × 3 = 6

```
      2 3 4
    ×   2 6
    1 4 0 4        (234 × 6)
    4 6 8 0        (234 × 20)
    6 0 8 4
```

→ So the answer must be **6.084**

49.2 ÷ 4 → approximation 48 ÷ 4 = 12

```
      1 2 3
  4)4 9 ¹2
```

→ So the answer must be **12.3**

Get started

When division questions contain decimals it is often difficult to make approximations. Look at these decimal divisions:

| 665.4 ÷ 0.6 | 632.43 ÷ 0.09 | 0.076 ÷ 0.0025 | 0.4221 ÷ 2.1 |

To make these easier to estimate, make both the numbers in the question 10, 100 or 1000 times larger, as the answer will be the same. Think about how 10 ÷ 1 and 100 ÷ 10 have the same answer, where both numbers in the first question have been made 10 times larger.

665.4 ÷ 0.6	632.43 ÷ 0.09	0.076 ÷ 0.0025	0.4221 ÷ 2.1
6654 ÷ 6	6324.3 ÷ 0.9	0.76 ÷ 0.025	4.221 ÷ 21
	63 243 ÷ 9	7.6 ÷ 0.25	
		76 ÷ 2.5	
about 1100		760 ÷ 25	*about 0.2*
	about 7000	*about 30*	

This only works for division, so don't do this if the question is a multiplication!

1 Change each of the divisions so that the number being divided by is a whole number. Then approximate the answer.

a) 241.6 ÷ 0.4

b) 323.6 ÷ 0.08

c) 0.063 ÷ 0.0015

_____

_____

_____

d) 607.8 ÷ 0.6

e) 426.3 ÷ 0.07

f) 0.429 ÷ 3.9

_____

_____

_____

Once the approximation has been made a written method can be used to find the exact answer. Use the calculation that involves dividing by a whole number (the last one in each list).

665.4 ÷ 0.6   632.43 ÷ 0.09   0.076 ÷ 0.0025   0.4221 ÷ 2.1

6654 ÷ 6   6324.3 ÷ 0.9   0.76 ÷ 0.025   4.221 ÷ 21

63 243 ÷ 9   7.6 ÷ 0.25

about 1100   76 ÷ 2.5   *about 0.2*

about 7000   760 ÷ 25

about 30

```
    1 1 0 9              7 0 2 7                  3 0 . 4              0 . 2 0 1
6 ) 6 6 5 ⁵4        9 ) 6 3 2 ²4 ⁶3      25 ) 7 6 0          21 ) 4 . 2 2 1
                                          7 5 0    (25 × 30)      4 . 2      (21 × 0.2)
                                          1 0 . 0                0 . 0 2 1
                                          1 0 . 0    (25 × 0.4)  0 . 0 2 1    (21 × 0.001)
                                                0                      0
```

Practice

1 Change each division question so that you divide by a whole number. Use a written method of division to answer the new questions. Remember to make an approximation first.

a) 385.2 ÷ 0.4   b) 2975.7 ÷ 0.7   c) 3.77 ÷ 0.13   d) 0.7434 ÷ 4.2

_____   _____   _____   _____

2 Find the exact answers for each of the calculations in question 1 of the Get started section.

a) _____   b) _____   c) _____

d) _____   e) _____   f) _____

How did I do?

I can use written methods to calculate with decimals.   ☐

I can approximate divisions by transforming to division by an integer.   ☐

✔

61

29: Using a calculator

In this unit you will revise:

▶ how to enter numbers into a calculator and interpret the display
▶ how to use the π and sign change, powers, roots and fraction keys and use brackets.

Make sure your pencil case has all the right equipment. You will be much better at using a calculator if you always use your own. Check with your teacher which type of calculator is best to have.

What you should know

There are two types of calculators:

There are simple ones that usually have only numbers and a few extra keys, like ON, +, −, ×, ÷, =, √, M+. These are called **arithmetic calculators** and are useful for simple calculations.

The second type are **algebraic calculators**. They have many more keys and can do several things at once. This is the type of calculator you need for school Maths from year 7 onwards.

When using a calculator to solve a problem, think carefully about the number shown on the display.

Is the question about money?

When a problem is about money in pounds, always write amounts with two digits after the decimal point. The display might show 5.4 but you must write £5.40.

Is it a time question?

When a problem is about time in hours, always remember 0.5 hours is half an hour (30 minutes), 0.25 hours is quarter of an hour (15 minutes) and 0.75 hours is three-quarter of an hour (45 minutes). The display might show 6.25 but this means 6 hours and 15 minutes NOT 6 hours and 25 minutes.

Do I need to round?

When a problem involves dividing, you sometimes need to round the answer up or down. If the question is 'How many £8.68 CDs can you buy with £50?' the display will show 5.760368664. Here you must round down the answer for it to make sense. You can only buy 5 CDs.

Get started

Check your calculator's manual as your calculator may operate in a different way to the one described here.

x^2	To square a number
$\sqrt{}$	To find the **square root** of a number
x^3	To cube a number
$\sqrt[3]{}$	To find the cube root of a number
$\wedge$ or x^y	To raise a number to a power

$(-)$ or $+/-$	To enter a negative number or change the sign
$($ $)$	To enter brackets
Ans	To use your previous answer
M+	To enter a number into the memory
π	To enter the number pi (sometimes you must use the SHIFT key)

1 Answer these questions using the keys on your calculator:

a) $6^3 =$ _____
b) $5^4 =$ _____
c) $8^7 =$ _____
d) $\sqrt{1\,550\,025} =$ _____
e) $\sqrt[3]{32\,768} =$ _____
f) $5^2 \times \pi =$ _____ (to 2 d.p.)
g) $424 - (-55 + 15)^2 =$ _____
h) $\sqrt{324} - (-677 + 125) =$ _____
i) $-54 \times (-67 - -95) =$ ____
j) $-92 \times (-47 + -281) =$ _____
k) $9^4 - (-33 + 24)^2 =$ _____
l) $3^5 - (-45 \times -48) =$ _____

To key a fraction or a mixed number into a calculator, use the $\boxed{a^{b/c}}$ key:

To enter $\frac{7}{8}$ → key 7 $\boxed{a^{b/c}}$ 8   The display shows 7 ⌐ 8

To enter $2\frac{3}{4}$ → key 2 $\boxed{a^{b/c}}$ 3 $\boxed{a^{b/c}}$ 4   The display shows 2 ⌐ 3 ⌐ 4

If you press the = sign after entering the fraction, it will give it in its simplest form:

Enter $\frac{16}{24}$ → key 16 $\boxed{a^{b/c}}$ 24 =   The display shows 2 ⌐ 3

❷ Use a calculator to find each fraction in its simplest form.

a) $\frac{140}{4900}$ _____   b) $\frac{375}{600}$ _____   c) $\frac{960}{2160}$ _____

To **convert a fraction to a decimal**, key in the fraction and press the = key. Then repress $\boxed{a^{b/c}}$.
The display will show the decimal:

Enter $2\frac{3}{4}$ → key 2 $\boxed{a^{b/c}}$ 3 $\boxed{a^{b/c}}$ 4 = $\boxed{a^{b/c}}$ The display shows 2.75

To **convert a decimal to a fraction,** key in the decimal and press the = key. Then repress $\boxed{a^{b/c}}$.
The display will show the fraction:

Enter 2.4 → key 2.4 = $\boxed{a^{b/c}}$ The display shows 2 ⌐ 2 ⌐ 5

❸ Use a calculator to convert these fractions to decimals:

a) $\frac{13}{16}$ _____   b) $\frac{375}{600}$ _____   c) $\frac{17}{32}$ _____

❹ Use a calculator to convert these decimals to fractions or mixed numbers in their simplest form

a) 0.348 _____   b) 9.0625 _____   c) 3.375 _____

Practice

❶ Answer these questions using the keys on your calculator:

a) $13^4 + \sqrt[3]{343}$ = _____

b) $(-37 + 41)^3 \times -\sqrt{25} \times \pi$ = _____ (to 2 d.p.)

c) $\frac{13}{16} + \frac{5}{24}$ = _____

d) $\frac{21}{18} \times \frac{27}{28}$ = _____

e) Write $\frac{4750}{8200}$ in its simplest form _____

f) Write $\frac{1701}{2187}$ in its simplest form _____

g) Write $\frac{11}{16}$ as a decimal _____

h) Write $\frac{972}{2187}$ as a decimal _____

How did I do?

I know how to enter numbers into a calculator and interpret the display.   □

I know how to use the π and sign change, powers, roots and fraction keys and use brackets.   □

✔

30: Simplifying expressions (1)

In this unit you will revise:

▶ how to simplify or transform an expression by collecting like terms
▶ how to collect like terms including those in subtractions.

 Start each revision session by trying to remember what you revised during your last one. If you have forgotten anything, go back and look at the topic again before starting a new topic.

What you should know

In Maths, letters are sometimes used to stand for numbers. It is quicker to write a letter, such as 'n', than to write out the words 'a number'. Here the letter 'n' stands for a number, the value of which is not yet known.

$n - 1$ is a short way of saying that 1 is subtracted from that number.

$n \times 9$ means the number is multiplied by 9.

n stands for a number. $2n$ means 2 lots of the number. $8n$ means 8 lots of the number.

Any letter of the alphabet can be used to stand for a number.

Get started

Simplifying means writing something more simply.

The **expression** $n + n + n$ can be written more simply as $3n$.

and $3n + n + 2n + 2n + n$ can be simplified as $9n$.

When an expression contains more than one letter you must find out how many of each letter there are. Don't mix the letters! Watch out also for whether to add or subtract:

$5a + 6b + 4b - 2a + a - b$ First count the 'a's $5a - 2a + a = 4a$

then count the 'b's $6b + 4b - b = 9b$

$5a + 6b + 4b - 2a + a - b = \mathbf{4a + 9b}$

This is called 'collecting like terms' which means grouping together things that are the same.

1 | **Simplify** these expressions by collecting like terms (the first one has been done for you):

a) $g + 3g + 4h - h = \mathbf{4g + 3h}$

b) $5m - 2m + 2n - n + 3m = $ _____

c) $6x + 5y - 5x - 2y = $ _____

d) $9e + f + f - f - 4e = $ _____

e) $6c + 3d + c - 4c - d = $ _____

f) $7j + 3k - 2j + k - 2k = $ _____

g) $5p + 2q - q - 2p - 3p = $ _____

h) $7s + t + 2s - 5s - 2t = $ _____

i) $4a - 5a + b - 2b + 2a = $ _____

Some expressions use letters to stand for numbers but also include numbers called **constants**.

2a + 7   The 7 here is a constant because it is a known number and it doesn't change.
          This expression means 2 lots of an unknown number and then add 7.

n + 3 + 2   This means 3 and 2 are added to a number, and can be simplified as n + 5.

When simplifying expressions with letters and numbers, first count up how many of each letter there are and then add up the constants. Write them separately and remember to watch out for whether to add or subtract, like this:

6a + 5b + 7 – 2a – 8b – 1   Count the 'a's, then the 'b's and then add the constants.

6a + 5b + 7 – 2a – 8b – 1 = **4a – 3b + 6**

Practice

1 **Simplify** these expressions by collecting like terms:

a) a + 3a + b + c – 2b + 3c + a – 4a = _____

b) 2p + 5q + q + r + 2r – p + p – 3q = _____

c) g + 3g + 3 + h + 4 – 2h – 2 = _____

d) m + 3 + 2m – 6 + 3n + n = _____

e) 4 + 2c + 3d – c – 2 – 3d = _____

f) 5s – 3t + 2 + 4t – 5 – 2s = _____

g) w + w – w + v – 2v + 7v + 2 + 6 – 5 = _____

h) 2x – 5y + y + 7 + 3x + 5x + 2y – 4 + 1 = _____

i) 2a + b + c + 3 + 2b – 3c – c + 4 + 6a – 5b + 2 – a + 2c = _____

2 Add the expressions in two bricks next to each other (the first one has been done for you). Simplify your answer and write it in the brick above. Keep going until you have finished the pyramid.

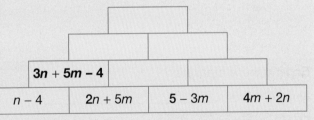

3 Find the perimeter of each shape and simplify the answer as much as possible.

a)
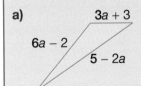
3a + 3
6a – 2
5 – 2a

_____

b)
2e – 10
e – 7   e – 7
25 – e

_____

c)
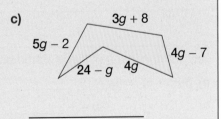
3g + 8
5g – 2
24 – g   4g
4g – 7

_____

How did I do?

I know how to simplify or transform an expression by collecting like terms. ☐

I can collect like terms including those in subtractions. ☐

31: Simplifying expressions (2)

In this unit you will revise:

> ▶ how to simplify an expression by collecting like terms, including brackets
>
> ▶ how to collect like terms including subtraction of brackets.

What you should know

Simplifying means writing something more simply. When simplifying an expression that contains more than one letter you must find out how many of each letter there are. Don't mix the letters! Watch out also for whether to add or subtract:

$5a + 6b + 4b - 2a + a - b$

First count the 'a's $5a - 2a + a = 4a$

then count the 'b's $6b + 4b - b = 9b$

$5a + 6b + 4b - 2a + a - b = \mathbf{4a + 9b}$

This is called **collecting like terms** which means grouping things that are the same together.

Get started

Brackets are often used to group things together. If the expression $(2y - 6)$ is multiplied by 3 it can be written as $(2y - 6) \times 3$ or $3 \times (2y - 6)$ but is more simply written as $3(2y - 6)$.

$3(2y - 6)$ can also be written **without** brackets. Changing an expression with brackets to one without brackets is called **expanding.** Here are two ways of expanding $3(2y - 6)$:

$3(2y - 6) = 3 \times 2y + 3 \times -6 = 6y - 18$

×	2y	−6
3	6y	−18

$3(2y - 6) = 6y - 18$

---

1   **Expand** these brackets:

a) $5(2a - 4) = $ _____

b) $7(2m + 3) = $ _____

c) $6(p + 5) = $ _____

d) $9(3y - 1) = $ _____

e) $11(2 - n) = $ _____

f) $10(7 - 2f) = $ _____

---

2   Say whether each of these statements is true or false:

a) $3(2g - 5) = 6g - 15$ _____

b) $9(r + 4) = 9r + 4$ _____

c) $11(2p + 1) = 22p + 1$ _____

d) $2(4s - 3) = 8s - 6$ _____

e) $2(6 - 5m) = 12 - 10m$ _____

f) $-8(q + 2) = -8q - 16$ _____

To simplify an expression with several brackets, first expand each bracket and then simplify:

Simplify: $3(2a + 5) + 2(a - 1) = 6a + 15 + 2a - 2 = 8a + 13$

It is very important, however, to watch out for when one bracket is subtracted from another, particularly when the second bracket has a subtraction sign in it. These two examples show how you must make sure that both parts of the second bracket are subtracted. Remember that when a negative is subtracted this can be thought of as an addition.

Simplify:

$3(2a + 5) - 2(a + 3) =$

$6a + 15 - (2a + 6) =$

both 2*a* and the 6 must be **subtracted**

$6a + 15 - 2a - 6 = 4a + 9$

$4(b + 4) - 3(b - 5) =$

$4b + 16 - (3b - 15) =$

both 3*b* and the −15 must be **subtracted** so when we have −−15 this makes an add!

$4b + 16 - 3b + 15 = b + 31$

Practice

1 Simplify:

a) $5(y + 3) + 2(4y + 1)$ _____

b) $4(a - 4) + 2(2a + 6)$ _____

c) $6(n + 3) + 2(3 - 2n)$ _____

d) $5(m - 1) + 3(6 - m)$ _____

e) $10(p + 4) - 4(2p + 1)$ _____

f) $6(3e - 1) - 3(5e + 2)$ _____

g) $9(2g + 3) - 4(2 - 3g)$ _____

h) $8(2y - 1) - 3(3y - 2)$ _____

2 Find the perimeter of each shape and simplify the answer as much as possible.

a)

$3(a + 3)$

$6(a - 2)$

$5 - 2a$

b)

$2(e - 5)$

$e - 7$ $e - 7$

$25 - e$

c)

$3(g + 3)$

$3(2g - 1)$ $4(g - 2)$

$4g$

$2(15 - g)$

_____   _____   _____

How did I do?

I know how to simplify an expression by collecting like terms, including brackets. ☐

I can collect like terms, including subtraction of brackets. ☐

32: Simplifying expressions (3)

In this unit you will revise:

▶ how to multiply and expand expressions with brackets

▶ how to transform expressions by taking out single-term common factors.

What you should know

Powers are used to show how many of the same number or letter are **multiplied** together. This is called index notation.

$$n \times n \times n \times n \times n \times n = n^6 \qquad a \times a \times a = a^3 \qquad c \times c \times c \times c \times c = c^5$$

Be careful not to confuse this with **adding** lots of the same number.

Multiplying	Adding
$5 \times 5 \times 5 = \mathbf{125}$	$5 + 5 + 5 = \mathbf{15}$
$2 \times 2 \times 2 = \mathbf{8}$	$2 + 2 + 2 = \mathbf{6}$
$n \times n \times n = \mathbf{n^3}$	$n + n + n = \mathbf{3n}$

Get started

Changing an expression with brackets to one without brackets is called **expanding.** Here are two ways of expanding expressions. Remember that everything inside the bracket must be multiplied by what is outside the bracket.

$$3y(5a - 2b) = 3y \times 5a + 3y \times -2b = 15ay - 6by$$

×	$5a$	$-2b$
$3y$	$15ay$	$-6by$

$$3y(5a - 2b) = 15ay - 6by$$

Notice that sometimes a letter becomes squared.

$$-2a(a - 3b) = -2a \times a + -2a \times -3b = -2a^2 + 6ab$$

×	a	$-3b$
$-2a$	$-2a^2$	$6ab$

$$-2a(a - 3b) = -2a^2 + 6ab$$

1 **Expand** these brackets:

a) $5b(2a - 4c) = $ _____

b) $7k(2p + 3) = $ _____

c) $6p(p + 5q) = $ _____

d) $2y(3y - 1) = $ _____

e) $10n(2 - n) = $ _____

f) $-2xy(x + 3y) = $ _____

g) $-6e(7f - 3e) = $ _____

h) $-4x(5x - 1) = $ _____

The opposite of expanding brackets is called **factorising**. **Factorising** means finding factors that divide into each part of the expression. In these examples you can see that the factors are taken outside the bracket.

Factorise:

$15ay + 6by$ *What are the factors that are common to 15ay and to 6by?*

3 divides into both and y is in both so 3y is taken outside the bracket.

$3y(\ldots + \ldots)$ *What must be inside the bracket that when expanded gives the original expression?*

$3y \times 5a$ is 15ay and $3y \times 2b$ is 6by.

$3y(5a + 2b)$ CHECK by expanding $\rightarrow$ $3y(5a + 2b) = 15ay + 6by$ ✓

2 Factorise these expressions by taking a factor outside a pair of brackets. One has been done for you.

a) $3a + 6 = \mathbf{3(a + 2)}$

b) $4a + 8 = $ _____

c) $5d + 15e = $ _____

d) $9c + 6d = $ _____

e) $2x + 8y = $ _____

f) $10p + 10q = $ _____

g) $4a - 12b = $ _____

h) $x^2 - x = $ _____

i) $10s - 8t = $ _____

j) $15x - 5x^2 = $ _____

k) $6t - 6 = $ _____

l) $8g - 18g^2 = $ _____

Practice

1 **Simplify** these expressions by expanding them first and then simplifying them:

a) $5(a - 4) + 5(2a - 1) = $ _____

b) $6(m - 3) + 2(3 - m) = $ _____

c) $7(p - 5) - 4(3p + 5) = $ _____

d) $8(2y - 1) - 3(2 - 3y) = $ _____

2 **Factorise** these expressions.
The first one has been done for you.

Without brackets	With brackets
$27n + 18$	$9(3n + 2)$
$8k + 20$	
$15g - 3h$	
$4f - 14ef$	
$24 + 3d$	
$15m - 5$	
$15n + 3n^2$	
$6xy + 4xy^2$	

How did I do?

✔

I can multiply and expand expressions with brackets. ☐

I can transform expressions by taking out single-term common factors. ☐

33: Equations (1)

In this unit you will revise:
- the meaning of the word equation
- how to construct and solve simple equations.

What you should know

An **equation** always has an equals sign. What is on one side of the equals sign is worth the same as what is on the other side.

Like: $2a = 6$ or $2y + 3 = 4y - 1$

2a is worth the same as 6   2y + 3 is worth the same as 4y − 1

When there is only one unknown in an equation it is possible to **solve the equation**.

Solving the equation means finding out what number the letter stands for. It is like cracking a code.

Look at each of these equations. Imagine a number is hidden underneath each letter. What number must this be to make each number sentence correct?

$\boxed{a} + 4 = 10$ $\boxed{b} - 2 = 7$ $5 \times \boxed{c} = 15$

a must be 6   *b* must be 9   *c* must be 3

Get started

Look at this puzzle:

I am thinking of a number. I multiply it by eight and add four to it. The answer is 44. What is the number?

This can be written as the equation **$8n + 4 = 44$**. The equation can be solved to find the number, *n*. There are two main ways that an equation can be solved: using ideas of balancing and using inverses. Both ways are shown below:

Both sides of an **equation** are worth the same – they **balance**.

$8n + 4 = 44$

The balancing rules

1 Whatever you do to one side of an equation, do it to the other so that both sides still balance. So you can add, subtract, multiply or divide one side of an equation – but you must do the same to the other side too!

2 Aim to get the **letter** on its own **on one side** and the **numbers** on **the other side**.

3 To get rid of something from one side, do the opposite. If it's an **add** then **subtract**, if it's a **times** then **divide** and vice versa.

$\begin{aligned} 8n + 4 &= 44 \\ -4 \quad &\quad -4 \end{aligned}$ (a) Get rid of the + 4 on the left. (Do the opposite – subtract 4 from both sides)

$\begin{aligned} 8n &= 40 \\ \div 8 \quad &\quad \div 8 \end{aligned}$ (b) 8n means *n* × 8. Get rid of the × 8. (Do the opposite – divide by 8 on both sides)

$n = 5$

1 Try following the balancing rules to solve these equations (use a separate sheet of paper):

a) $2a + 4 = 14$ b) $7y - 2 = 33$ c) $5f - 1 = 19$ d) $3p + 2 = 17$

e) $6d + 9 = 51$ f) $4c - 5 = 27$ g) $5b - 5 = 45$ h) $3e + 8 = 26$

The inverse rules

The idea of this method is to work backwards, using **inverses.** Addition and subtraction are inverses. Multiplication and division are inverses.

1 Think of this equation as a trail of instructions, <u>starting with the letter</u>.

$8n + 4 = 44$

Start with n   →   **multiply it by 8**   →   **then add 4**   →   **to get to 44**

2 Now write this backwards, starting at 44.

to get to n   ←   **divide by 8**   ←   **subtract 4**   ←   **Start with 44**

Notice that the order is reversed and the **inverse** is used for each part.

$(44 - 4) \div 8 = 5$ So $n = 5$

2 Try following the inverse rules to solve these equations (use a separate sheet of paper):

a) $2a + 3 = 19$ b) $3y + 15 = 24$ c) $7f - 12 = 16$ d) $4p + 2 = 14$

e) $3d + 5 = 35$ f) $4c - 4 = 28$ g) $5b - 5 = 35$ h) $6e + 8 = 32$

Do you prefer the method of balancing or the inverse method? It doesn't matter which way you use as long as you can get to the right answer every time!

Practice

1 Write an equation for each puzzle and solve it, using whichever method you prefer:

a) I am thinking of a number. I multiply it by two and add seven to it. The answer is 19.
   What is the number?

   _____

b) I am thinking of a number. I multiply it by five and add ten to it. The answer is 25.
   What is the number?

   _____

c) I am thinking of a number. I multiply it by three and subtract five from it. The answer is 16.
   What is the number?

   _____

d) I am thinking of a number. I multiply it by four and subtract eight from it. The answer is 20.
   What is the number?

   _____

How did I do?

✔

I know what an equation is. ☐

I can write an equation. ☐

I can solve a simple equation. ☐

34: Equations (2)

Don't leave revision to just before a test or exam. Students who do well have usually worked hard throughout the year.

In this unit you will revise:

▶ how to solve simple equations with and without brackets
▶ how to solve simple equations with negative signs and answers.

What you should know

An **equation** always has an equals sign. What is on one side of the equals sign is worth the same as what is on the other side.

For example: $2a + 4 = 6$ or $2y + 3 = 4y - 1$

2a + 4 is worth the same as 6   2y + 3 is worth the same as 4y – 1

Solving an equation means finding out what number a letter stands for. It is like cracking a code.

Get started

The equation **4 − 4n = 12 + n** can be solved to find the number, n.

Here is one way of solving it.

The balancing rules

Both sides of an **equation** are worth the same – they **balance.**

1 Whatever you do to one side of an equation, do it to the other so that both sides still balance. So you can add, subtract, multiply or divide one side of an equation – but you must do the same to the other side too!

2 Aim to get the **letter** on its own **on one side** and the **numbers** on **the other side.**

3 To get rid of something from one side, do the opposite. If it's an **add** then **subtract**, if it's a **times** then **divide** and vice versa.

$4 - 4n = 12 + n$
$\quad + 4n \qquad + 4n$
(a) Get rid of the −4n on the left (Do the opposite – add 4n to both sides)

$\quad 4 = 12 + 5n$
$\quad -12 \qquad -12$
(b) Get rid of the 12 on the right (Do the opposite – subtract 12 from both sides)

$\quad -8 = 5n$
$\quad \div 5 \quad \div 5$
(c) 5n means n × 5. Get rid of the ×5 (Do the opposite – divide by 5 on both sides)

$\quad -1.6 = n$

1

Solve these equations. You may use a calculator.

a) $m - 14 = -32$ _____

b) $-2y - 2 = 33$ _____

c) $42 - 4f = 19$ _____

d) $29 + r = 5 - 3r$ _____

e) $5p - 1 = -19 + p$ _____

f) $12 - 7q = 16 + q$ _____

g) $28 + n = 8 - 3n$ _____

h) $4e - 8 = -11 - 2e$ _____

i) $-1 = 8p + 8$ _____

An equation with **brackets** can be solved by first expanding the brackets and then finding the value of the letter.

$$2(g + 4) = 24$$
$$2g + 8 = 24$$
$$2g = 16$$
$$g = 8$$

❷

Solve each of these equations:

a) $4(h - 1) = -6$ _____

b) $5(k + 3) = -8$ _____

c) $8(c - 4) = -16$ _____

d) $-12 = 5(5 - g)$ _____

e) $-9 = 4(6 - 2x)$ _____

f) $-7 = 4(4 - p)$ _____

Practice

❶

You may use a calculator to help you solve these equations. Round answers to 3 d.p. if necessary.

a) $4y + 12 = -4$

b) $10 = 12 - 4f$

c) $2 = 5 - 4g$

d) $60 + 3b = 5 - 5b$

e) $-6 + 4y = 8y - 2$

f) $-13 - 2e = -4e - 8$

g) $3(m - 2) = 41$

h) $53 = 8(n + 4)$

i) $6(3p - 7) = 55$

j) $2(h - 3) = -6 + h$

k) $4(6 - j) = 12 - j$

l) $5(2k - 1) = 38 + k$

❷

Use a calculator to help you solve these puzzles. The area of each rectangle is shown in the centre of the rectangle and all lengths are in centimetres. Find the value of the unknown letter each time.

a) $4 - 5n$

8 | Area = 75 cm²

b) $4m - 9$

5 | Area = 95 cm²

c) $9 - 4p$

5 | Area = 21 cm²

d) $7 - 2q$

4 | Area = 62 cm²

_____ _____ _____ _____

How did I do?

I can solve simple equations with and without brackets. ☐

I can solve simple equations with negative signs and answers. ☐

35: Formulae and substituting (1)

In this unit you will revise:

 ▶ what 'substituting' means

 ▶ how to substitute numbers into an expression or formula.

! When using letters in Maths, be careful to write them clearly. It is easy to confuse the letter b with the number 6, z for 2 and s for 5 unless your handwriting is clear.

What you should know

To **substitute** means to exchange (or replace) one thing for another. In sport, players are substituted. In Maths, numbers are substituted for letters.

The expression $3y + 6$ means '*3 lots of a number and add 6*'. Remember that $3y$ means $3 \times y$.

You can substitute any number for the letter y: $3y + 6$

If **y is 5** then find '*3 lots of 5 and add 6*' $3 \times 5 + 6 = 15 + 6 = 21$

If **y is 8** then find '*3 lots of 8 and add 6*' $3 \times 8 + 6 = 24 + 6 = 30$

Get started

A **formula** is a way of writing a mathematical rule that helps you to find answers quickly. Here is a formula you may already know, written in words and using letters:

Area of a rectangle = length × width $A = l \times w$

Area is the amount of surface that a 2-D shape covers. This formula is useful because you can find the area of any rectangle quickly by **substituting** its length and width into the formula.

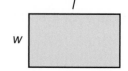

Any length and width can be substituted: $A = l \times w$

If **l is 4 cm** and **w is 3 cm**

$A = 4 \times 3 = 12$

This means the area is 12 cm².

If **l is 10 cm** and **w is 7 cm**

$A = 10 \times 7 = 70$

This means the area is 70 cm².

1 Find the area of each rectangle, **substituting** the given lengths and widths:

a) If **l is 8 cm** and **w is 5 cm**

$A = l \times w$

$A = $ _____ cm²

b) If **l is 9 cm** and **w is 6 cm**

$A = l \times w$

$A = $ _____ cm²

c) If **l is 8 cm** and **w is 7 cm**

$A = l \times w$

$A = $ _____ cm²

This formula can help you to find the perimeter (P) of a rectangle: $P = 2(l + w)$

Perimeter is the distance around the edge of a shape.

Remember to do the part in brackets first, so add the length and width and then double the answer.

Any length and width can be substituted: $P = 2(l + w)$

If **l is 4 cm** and **w is 3 cm**

$P = 2(4 + 3) = 2 \times 7 = 14$

This perimeter is 14 cm.

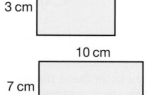

2 Find the perimeter of each rectangle, **substituting** the given lengths and widths:

a) If *l* is **8 cm** and *w* is **5 cm**

$P = 2(l + w)$

$P =$ _____ cm

b) If *l* is **9 cm** and *w* is **6 cm**

$P = 2(l + w)$

$P =$ _____ cm

c) If *l* is **8 cm** and *w* is **10 cm**

$P = 2(l + w)$

$P =$ _____ cm

Practice

1 **Substitute** to find the value of each expression:

a) If $y = 2$, find the value of $7y$.

$7y =$ _____

b) If $m = 5$, find the value of $8m$.

$8m =$ _____

c) If $k = 11$, find the value of $8k + 1$.

$8k + 1 =$ _____

d) If $x = 7$, find the value of $9x + 5$.

$9x + 5 =$ _____

e) If $g = 3$, find the value of $5g + 4$.

$5g + 4 =$ _____

f) If $q = 4$, find the value of $10q - 2$.

$10q - 2 =$ _____

2 What is the value of the expression $4y - 2$, when y equals 8? _____

3 You may use a calculator for this question.

This formula shows the relationship between:

speed, *s*, in miles per hour   distance, *d*, in miles   and time, *t*, in hours

$$s = d \div t$$

a) Use the formula to find the speed of a train that travels 240 miles in 3 hours.

$s =$ _____ miles per hour

b) Use the formula to find the speed of a train that travels 485 miles in 5 hours.

$s =$ _____ miles per hour

How did I do?

I know what 'substituting' means.

I can substitute numbers into an expression or formula.

✔

In this unit you will revise:

▶ that algebraic operations follow the same order as arithmetic operations

▶ how to substitute integers into expressions involving small powers

▶ how to substitute integers into simple formulae and to find unknown values.

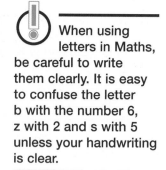 When using letters in Maths, be careful to write them clearly. It is easy to confuse the letter b with the number 6, z with 2 and s with 5 unless your handwriting is clear.

What you should know

To **substitute** means to exchange (or replace) one thing for another. In sport, players are substituted. In Maths, numbers are substituted for letters.

Get started

It is important to know that the order of doing calculations (**BODMAS** – see page 24) also applies to substitution. The **O** in **BODMAS** stands for **Other** operations such as using powers and roots. When an expression involves squares, cubes or roots, remember to work them out before division, multiplication, addition and subtraction.

If y is 5, then the value of $2y^2$ is found by first squaring 5 and then multiplying by 2, not the other way around.

$2y^2 = 2 \times 25 = 50$

The following expression has brackets, squaring, multiplication (by 2) and addition: $2(y - 1)^2 + 6$

If y is 5, then the value of the expression is found by working out the part in brackets first, then doing the squaring, then the multiplication and finally the addition.

$y = 5$ $\qquad 2(y - 1)^2 + 6 =$

$\qquad\qquad 2(5 - 1)^2 + 6 =$

$\qquad\qquad\quad 2(4)^2 + 6 =$

$\qquad\qquad\quad 2 \times 16 + 6 =$

$\qquad\qquad\qquad 32 + 6 = 38$

1 Find the value of each expression, if **y = 2**.

a) $2(y + 3)^2 - 10$

b) $10 - 2y^2$

c) $(y - 1)^3$

d) $(2y \times 2)^2 + 36$

e) $4y^2 \times (6 - 2)$

f) $5y^3 + 3 \times 2$

g) $10 + 5y^2$

h) $(3 + y^2) \times 2$

i) $1 + \dfrac{y^2}{4}$

Some expressions or formulae have more than one letter to substitute, like this: $2(1 + b^3) + 2a^2$

If $a = 3$ and $b = 2$ the value of the expression is:

$2(1 + 2^3) + 2 \times 3^2 =$

$2(1 + 8) + 2 \times 9 =$

$2 \times 9 + 2 \times 9 = 18 + 18 = \mathbf{36}$

The following formula shows a relationship between the number of faces, F, edges, E, and vertices, V, of polyhedrons (3-D shapes with straight sides):

$E = F + V - 2$

By substituting the number of faces and vertices, the number of edges can be found.

❷ Use the formula $E = F + V - 2$ to find the number of edges of each shape.

a) Cuboid: $F = 6$ and $V = 8$,

  $E =$ _____

b) Triangular prism: $F = 5$ and $V = 6$,

  $E =$ _____

c) Square pyramid: $F = 5$ and $V = 5$,

  $E =$ _____

d) Hexagonal prism: $F = 8$ and $V = 12$,

  $E =$ _____

e) Tetrahedron: $F = 4$ and $V = 4$,

  $E =$ _____

f) Pentagonal pyramid: $F = 6$ and $V = 6$,

  $E =$ _____

Practice

❶ This grid shows different expressions which use the letters a and b. Substitute the following values of a and b into each expression.

Write the value of each expression in the corresponding sections of the grids below.

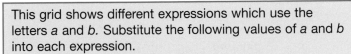

$2b^3 + 3$	$3(a^2 + b^3)$	$1 - a^2$
$a^2 + 3b^3 + 5$	$2(1 - b^3 - a^2)$	$3a^2 - 3$
$a^2 - 4$	$a^2 + 2$	$b^3 + 6$

a) Let $a = 3$ and $b = 2$

19		

b) Let $a = 4$ and $b = 1$

c) Let $a = 5$ and $b = 3$

❷ The formula for the **surface area**, S, of a cuboid with length, l, breadth, b, and height, h, is:

$S = 2bl + 2lh + 2hb$

Find the surface area for a cuboid with these dimensions:

a) $l = 6\,cm$, $b = 5\,cm$, $h = 10\,cm$ _____

b) $l = 7\,cm$, $b = 2\,cm$, $h = 5\,cm$ _____

c) $l = 5\,cm$, $b = 3\,cm$, $h = 7\,cm$ _____

d) $l = 9\,cm$, $b = 6\,cm$, $h = 14\,cm$ _____

How did I do?

I know that algebraic operations follow the same order as arithmetic operations.

I can substitute integers into expressions involving small powers.

I can substitute integers into simple formulae and find unknown values.

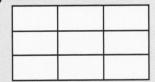

37: Formulae and substituting (3)

In this unit you will revise:
- using formulae from Mathematics and other subjects
- substituting numbers into expressions and formulae.

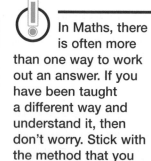

In Maths, there is often more than one way to work out an answer. If you have been taught a different way and understand it, then don't worry. Stick with the method that you understand – but make sure that you get the right answers every time and that your method doesn't take too long.

What you should know

To **substitute** means to exchange (or replace) one thing for another. In sport, players are substituted. In Maths, numbers are substituted for letters.

The expression $3y^2 + 6$ means '3 lots of a number squared and add 6'. Remember that $3y^2$ means $3 \times y^2$. The value of $3y^2$ is found by first squaring y and then multiplying by 3, not the other way around.

You can substitute any number for the letter y: $3y^2 + 6$

If **y is 5** then find '3 lots of 5^2 and add 6' $3 \times 25 + 6 = 75 + 6 = 81$

Get started

Temperature can be measured in degrees Celsius (°C) or in degrees Fahrenheit (°F). This formula shows the relationship between the two sets of units, where C stands for degrees Celsius and F for degrees Fahrenheit.

$$F = \frac{9}{5}C + 32$$

Substitute $C = 25$ to find 25 °C in Fahrenheit $F = \frac{9}{5}(25) + 32 = 45 + 32 = 77\ °F$

1

Use the formula $F = \frac{9}{5}C + 32$ to convert these temperatures from degrees Celsius to degrees Fahrenheit.

Give your answers to the nearest degree.

a) 5 °C = _____ °F	b) 15 °C = _____ °F	c) 20 °C = _____ °F
d) 32 °C = _____ °F	e) –10 °C = _____ °F	f) –30 °C = _____ °F
g) 17 °C = _____ °F	h) 23 °C = _____ °F	i) –28 °C = _____ °F
j) 37 °C = _____ °F	k) –22 °C = _____ °F	l) –24 °C = _____ °F

The formula above can be rewritten to make C the subject of the formula.

$$C = \frac{5}{9}(F - 32)$$

2

Use this formula to convert temperatures from degrees Fahrenheit to degrees Celsius, giving your answers to the nearest degree.

a) 50 °F = _____ °C	b) 95 °F = _____ °C	c) 104 °F = _____ °C
d) 23 °F = _____ °C	e) 5 °F = _____ °C	f) –13 °F = _____ °C
g) 32 °F = _____ °C	h) 47 °F = _____ °C	i) 53 °F = _____ °C
j) 75 °F = _____ °C	k) –20 °F = _____ °C	l) –24 °F = _____ °C

Here are some formulae used in Maths and in Science:

$P = 2(l + w)$ P = perimeter of a rectangle, l = length, w = width

$A = \pi r^2$ A = area of a circle, π = pi = 3.14 and r = radius

$S = \dfrac{D}{T}$ S = average speed, D = distance, T = time

$F = ma$ F = force, m = mass, a = acceleration

$V = l^3$ V = **volume** of a cube, l = length of a side

$c = \sqrt{(a^2 + b^2)}$ c = hypotenuse of a right-angled triangle, a and b are the shorter two sides

$S = 2bl + 2lh + 2hb$ S = **surface area** of a cuboid, l = length, b = breadth, h = height

When substituting, remember to use the order of BODMAS (see page 22), which reminds you to do the part in brackets first, then use any powers, then multiplication and division before finally adding and subtracting.

Find the area, A, for a circle with a radius of 5 cm $\boldsymbol{A = \pi r^2}$ $A = 3.14 \times 5^2 = 3.14 \times 25 = 78.5 \text{ cm}^2$

Practice

1 Substitute into the formulae above to find the missing values.

a) Find the area, A, for a circle with a radius of 4 cm. $A =$ _____ cm²

b) Find the volume, V, of a cube with sides of length 5 cm. $V =$ _____ cm³

c) Find the perimeter, P, of a rectangle of length 8 cm and width 5 cm. $P =$ _____ cm

d) Find the force, F, for a mass, m, of 9 kg, and acceleration, a, of 8 m s⁻². $F =$ _____ N

e) Find the average speed, S, of an object travelling 15 km in 3 hours. $S =$ _____ km h⁻¹

f) Find the hypotenuse, c, of a right-angled triangle with shorter lengths, a and b, of 3 cm and 4 cm. $c =$ _____ cm

g) Find the surface area, S, of a cuboid of length 3 cm, breadth 5 cm and height 2 cm. $S =$ _____ cm²

2 This grid shows different expressions which use the letters a and b. Substitute the following values of a and b into each expression. Write the value of each expression in the corresponding section.

Let $a = 3$ and $b = 2$

$5b^3 + 3a$	$3(a^2 + b^3)$	$\dfrac{10 - b^2}{a}$
$a^2 + 3b^3 - 5$	$2(1 + b^3 - a^2)$	$4a^2 - 3b$
$\dfrac{a^2 - 4}{b - 1}$	$\dfrac{a^2 + 3}{b^2}$	$\dfrac{a^3}{b^3 + 5b}$

How did I do?

✔

I can use formulae from Mathematics and other subjects. ☐

I can substitute numbers into expressions and formulae. ☐

38: Trial and improvement

In this unit you will revise:
- using a calculator to estimate square roots and cube roots
- using systematic trial and improvement methods.

What you should know

Squaring a number means multiplying it by itself. Any number can be squared, including decimals like these:

$4.75^2 = 4.75 \times 4.75 = 22.5625$ $2.9^2 = 2.9 \times 2.9 = 8.41$

Square numbers are numbers made by squaring whole numbers.
These are square numbers: 1, 4, 9, 16, 25, 36, 49, 64, 81, 100, ...

Finding the **square root** ($\sqrt{\ }$) is the opposite of squaring. You are finding what number has been multiplied by itself to get the given number, like this:

$\sqrt{22.5625} = 4.75$ $\sqrt{8.41} = 2.9$

Cubing a number means multiplying three of that number together. Any number can be cubed, including decimals like these:

$4.75^3 = 4.75 \times 4.75 \times 4.75 = 107.171\,875$ $2.9^3 = 2.9 \times 2.9 \times 2.9 = 24.389$

Cubic numbers are numbers made by cubing whole numbers. These are cubic numbers: 1, 8, 27, 64, 125, ...

Finding the **cube root** ($\sqrt[3]{\ }$) is the opposite of cubing. You are finding what number has been cubed to get the given number, like this:

$\sqrt[3]{107.171\,875} = 4.75$ $\sqrt[3]{24.389} = 2.9$

Get started

When finding the square root of a number that isn't a square number, always make an estimate as to which whole numbers it lies between.

$\sqrt{22} \rightarrow$ 22 lies between the square numbers 16 (which is 4×4) and 25 (which is 5×5) so the answer must lie between 4 and 5.

1 Which two whole numbers must each square root lie between? Do not use a calculator.

a) $a = \sqrt{75}$ a must lie between _____ and _____

b) $b = \sqrt{55}$ b must lie between _____ and _____

c) $c = \sqrt{86}$ c must lie between _____ and _____

d) $d^2 = 42$ d must lie between _____ and _____

When finding the cube root of a number that isn't a cubic number, make an estimate as to which whole numbers it lies between, in a similar way.

$\sqrt[3]{107} \rightarrow$ 107 lies between the cubic numbers 64 (which is 4^3) and 125 (which is 5^3) so the answer must lie between 4 and 5.

2 Which two whole numbers must each cube root lie between? Do not use a calculator.

a) $a = \sqrt[3]{22}$ a must lie between _____ and _____

b) $b = \sqrt[3]{35}$ b must lie between _____ and _____

c) $c = \sqrt[3]{7}$ c must lie between _____ and _____

d) $d^3 = 50$ d must lie between _____ and _____

Once you have made an estimate, you can begin to use **trial and improvement** methods to get closer to the actual answer.

Estimate the value of x to 2 decimal places $x^3 = 50$

x must lie between 3 and 4, so start with 3.5. Use a calculator to cube 3.5. The answer is too small, so choose a larger number such as 3.7 and continue on the next line of the table.

$x^3 = 50$

x	x^3	too large/small?	
3.5	42.875	too small	→ choose a number larger than 3.5 such as 3.7
3.7	50.653	too large	→ choose a number smaller than 3.7 but larger than 3.5
3.6	46.656	too small	→ choose a number larger than 3.6 but smaller than 3.7
3.65	48.627 125	too small	→ choose a number larger than 3.65 but smaller than 3.7
3.68	49.836 032	too small	→ choose a number larger than 3.68 but smaller than 3.7
3.69	50.243 409	too large	→ choose a number smaller than 3.69 but larger than 3.68
3.685	50.039 44...	too large	→ This tells you that it is closer to 3.68 than 3.69

You can draw a number line to help you choose values:

Practice

1 Estimate the value of x to 2 decimal places. Use as many of the rows of the table as you need.

$x^3 = 12$

x	x^3	too large/small?

x	x^3	too large/small?

2 Estimate the value of x to 2 decimal places. Use as many of the rows of the table as you need.

$x^3 + x = 80$

x	x^3	$x^3 + x$	too large/small?
4	64	68	too small
5	125	130	too large

x	x^3	$x^3 + x$	too large/small?

How did I do?

✔

I can use a calculator to estimate roots.   ☐

I can use methods of trial and improvement.   ☐

39: Functions (1)

Don't leave revision to just before a test or exam. Students who do well have usually worked hard throughout the year.

In this unit you will revise:
- how to express simple functions in words and using symbols
- how to represent simple functions in mappings.

What you should know

Function machines can be used to turn one number into another. A function machine is shown below. The table to the right shows numbers put into the machine (INPUT) and the numbers that come out (OUTPUT).

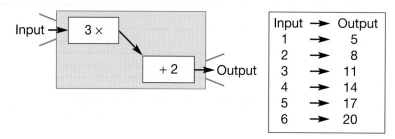

Input	Output
1	→ 5
2	→ 8
3	→ 11
4	→ 14
5	→ 17
6	→ 20

You should be able to input any small number and find the output number.

Get started

Functions can be described in words or using symbols.

The function above can be described in words as '*Multiply by three and then add two*'.

To describe it using symbols, imagine you were putting the letter x into the machine. What would come out?

x turns into '3 lots of x add 2'

This is written as: $x \rightarrow 3x + 2$

1. Write these functions using symbols. One has been done for you.

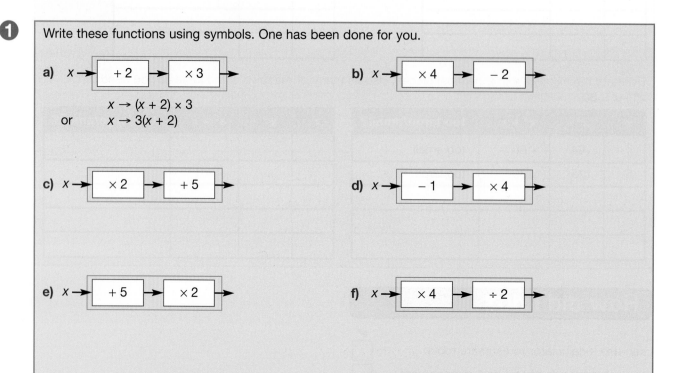

a) $x \rightarrow \boxed{+2} \rightarrow \boxed{\times 3} \rightarrow$

        $x \rightarrow (x + 2) \times 3$
or $x \rightarrow 3(x + 2)$

b) $x \rightarrow \boxed{\times 4} \rightarrow \boxed{-2} \rightarrow$

c) $x \rightarrow \boxed{\times 2} \rightarrow \boxed{+5} \rightarrow$

d) $x \rightarrow \boxed{-1} \rightarrow \boxed{\times 4} \rightarrow$

e) $x \rightarrow \boxed{+5} \rightarrow \boxed{\times 2} \rightarrow$

f) $x \rightarrow \boxed{\times 4} \rightarrow \boxed{\div 2} \rightarrow$

Functions can also be shown on **mapping diagrams**. Two lines make up a mapping diagram, one for the input number and the other for the output number. Arrows are used to join each input with its related output number, like this:

$x \rightarrow 3x - 2$

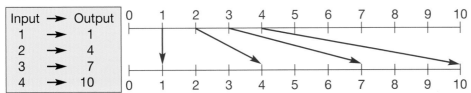

2 Complete this input/output list for the function $x \rightarrow 3x$ and complete the mapping diagram using the inputs and outputs in your list.

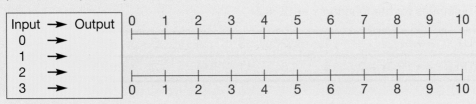

Practice

1 Write an input/output list and complete a mapping diagram for each of these functions:

a) $x \rightarrow x + 5$

b) $x \rightarrow 2x + 2$

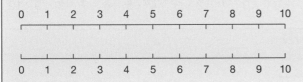 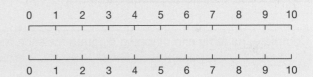

c) $x \rightarrow 2x - 1$

d) $x \rightarrow x + 3$

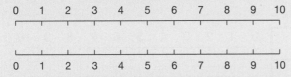 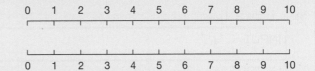

2 Tick the functions above that produce mapping diagrams with **parallel** arrows.

3 Tick which of the functions below you think will produce mapping diagrams with **parallel** arrows.

$x \rightarrow x - 5$ $x \rightarrow 4x$ $x \rightarrow x + 4$ $x \rightarrow 5x$ $x \rightarrow 6x + 1$

How did I do?

I know how to express simple functions in words and using symbols. ☐

I can represent simple functions in mappings. ☐

40: Functions (2)

In this unit you will revise:

- how simple functions can be expressed using symbols
- how to represent functions in mapping diagrams
- how to recognise inverse functions.

In an exam, try to give yourself time to go back and check answers. You can lose valuable marks with a careless mistake. Make sure your answers are clear and readable.

What you should know

A **function** turns one number into another. Functions can be described in words, such as *'Multiply by three and then add two',* or using the symbols: $x \rightarrow 3x + 2$

This table shows some outcomes for the function $x \rightarrow 3x + 2$

INPUT	x	1	2	3	4	5	6
OUTPUT	$x \rightarrow 3x + 2$	5	8	11	14	17	20

Get started

Functions can be shown on **mapping diagrams**. Two lines make up a mapping diagram, one for the input number and the other for the output number. Arrows are used to join each input with its related output number, like this: $x \rightarrow 3x - 2$

INPUT	1	2	3	4
OUTPUT	1	4	7	10

1 Complete the table and mapping diagram for each function.

a) $x \rightarrow 2x - 1$

INPUT	x	
OUTPUT	$x \rightarrow 2x - 1$	

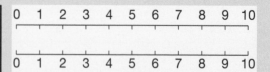

b) $x \rightarrow 3(x - 1)$

INPUT	x	
OUTPUT	$x \rightarrow 3(x - 1)$	

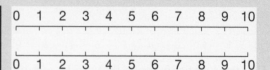

c) $x \rightarrow 10 - x$

INPUT	x	
OUTPUT	$x \rightarrow 10 - x$	

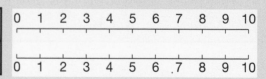

d) $x \rightarrow 10 - 2x$

INPUT	x	
OUTPUT	$x \rightarrow 10 - 2x$	

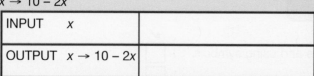
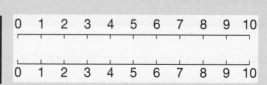

This mapping diagram shows two functions performed one after another. The first function is $x \rightarrow 2x - 1$ and the second is $x \rightarrow \dfrac{x + 1}{2}$.

The outputs of the first function are used as the inputs of the second function.

$x \rightarrow 2x - 1$

$x \rightarrow \dfrac{x + 1}{2}$

Notice that the final outputs of the second function are the same as the original inputs of the first function.

Because of this, it is said that $x \rightarrow \dfrac{x + 1}{2}$ is the **inverse function** of $x \rightarrow 2x - 1$.

An inverse function takes the final outputs back to the original inputs.

Here are pairs of inverse functions: $x \rightarrow 3x - 1$ and $x \rightarrow \dfrac{x + 1}{3}$

$x \rightarrow 2x + 4$ and $x \rightarrow \dfrac{x - 4}{2}$

$x \rightarrow 2(x + 4)$ and $x \rightarrow \frac{1}{2}x - 4$

$x \rightarrow 4(x - 2)$ and $x \rightarrow \frac{1}{4}x + 2$

Practice

1 Complete a two-tiered mapping diagram for each pair of functions.

a) Show the function $x \rightarrow 3x - 2$ followed by the function $x \rightarrow \dfrac{x + 2}{3}$ below.

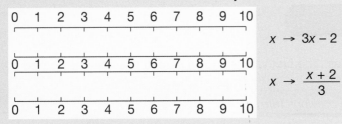

$x \rightarrow 3x - 2$

$x \rightarrow \dfrac{x + 2}{3}$

Are these inverses?

Yes ☐   No ☐

b) Show the function $x \rightarrow 10 - x$ followed by the function $x \rightarrow 10 - x$ below.

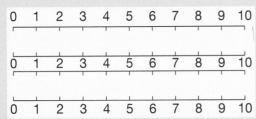

$x \rightarrow 10 - x$

$x \rightarrow 10 - x$

Are these inverses?

Yes ☐   No ☐

c) A function that has an inverse that is the same as itself is called a 'self-inverse' function.

Is the function $x \rightarrow 10 - x$ a self-inverse function?   Yes ☐   No ☐

How did I do?

✔

I know how simple functions can be expressed using symbols.   ☐

I can represent functions in mapping diagrams.   ☐

I can recognise inverse functions.   ☐

41: Sequences (1)

In this unit you will revise:

▶ how to describe simple sequences

▶ how to generate the terms of a simple sequence given a rule.

What you should know

Numbers arranged in a special order are called **sequences**.

Each number in a sequence is called a **term**. It is important to be able to say which term in a sequence you are talking about.

1, 4, 9, 16, 25, 36, ...

The third term in this sequence is 9.

The fifth term in this sequence is 25.

I think the tenth term in this sequence will be 100.

Sequences can be ascending or descending. **Ascending** sequences are those where the **terms** in the sequence get larger. **Descending** sequences are those where the **terms** in the sequence get smaller.

Sequences can increase (go up) or decrease (go down) by the same sized steps, like these:

1, 3, 5, 7, 9, 11, ...   8, 6, 4, 2, 0, –2, –4, ...

Or they can increase or decrease by different sized steps, like these:

1, 4, 9, 16, 25, 36, ...   32, 16, 8, 4, 2, 1, ...

Get started

There are two ways of describing sequences. The first way is shown here. It is sometimes called the '**term-to-term**' rule.

Explain how each term is different from the previous term:

3, 7, 11, 15, 19, 23, ... The first term is 3. Each term increases by 4.

1, 10, 100, 1000, 10 000, ... The first term is 1. Each term is multiplied by 10.

1 Write the first **eight** terms of these sequences:

a) The first term is 7. Each term increases by 2. _____

b) The first term is 84. Each term decreases by 5. _____

c) The first term is 1. Each term is multiplied by 2. _____

d) The first term is 512. Each term is divided by 2. _____

2 Describe each sequence. State the first term and say how each term increases or decreases.

a) 4, 7, 10, 13, 16, 19, ... The first term is _____. Each term _____ by _____.

b) 7, 12, 17, 22, 27, 32, ... The first term is _____. Each term _____ by _____.

c) 100, 75, 50, 25, 0, –25, ... The first term is _____. Each term _____ by _____.

d) 8, 6, 4, 2, 0, –2, –4, –6, ... The first term is _____. Each term _____ by _____.

The second way to describe sequences is to explain how you can work out each term from where it is in the sequence, its position. This is sometimes called the '**position-to-term**' rule. Write position numbers, starting at 1, above the sequence.

position number:	**1** **2** **3** **4** **5** **6**	Multiply the position number by 4 and subtract 1.		

terms of sequence: 3, 7, 11, 15, 19, 23, ...

1st term	**2nd term**	**3rd term**	**4th term**	**5th term**
1 × 4 − 1 = 3	**2** × 4 − 1 = 7	**3** × 4 − 1 = 11	**4** × 4 − 1 = 15	**5** × 4 − 1 = 19 ...

❸ Write the first **five** terms of these sequences:

a) Multiply the position number by 2 and add 3.

position number:	<u>1</u>	<u>2</u>	<u>3</u>	<u>4</u>	<u>5</u>	
terms of sequence:	_____	_____	_____	_____	_____	...

b) Multiply the position number by 5 and subtract 4.

position number:	<u>1</u>	<u>2</u>	<u>3</u>	<u>4</u>	<u>5</u>	
terms of sequence:	_____	_____	_____	_____	_____	...

c) Multiply the position number by 2 and subtract the answer from 10.

position number:	<u>1</u>	<u>2</u>	<u>3</u>	<u>4</u>	<u>5</u>	
terms of sequence:	_____	_____	_____	_____	_____	...

Practice

❶ Generate (write) the first **six** terms of these sequences:

a) The first term is 7. Each term increases by 11. _____

b) The first term is 100. Each term decreases by 15. _____

c) The first term is 4. Each term doubles. _____

d) The first term is 0. Each term decreases by 2 _____

❷ Count how many squares each shape is made from to create a sequence.

a) _____   _____   _____   _____   _____

b) Write the term-to-term rule for this sequence.

The first term is _____ . Each term _____ by _____ .

c) Which of these rules is the position-to-term rule for the sequence? Tick the correct rule.

Multiply the position number by 5 and subtract 1. Multiply the position number by 4.

Multiply the position number by 8 and subtract 4. Multiply the position number by 3.

How did I do?

I know how to describe simple sequences. ☐

I can generate the terms of a sequence given a rule. ☐

42: Sequences (2)

In this unit you will revise:
- describing sequences using term-to-term and position-to-term rules
- how to find the *n*th term of a simple sequence.

> When making your own revision notes, use different colours to show different things.

What you should know

Each number in a **sequence** is called a **term.**

1, 4, 9, 16, 25, 36, ... The **third term** in this sequence is **9**.

The **fifth term** in this sequence is **25**.

Sequences can be described in two ways; using the **term-to-term** or the **position-to-term** rule.

The **term-to-term** rule describes the first term and explains how each term is different from the previous term. *3, 7, 11, 15, 19, 23, ... The first term is 3. Each term increases by 4.*

The **position-to-term** rule explains how you can work out each term from where it is in the sequence, its position. It is the more useful way of describing sequences as you can use it to predict other numbers in the sequence.

position number (*n*): **1 2 3 4 5 6** *Multiply the position number by 4 and subtract 1*
terms of sequence: 3, 7, 11, 15, 19, 23, ... *or more simply* nth term = $4n - 1$

Each term can be generated from the **position-to-term** rule:

1st term $1 \times 4 - 1 = 3$ **2nd term** $2 \times 4 - 1 = 7$ **3rd term** $3 \times 4 - 1 = 11$ and so on

We can use the **position-to-term** rule to predict other numbers in the sequence, like this:

10th term $10 \times 4 - 1 = 39$ → the 10th number in the sequence will be 39.

Get started

Working out the **position-to-term** rule of a sequence is also sometimes called **finding the *n*th term.**

Find the rule for the nth term of this sequence: *7, 9, 11, 13, 15, 17, ...*

1 Find the difference between adjacent (next-door) numbers in the sequence:

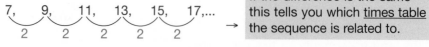

terms of sequence: 7, 9, 11, 13, 15, 17,...
difference   2   2   2   2   2

→ If the difference is the same this tells you which <u>times table</u> the sequence is related to.

2 Write out the related <u>times table</u> under the sequence.

3 Then compare each number in the times table with the related number in the sequence.

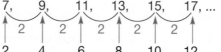

terms of sequence: 7, 9, 11, 13, 15, 17, ...
difference   2   2   2   2   2
2 times table = 2*n* 2, 4, 6, 8, 10, 12, ...

→ Notice that each number is 5 more than 2*n*.

4 Write the rule in symbols, with the times tables number showing the number of *n* (such as 2*n* for the 2 times table). nth term = $2n + 5$

5 Check by substituting the number 1 into the rule, then the number 2 and so on. It should make the sequence   1st term = $(2 \times 1) + 5 = 7$ 2nd term = $(2 \times 2) + 5 = 9$ ✓

1 Find the rule for the *n*th term for each sequence.

a) terms of sequence: 4, 7, 10, 13, 16, 19...

*n*th term = _____

b) terms of sequence: 4, 9, 14, 19, 24, 29...

*n*th term = _____

c) terms of sequence: 1, 5, 9, 13, 17, 21...

*n*th term = _____

d) terms of sequence: 7, 12, 17, 22, 27, 32...

*n*th term = _____

Practice

1 Count the total number of squares in each shape and create a sequence. Then find the rule for the *n*th term of the sequence. One has been started for you.

a)

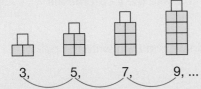

3,   5,   7,   9, ...

*n*th term = _____

b)

*n*th term = _____

c)

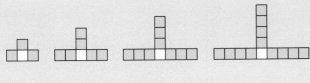

*n*th term = _____

d)

*n*th term = _____

How did I do?

I can describe sequences using term-to-term and position-to-term rules.

I can find the *n*th term of a simple sequence.

✔

43: Straight line graphs (1)

In this unit you will revise:
- how to use a rule to generate co-ordinate pairs
- how to plot straight line graphs.

 When making your own revision notes, use different colours to show different things. Write some notes about straight line graphs. You could use one colour each time you write an *x* co-ordinate and a different colour for the *y* co-ordinate.

What you should know

Co-ordinates are written as pairs of numbers inside brackets, like (**3**, **2**). The first number tells you how many across from zero to move and the second number tells you how many up or down to move.

The first number is called the ***x* co-ordinate** and the second number is called the ***y* co-ordinate**, (***x***, ***y***).

It is useful to remember the phrase 'Along the corridor and up or down the stairs' to remind you to move across first.

Get started

Sets of co-ordinates can be generated by following a rule, written in words or using letters:

Rule in words   '*Multiply the x co-ordinate by 2 and add 1 to make the y co-ordinate*'

Rule using letters $2x + 1 = y$

Choose a value to be the *x* co-ordinate, work out the related *y* co-ordinate and then write the pair of co-ordinates in brackets:

For the rule: $\underline{2x + 1 = y}$

If **x = 2** → $2 \times 2 + 1 = 5$ So *y* = 5   (**2, 5**)

If **x = 3** → $2 \times 3 + 1 = 7$ So *y* = 7   (**3, 7**)

If **x = 5** → $2 \times 5 + 1 = 11$ So *y* = 11   (**5, 11**)

If **x = 8** → $2 \times 8 + 1 = 17$ So *y* = 17   (**8, 17**)

When the co-ordinates made using this rule are plotted on a graph you will see that they form a straight line. The pairs of co-ordinates of **every** point that lies on this straight line can be generated using the same rule, $2x + 1 = y$. The rule is called the **equation** of the straight line or its **linear equation**.

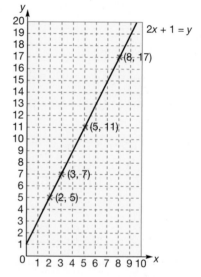

1

Generate pairs of sequences for this rule: '*Multiply the x co-ordinate by 3 and subtract 2 to make the y co-ordinate*'.

$$\underline{3x - 2 = y}$$

a) If **x = 5** → $3 \times 5 - 2 =$ _____   So *y* = ____   (____ , ____)

b) If **x = 1** → $3 \times 1 - 2 =$ _____   So *y* = ____   (____ , ____)

c) If **x = 4** → $3 \times 4 - 2 =$ _____   So *y* = ____   (____ , ____)

d) If **x = 2** → $3 \times 2 - 2 =$ _____   So *y* = ____   (____ , ____)

❷ Now plot the co-ordinates on the graph below and join them with a line. Label the line with the equation $3x - 2 = y$.

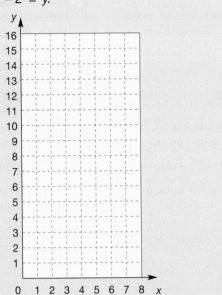

To use less space, co-ordinates can be written into a table like this:

$x + 4 = y$

x	1	2	3	4	5
y	5	6	7	8	9

These produce the pairs of co-ordinates (1, 5), (2, 6), (3, 7), (4, 8) and (5, 9).

Practice

❶

a) Fill in the missing y co-ordinates in the table for the rule $2x - 3 = y$ and write the set of co-ordinates produced.

$2x - 3 = y$

x	2	3	4	5	6
y	1				

(   ) (   ) (   ) (   ) (   )

b) Plot the pairs of co-ordinates on this graph and label the line correctly.

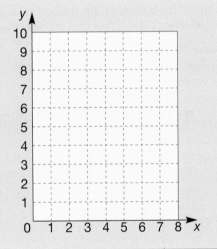

❷ Jamie writes some co-ordinate pairs using the rule $5x - 1 = y$.

These are the pairs of co-ordinates he wrote.

(1, 4)   (3, 14)   (10, 51)   (5, 24)   (2, 6)   (6, 29)

Circle the two that are incorrect.

How did I do?

I can use a rule to generate pairs of co-ordinates. ☐

I can plot straight line graphs. ☐

✔

44: Straight line graphs (2)

In this unit you will revise:
- how straight lines can be described using an equation
- how to recognise straight line graphs parallel to the *x* axis or *y* axis.

When making your own revision notes, use different colours to show different things. Write some notes to help you remember the equations of vertical and horizontal lines.

What you should know

Co-ordinates are written as pairs of numbers inside brackets, like (**3**, **2**). The first number tells you how many across from zero to move and the second number tells you how many up or down to move.

The first number is called the **x co-ordinate** and the second number is called the **y co-ordinate**, (*x*, *y*).

It is useful to remember the phrase 'Along the corridor and up or down the stairs' to remind you to move across first.

Get started

Look carefully at the co-ordinates in this list:

(3, 4) (−2, 4) (5, 4) (0, 4) (−5, 4) (4, 4) (−3, 4) (−4, 4)

What do they have in common?

Notice that each pair of co-ordinates has 4 as its *y* co-ordinate.

When these co-ordinates are plotted on a grid a **horizontal** line is produced. We describe this line using the equation **y = 4**. Notice that the line passes through the *y* axis at 4.

All horizontal lines on a grid are called
'*y* = a number'. To find what the number is, see where the line crosses the *y* axis.

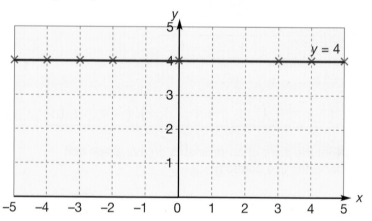

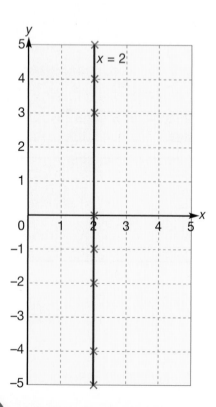

What do the co-ordinates in this list have in common?

(2, −5) (2, 4) (2, −2) (2, 0) (2, −1) (2, 5) (2, −4) (2, 3)

Notice that each pair of co-ordinates has 2 as its *x* co-ordinate.

When these co-ordinates are plotted on a grid a **vertical** line is produced. We describe this line using the equation **x = 2**. Notice that the line passes through the *x* axis at 2.

All vertical lines on a grid are called '*x* = a number'. To find what the number is, see where the line crosses the *x* axis.

1 Write the equation of each of these lines. One has been done for you.

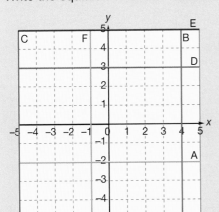

Line A $y = -2$

Line B _____

Line C _____

Line D _____

Line E _____

Line F _____

It is easy to make mistakes when describing the *x* or *y* axis itself!

These are some of the co-ordinates that lie along the **x axis**: (1, 0) (4, 0) (–3, 0) (5, 0) (–2, 0)

Notice that it is the *y* co-ordinates that are always zero, so the **x axis** is the line **y = 0**.

These are some of the co-ordinates that lie along the **y axis**: (0, 4) (0, –2) (0, 1) (0, –3) (0, 5)

Notice that it is the *x* co-ordinates that are always zero, so the **y axis** is the line **x = 0**.

Practice

1 Draw and label each of these lines on the grid:

Line A $x = -1$

Line B $y = 0$

Line C $y = -5$

Line D $y = 4$

Line E $x = 3$

Line F $x = 0$

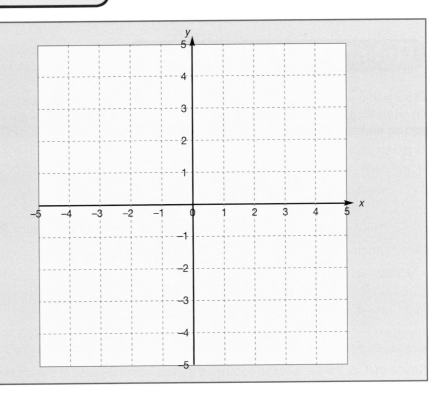

How did I do?

I can describe vertical and horizontal lines using an equation. ☐

I can recognise straight line graphs parallel to the *x* axis or *y* axis. ☐

45: Straight line graphs (3)

In this unit you will revise:

▶ how to rearrange functions into the form $y = mx + c$

▶ how to find the gradient and intercept of lines of linear functions.

What you should know

Functions can be drawn as lines on a co-ordinate grid. Linear functions are those that produce straight lines. All **horizontal** lines on a grid are called '**y = a number**'. To find what the number is, see where the line crosses the y axis.

All **vertical** lines on a grid are called '**x = a number**'. To find what the number is, see where the line crosses the **x axis**.

All **diagonal** lines on a grid have functions that include x and y. The functions can be arranged into the form '**y = mx + c**', where m and c are numbers.

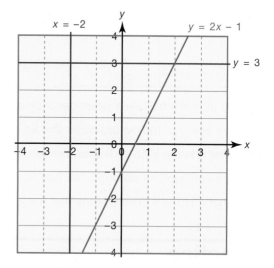

Get started

In the same way that you can change equations when you try to solve them (see the balancing method on page 28) the function of a line can be rearranged. The function $y - 2x + 1 = 0$ can be rearranged by adding and subtracting the same thing from both sides:

$$y - 2x + 1 = 0$$
$$ + 2x + 2x$$

$$y + 1 = 2x$$
$$-1 -1$$

$$y = 2x - 1 \quad \rightarrow \quad y - 2x + 1 = 0 \text{ is the same function as } y = 2x - 1$$

Here is another example:

$$y + 3x - 4 = 0$$
$$ - 3x - 3x$$

$$y - 4 = -3x$$
$$+4 +4$$

$$y = -3x + 4 \quad \rightarrow \quad y + 3x - 4 = 0 \text{ is the same function as } y = -3x + 4$$

Notice that as the term of the sequence moves from one side of the equals sign to the other its sign changes, so what is $+3x$ on one side is $-3x$ on the other. What is -4 on one side is $+4$ on the other.

❶

Rearrange these functions to the form $y = mx + c$ where m and c are numbers.

a) $y - 4x - 6 = 0$ $y = $ _____   **b)** $y + 2x - 7 = 0$ $y = $ _____

c) $y + 9x + 5 = 0$ $y = $ _____   **d)** $y - x + 5 = 0$ $y = $ _____

e) $y - 5x - 1 = 0$ $y = $ _____   **f)** $y + x - 2 = 0$ $y = $ _____

All straight lines on a co-ordinate grid are vertical, horizontal or diagonal. The diagonal lines have functions in the form **y** = m**x** + c where m and c are numbers.

● The gradient of the straight line on the graph (how steep it is) is the value of m.

● The point where the line crosses the y axis (the intercept) is the value of c.

$y = 2x + 1$ → m is 2 and c is 1

$y = -2x - 2$ → m is −2 and c is −2

$y = x - 3$ → m is 1 and c is −3

$y = 3x$ → m is 3 and c is 0

The line $y = 3x + 4$ has a gradient of 3 and its intercept with the y axis is at the y co-ordinate 4.

A positive gradient means that the line slopes up to the right. A negative gradient means that it slopes up to the left. When two lines have the same gradient they are **parallel** to each other.

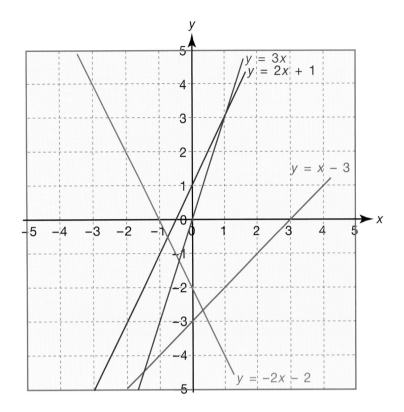

2 State the gradient and the y co-ordinate of the intercept of the line for each of these functions:

a) $y = -4x + 1$

gradient = _____ intercept = _____

b) $y = 3x - 7$

gradient = _____ intercept = _____

c) $y = 7x$

gradient = _____ intercept = _____

d) $y = x + 5$

gradient = _____ intercept = _____

Practice

1 Rearrange each of these functions into the form $y = mx + c$ and state its gradient and intercept:

a) $y - 3x + 4 = 0$ y = _____

gradient = _____ intercept = _____

b) $y - x - 2 = 0$ y = _____

gradient = _____ intercept = _____

c) $y + 6x - 5 = 0$ y = _____

gradient = _____ intercept = _____

d) $y + x = 0$ y = _____

gradient = _____ intercept = _____

How did I do?

I can rearrange functions into the form $y = mx + c$.

I can find the gradient and intercept of lines of linear functions.

46: Distance–time graphs

In this unit you will revise:

▶ how to interpret distance–time graphs

▶ how to calculate the speed from a distance–time graph

▶ how to construct a simple distance–time graph.

What you should know

A **distance–time** graph has time marked on the horizontal axis and distance up the vertical axis. It shows information about how something has travelled. When looking at a distance–time graph always take care to read the numbers on the axes.

On a distance–time graph, as time always moves forward, the line always starts on the left and moves across towards the right. It can go up or down or stay level, but the line moves across to the right.

Get started

When interpreting distance–time graphs:

● read the numbers on the axes carefully

● look for horizontal sections of the line – these show periods when the object stopped travelling

● look at the steepness of each section of the line – the steeper the line, the faster the object is travelling

● look for sections where the line is going down to the right (negative gradient) – this means that the object is moving back towards its starting point, such as returning home.

1 Each graph shows a different journey made by a man. Tell the story of each journey in as much detail as you can (either write a short description on a separate sheet of paper or describe the journeys verbally to an adult).

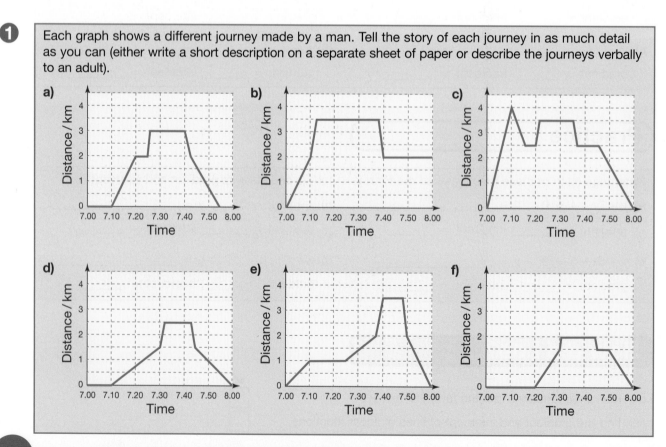

Use the following formula to work out the average speed for sections of a journey shown on a distance–time graph.

$$\text{Average speed} = \frac{\text{distance travelled}}{\text{time taken}}$$

For the first section, the average speed is found by dividing 20 miles by 60 minutes (1 hour). It is best to use the time in hours so that the speed is given in miles per hour (m.p.h.).

Average speed = 20 ÷ 1 = 20 m.p.h.

For the last section, the average speed is found by dividing 20 miles by 15 minutes ($\frac{1}{4}$ hour).

Average speed = $20 \div \frac{1}{4}$ = 80 m.p.h.

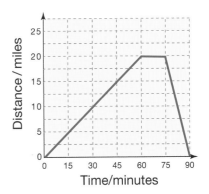

Practice

1 On this grid, plot a distance–time graph for this man's journey.

I drove from my home to Scarborough (30 km) in 30 minutes. I spent 15 minutes at a friend's house. I drove back – it took 45 minutes to get home.

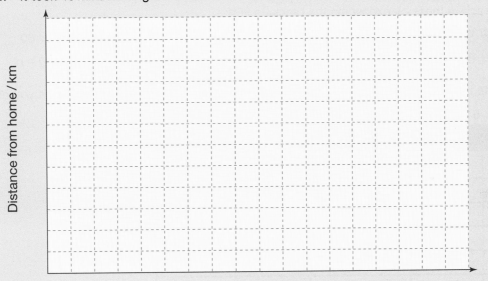

Time/minutes

2 Approximately how far from home was the man:

a) 10 minutes after leaving home? _____ km   **b)** 1$\frac{1}{4}$ hours after leaving home? _____ km

3 (Give two answers to each). After approximately how many minutes was he:

a) 20 km from home? _____ _____   **b)** 15 km from home? _____ _____

c) 25 km from home? _____ _____   **d)** 5 km from home? _____ _____

4 Find the average speed for both parts of his journey. _____ km h⁻¹   _____ km h⁻¹

How did I do?

I can interpret and construct distance–time graphs.   ☐

I can calculate the speed from a distance–time graph.   ☐

1 Write the value of each expression.

a) $-4^2 + (-4)^2 =$ _____

b) $-2^2 \times (-3)^2 =$ _____

c) $-8^2 \div (-4)^2 =$ _____

d) $(-6)^2 \div (-3)^2 =$ _____

e) $-5^2 \div (-5)^2 =$ _____

f) $(-8)^2 \div (-4)^2 =$ _____

g) $\dfrac{(8-3)^2(7-\sqrt{36})}{\sqrt{(9-5)}} =$ _____

h) $\dfrac{(5-2)^2(8-\sqrt{25})}{(1+2)^2} =$ _____

i) $8 + 3 \times (10-7)^2 - 5 \times \sqrt{49} =$ _____

j) $(6+3)^2 - 4^3 \div 2 + (5-4)^3 =$ _____

2 Write the value of each expression if $b = 2$.

a) $4b^2 - 16 =$ _____

b) $4(b^2 - 16) =$ _____

c) $(4b)^2 - 16 =$ _____

3 Use a written method to answer these questions. Remember to make an approximation first.

a) $2408 \div 4$ _____

b) $29\,757 \div 7$ _____

c) $784 \div 14$ _____

d) $21.16 \div 23$ _____

4 Simplify:

a) $4(y + 2) + 2(5y + 1)$ _____

b) $3(a - 5) + 4(3a + 6)$ _____

c) $8(n + 2) + 5(3 - 2n)$ _____

d) $7(m - 2) + 3(5 - m)$ _____

5 Solve each of these by expanding the brackets first:

a) $8(h - 1) = 34$ _____

b) $4(k + 3) = -6$ _____

c) $5(c - 2) = 60$ _____

d) $-7 = 8(g + 7)$ _____

e) $-25 = 5(17 - x)$ _____

f) $34 = 2(42 - p)$ _____

6 Estimate the value of x to 2 decimal places. Use as many of the rows of the table as you need.

$x^3 - x = 51.5$

x	x³	x³ – x	too large/small?
3	27	24	too small
4	64	60	too large

7 This grid shows different expressions which use the letters a and b. Substitute the following values of a and b into each expression. Write the value of each expression in the corresponding section.

Let $a = 3$ and $b = 2$

$3b^3 + 3a$	$4(a^2 + b^3)$	$\dfrac{5 + b^2}{a}$
$a^3 + 3b^2 - 4$	$3(1 - b^3 - a^2)$	$3a^2 - 4b$
$\dfrac{a^2 - 3}{b - 1}$	$\dfrac{a^3 + 1}{b^2}$	$\dfrac{a^2}{b^2 + 3b}$

8 Find the rule for the *n*th term for each sequence.

   a) terms of sequence: 5, 8, 11, 14, 17, 20, ...

                                                 *n*th term = _____

   b) terms of sequence: 4, 10, 16, 22, 28, 34, ...

                                                 *n*th term = _____

9 Rearrange each of these functions into the form $y = mx + c$ and state its gradient and intercept.

   a) $y - 2x + 7 = 0$ _____   **b)** $y + x - 3 = 0$ _____

       gradient = _____ intercept = _____   gradient = _____ intercept = _____

   c) $y - 6x - 2 = 0$ _____   **d)** $y - x = 0$ _____

       gradient = _____ intercept = _____   gradient = _____ intercept = _____

10 On this grid, plot a distance–time graph for this girl's journey.

I walked from my home to Whitby (1 km) in 10 minutes. I spent 20 minutes in a shop. I walked another kilometre further away from my home which took 10 minutes and was then driven back home. This took 5 minutes.

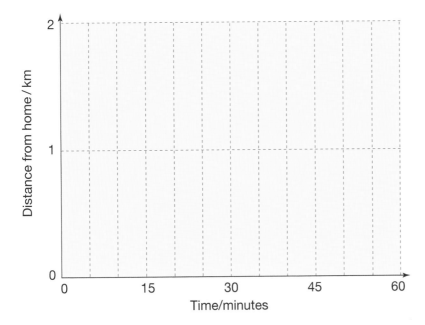

11 Approximately how far from home was the girl:

   a) 7.5 minutes after leaving home? _____ km

   b) 25 minutes after leaving home? _____ km

12 (Give two answers to each). After approximately how many minutes was she:

   a) $1\frac{1}{2}$ km from home? _____ _____

   b) $\frac{1}{2}$ km from home? _____ _____

1 Use the commutative and/or associative laws to help you answer these addition questions using mental methods. Group or reorder the numbers whichever way you think is easiest.

a) $7.6 + 23.8 + 2.4 =$ _____

b) $7.9 + 6.2 + 3.1 =$ _____

c) $1.9 + 23.2 + 7.8 =$ _____

d) $0.32 + 0.38 + 0.17 =$ _____

e) $459 + 184 + 316 =$ _____

f) $6.24 + 7.36 + 2.32 =$ _____

2 Use the commutative and/or associative laws to help you answer these multiplication questions using mental methods. Group or reorder the numbers whichever way you think is easiest.

a) $3.5 \times 0.6 \times 2 =$ _____

b) $25 \times 26 \times 8 =$ _____

c) $7.5 \times 2 \times 8 =$ _____

d) $4 \times 7.5 \times 8 =$ _____

e) $3.8 \times 0.2 \times 5 =$ _____

f) $18 \times 4 \times 0.5 =$ _____

g) $11 \times 7.5 \times 4 =$ _____

h) $4 \times 4.5 \times 3.5 =$ _____

i) $3.5 \times 8 \times 2 =$ _____

3 Use the distributive law to help you answer these questions:

a) 7.2×12 _____   b) 32×1.2 _____

c) 0.6×1.7 _____   d) 3.7×1.3 _____

4 Change each division question so that you divide by a whole number. Use a written method of division to answer the new questions. Remember to make an approximation first.

a) $136.2 \div 0.4$ b) $840.4 \div 0.4$

c) $8.32 \div 0.32$ d) $20.16 \div 3.6$

5 Answer these questions using the keys on your calculator:

a) $9^4 + \sqrt[3]{343} =$ _____

b) $(-42 + 12)^3 \times -\sqrt{25} \times \pi =$ _____ (to 2 d.p.)

c) $\frac{9}{16} + \frac{3}{24} =$ _____   d) $\frac{25}{18} \times \frac{23}{28} =$ _____

e) Write $\frac{3650}{5200}$ in its simplest form _____

f) Write $\frac{504}{952}$ in its simplest form _____

g) Write $\frac{5}{8}$ as a decimal _____   h) Write $\frac{127}{200}$ as a decimal _____

6 **Expand** these brackets:

a) $3b(4a - 2c) =$ _____   b) $5k(2m + 6) =$ _____

c) $5p(p + 6q) =$ _____   d) $6y(2y - 1) =$ _____

7 **Simplify** these expressions by expanding them first and then simplifying them:

a) $4(a - 4) + 4(2a - 1) = $ _____

b) $3(m - 3) + 5(3 - m) = $ _____

c) $8(p - 5) - 5(3p + 5) = $ _____

d) $6(2y - 1) - 2(2 - 3y) = $ _____

8 **Factorise** these expressions:

Without brackets	With brackets		Without brackets	With brackets
$27n + 18$	$9(3n + 2)$		$18 + 3d$	
$10k + 15$			$15m - 10$	
$12g - 3h$			$3n + 3n^2$	
$6f - 18ef$			$8xy + 4xy^2$	

9 Use a calculator to help you solve these equations:

a) $6y + 12 = 30$

b) $0 = 18 - 6f$

c) $2 = 5 - 2g$

d) $15 + 3b = 8 - 5b$

e) $-12 + 4y = 3y - 2$

f) $-21 - 2e = -7e - 3$

g) $6(m - 2) = 65$

h) $46 = 4(n + 4)$

i) $5(8p - 7) = 44$

j) $6(h - 3) = -8 + h$

k) $4(7 - j) = 18 - j$

l) $5(4k - 1) = 22 + 2k$

10 Complete a two-tiered mapping diagram to show the function $x \rightarrow 2x + 1$ followed by the function $x \rightarrow \dfrac{x - 1}{2}$.

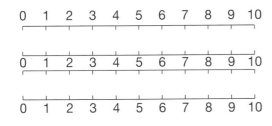

$x \rightarrow 2x + 1$

$x \rightarrow \dfrac{x - 1}{2}$

Are these inverses?

Yes ☐   No ☐

49: Measurement (1)

In this unit you will revise:

▶ the names and abbreviations of units of measurement

▶ reading and interpreting scales on a range of measuring instruments.

> **When** measuring, it is very important that you take care and make as accurate a reading as you can. Don't just say 'It is about 3 cm'. Find out whether it is 2.9 cm or 3.1 cm.

What you should know

When you are measuring, it is important to know:

● what <u>instruments</u> can be used to measure things

● what <u>units</u> are used and their abbreviations (the shorthand used to write them, such as **mm** for millimetres).

You will need to know these:

Measurement	Units	Instruments
Length including height, width, depth, perimeter, distance	millimetres **mm** centimetres **cm** metres **m** kilometres **km**	ruler, tape measure, trundle wheel, metre stick ...
Time	seconds, minutes, hours, days, weeks, years, decades, centuries, millenniums	watch, clock, timer, stopwatch ...
Capacity	millilitres **ml** centilitres **cl** litres **l**	measuring jugs, cylinders
Mass (Weight)	grams **g** kilograms **kg**	balance, kitchen and bathroom scales
Area	square centimetres **cm²** square metres **m²**	squares, grids, ruler, metre stick
Volume	cubic centimetres **cm³** cubic metres **m³**	cubes, ruler, metre stick
Angle	degrees °	protractor/angle measurer
Temperature	degrees Celsius **°C**	thermometer

Get started

When reading scales on measuring instruments look carefully at the adjacent numbers on the scale (the numbers next to each other) and follow these steps:

● **Step 1**: Choose two adjacent numbers on the scale and find the difference between them.

● **Step 2**: Count how many small intervals (spaces) there are between these numbers. Note it is the <u>intervals</u> you must count, <u>not</u> the number of marks on the scale.

● **Step 3**: Work out, by dividing, how much each of these intervals is worth.

● **Step 4**: Now use your answer to work out the marked value.

What number is the arrow pointing to?

600   700   ↓   800

- **Step 1:** 700 and 800. Difference = 100
- **Step 2:** 5 intervals (spaces) between 700 and 800
- **Step 3:** 100 ÷ 5 = 20
- **Step 4:** Each interval is worth 20, so the arrow is pointing to **740** (700 + 20 + 20).

1 What number is the arrow pointing to? _____ 1000   ↓   2000

2 What number is the arrow pointing to? _____ 250   ↓ 300   350

Practice

1 What number is the arrow pointing to on each scale? Remember to write the unit each time.

a) _____ 240 g   ↓   250 g

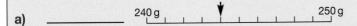

b) _____

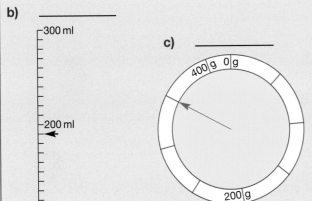

c) _____

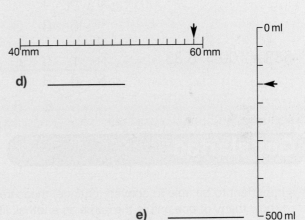

d) _____

40 mm   ↓ 60 mm

e) _____

2 The largest number on some kitchen scales has fallen off.

The potatoes in the scales weigh 450 grams.

Which of these boxes shows the number that has fallen off?

Tick that box.

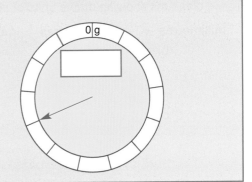

| 453 g | 480 g | 500 g |
| 600 g | 800 g | 1000 g |

How did I do?

I know the names and abbreviations of units of measurement.   ✔ ☐

I can read and interpret scales.   ☐

50: Measurement (2)

In this unit you will revise:
- ▶ the relationships between units of measurement
- ▶ how to convert one metric unit to another.

What you should know

When multiplying numbers by 10, 100 or 1000 move each digit one, two or three places to the **left**:

529 × 10 = 5290

Th	H	T	U
	5	2	9
5	2	9	0

0.85 × 100 = 85

H	T	U . t	h
		0 . 8	5
	8	5 .	

Dividing is the opposite of multiplying, so, when dividing by 10, 100 and 1000, move each digit to the **right**. Sometimes this means the answer will be a decimal.

683 ÷ 10 = 68.3

H	T	U . t
6	8	3 .
	6	8 . 3

683 ÷ 100 = 6.83

H	T	U . t	h
6	8	3 .	
		6 . 8	3

Get started

It is important to be able to convert (change) measurements from one unit to another. To do this you must know how many of one unit is the same as another, like 100 cm = 1 m or 1000 g = 1 kg.

These diagrams showing metric units of length can help you:

millimetres ⟷ centimetres	centimetres ⟷ metres	metres ⟷ kilometres
10 mm = 1 cm	100 cm = 1 m	1000 m = 1 km
× 10	× 100	× 1000

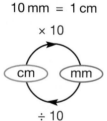
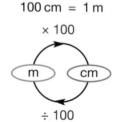

÷ 10	÷ 100	÷ 1000

27 cm → 27 × 10 = 270 mm

1

Convert these measurements to the units shown.

a) 48 cm = _____ mm

b) 137 cm = _____ m

c) 54 mm = _____ cm

d) 125 mm = _____ cm

e) 1400 m = _____ km

f) 1760 m = _____ km

g) 5362 m = _____ km

h) 467 m = _____ km

i) 0.62 m = _____ cm

These diagrams show metric units of mass and capacity:

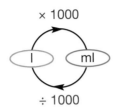

grams ←——→ kilograms	millilitres ←——→ litres
1000 g = 1 kg	1000 ml = 1 l
× 1000	× 1000
kg g	l ml
÷ 1000	÷ 1000

1500 g → 1500 ÷ 1000 = 1.5 kg

❷ Convert these measurements to the units shown:

a) 1200 g = _____ kg

b) 1640 g = _____ kg

c) 4362 g = _____ kg

d) 866 g = _____ kg

e) 3.5 kg = _____ g

f) 5.33 kg = _____ g

g) 1.584 l = _____ ml

h) 1647 ml = _____ l

i) 16.67 l = _____ ml

Practice

❶ Convert these measurements to the units shown. Try not to look at the diagrams.

a) 6263 m = _____ km

b) 57 mm = _____ cm

c) 0.8 m = _____ cm

d) 736 g = _____ kg

e) 350 ml = _____ l

f) 0.12 kg = _____ g

❷ The potatoes on some scales weigh 450 grams. Write this mass in kilograms.

_____ kg

❸ There are 1.7 litres of water in a container. Write this amount in millilitres.

_____ ml

❹ A dog weighs 10 kg. A person weighs 60 000 g. How many times heavier is the person than the dog?

_____

How did I do?

✔

I know the relationships between units of measurement. ☐

I can convert one metric unit to another. ☐

51: Measurement (3)

In this unit you will revise:

▶ metric units of measurement
▶ imperial units of measurement
▶ how to convert between metric and imperial units.

> **!** When measuring, it is very important that you take care and make as accurate a reading as you can. Don't just say 'It is about 3 cm'. Find out whether it is 2.9 cm or 3.1 cm.

What you should know

The units of measurement in the table below are called metric units. To convert one metric unit to another you multiply by 10, 100, 1000 or some other power of 10.

Measurement	Metric units	Relationships between units
Length including height, width, depth, perimeter, distance	millimetres **mm** centimetres **cm** metres **m** kilometres **km**	10 mm = 1 cm 100 cm = 1 m 1000 m = 1 km
Mass	grams **g** kilograms **kg**	1000 g = 1 kg
Capacity	millilitres **ml** centilitres **cl** litres **l**	10 ml = 1 cl 100 cl = 1 l

Get started

Other measuring units, called **imperial units**, are also sometimes used. These were the only units used many years ago, but then metric units were introduced (because they are easier!).

Here are some imperial units of length, mass and capacity you should know:

Measurement	Imperial units	Relationships between units
Length including height, width, depth, perimeter, distance	inches feet yards miles	12 inches = 1 foot 3 feet = 1 yard 1760 yards = 1 mile
Mass	ounces pounds stones	16 ounces (oz) = 1 pound 14 pounds (lb) = 1 stone
Capacity	pints gallons	8 pints = 1 gallon

1 Try to fill in the missing values without looking at the table on the previous page.

a) 1 foot = _____ inches

b) 1 mile = _____ yards

c) 1 stone = _____ pounds

d) 1 gallon = _____ pints

e) 1 pound = _____ ounces

f) 1 yard = _____ feet

It is important to have a rough idea of how many of one **metric** unit makes up an **imperial** unit, and vice versa.

The symbol ≈ means approximately equal to.

To convert from one unit to another, find the relationship between the two units in the table and use a calculator to multiply, like this:

Imperial to Metric	Metric to imperial
Length	**Length**
1 inch ≈ 2.54 cm	1 cm ≈ 0.4 inches
1 foot ≈ 30 cm	1 m ≈ 3.3 feet
1 yard ≈ 91 cm	1 m ≈ 1.1 yards
1 mile ≈ 1.6 km	1 km ≈ 0.62 miles
Mass	**Mass**
1 ounce ≈ 28 g	1 g ≈ 0.035 ounces
1 pound ≈ 454 g	1 kg ≈ 2.2 pounds
1 stone ≈ 6.35 kg	1 kg ≈ 0.16 stones
Capacity	**Capacity**
1 pint ≈ 568 ml	1 l ≈ 1.75 pints
1 gallon ≈ 4.55 l	1 l ≈ 0.22 gallons

240 m ≈ _____ *yards*

metres → yards   1 m ≈ 1.1 yards   Multiply 240 m by 1.1 = **264** yards

2 Convert these measurements to the units shown. One has been done for you.

a) 240 m ≈ **264** yards

b) 1600 yards ≈ _____ m

c) 47 litres ≈ _____ pints

d) 37 pints ≈ _____ litres

e) 42 kg ≈ _____ pounds

f) 78 pounds ≈ _____ kg

g) 77 pints ≈ _____ litres

h) 1 km ≈ _____ yards

i) 700 g ≈ _____ pounds

(**Practice**)

1 Convert each measurement in the sentence to the unit shown.

a) Take the turning on the right about 500 yards down this road. _____ m

b) When I was 19 years old I used to weigh about 126 pounds. _____ kg

c) A milk float is carrying 200 pints of milk. _____ l

d) A puppy's mass is 4.5 kg. _____ pounds

e) A large fish tank holds about 910 litres of water. _____ gallons

How did I do?

✔

I know metric and imperial units of measurement. ☐

I can convert between metric and imperial units. ☐

52: Measurement (4)

In this unit you will revise:

▶ metric units of measurement
▶ how to convert between metric units of area and volume.

What you should know

The units of measurement in the table below are called metric units. To convert one metric unit to another you multiply by 10, 100, 1000 or some other power of 10.

Measurement	Metric units	Relationships between units
Area	square millimetres **mm²** square centimetres **cm²** square metres **m²**	$100\,mm^2 = 1\,cm^2$ $10\,000\,cm^2 = 1\,m^2$
Volume	cubic millimetres **mm³** cubic centimetres **cm³** cubic metres **m³**	$1000\,mm^3 = 1\,cm^3$ $1\,000\,000\,cm^3 = 1\,m^3$

Get started

The lengths of sides of this square might be described in centimetres (cm) or millimetres (mm). Its **area** can be described in square centimetres (cm²) or square millimetres (mm²).

1 cm

1 cm ☐

Area = 1 cm × 1 cm = 1 cm²

10 mm

10 mm ☐

Area = 10 mm × 10 mm = 100 mm²

Notice that the number of square millimetres is **100** times larger than the number of square centimetres, even though there are 10 millimetres in 1 centimetre. This is because area is 2-dimensional (10 × 10).

Also the number of square **centimetres** is **10 000** times larger than the number of square **metres**, even though there are 100 centimetres in 1 metre. This is because area is 2-dimensional (100 × 100).

These diagrams can help you to convert from one unit of area to another:

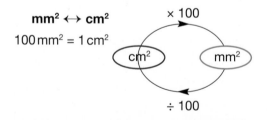

mm² ↔ cm²

$100\,mm^2 = 1\,cm^2$

× 100

cm²   mm²

÷ 100

cm² ↔ m²

$10\,000\,cm^2 = 1\,m^2$

× 10 000

m²   cm²

÷ 10 000

❶ Convert these areas to the units shown.

a) 8 cm² = _____ mm²

b) 37 cm² = _____ mm²

c) 500 mm² = _____ cm²

d) 125 m² = _____ cm²

e) 14 m² = _____ cm²

f) 140 000 cm² = _____ m²

The lengths of sides of this cube might be described in centimetres (cm) or millimetres (mm). Its **volume** can be described in cubic centimetres (cm³) or cubic millimetres (mm³).

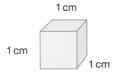

Volume = 1 cm × 1 cm × 1 cm = 1 cm³

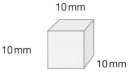

Volume = 10 mm × 10 mm × 10 mm = 1000 mm³

Notice that the number of cubic millimetres is **1000** times larger than the number of cubic centimetres, even though there are 10 millimetres in 1 centimetre. This is because volume is 3-dimensional (10 × 10 × 10).

Also the number of cubic **centimetres** is **1 000 000** (one million) times larger than the number of cubic **metres**, even though there are 100 centimetres in 1 metre. This is because volume is 3-dimensional (100 × 100 × 100).

These diagrams can help you to convert from one unit of volume to another:

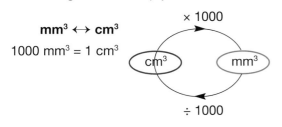

mm³ ↔ cm³

1000 mm³ = 1 cm³

× 1000

÷ 1000

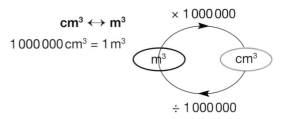

cm³ ↔ m³

1 000 000 cm³ = 1 m³

× 1 000 000

÷ 1 000 000

Practice

① Convert these volumes to the units shown:

a) 8 cm³ = _____ mm³

b) 37 cm³ = _____ mm³

c) 50 000 mm³ = _____ cm³

d) 125 m³ = _____ cm³

e) 14 m³ = _____ cm³

f) 2 000 000 cm³ = _____ m³

② Convert these areas to the units shown:

a) 16 cm² = _____ mm²

b) 22 cm² = _____ mm²

c) 50 mm² = _____ cm²

d) 7 m² = _____ cm²

e) 23 m² = _____ cm²

f) 500 000 cm² = _____ m²

③ These measurements include lengths, areas and volumes. Convert these measurements to the units shown:

a) 16 cm = _____ mm

b) 22 mm = _____ cm

c) 6000 mm² = _____ cm²

d) 260 m³ = _____ cm³

e) 14 m² = _____ cm²

f) 2 000 000 mm³ = _____ cm³

g) 7 m = _____ cm

h) 23 000 cm² = _____ m²

i) 14 million cm³ = _____ m³

j) 4 m³ = _____ cm³

k) 1400 cm = _____ m

l) 8 million mm³ = _____ cm³

How did I do?

I know metric units of measurement. ☐

I can convert between metric units of area and volume. ☐

✔

53: Perimeter and area

In this unit you will revise:

▶ the formula for the perimeter of a rectangle
▶ how to deduce and calculate the perimeter of shapes made from rectangles
▶ the formula for the area of a rectangle
▶ how to calculate the area of shapes made from rectangles.

Always have a rough idea of what your expected answer might be, before doing a calculation. This is especially important if you are using a calculator.

What you should know

Perimeter is the distance around the edge of a flat shape. To find the perimeter of straight-sided shapes, add the lengths of all the sides of the shape.

Perimeter is measured in units of length like centimetres (cm) or metres (m).

This formula can help you to find the perimeter (P) of a rectangle,

where l is its length and w is its width: $P = 2(l + w)$

Area is the amount of surface that a shape covers or the space inside the outline of a 2-D shape.

Area is measured in square units like square centimetres (cm^2) or square metres (m^2).

The area of a rectangle can be found by counting the number of squares it covers. Here the rectangle has 12 squares.

A quicker way of finding the area of a rectangle is to multiply the length by the width. The rectangle here has 3 rows with 4 squares in each. 3×4 is 12 so the area is 12 squares.

This formula can help you to find the area (A) of a rectangle,

where l is its length and w is its width: $A = l \times w$

Get started

When finding the perimeter and area of a shape made from more than one rectangle, you may need to work out the lengths of unmarked sides.

The length of the unmarked blue dotted side can be found by adding the lengths of the sides opposite, like this:

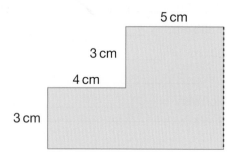

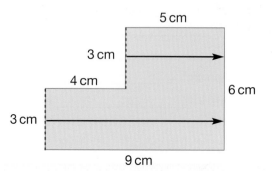

Can you see how the 9 cm length was found?

The perimeter is $3 + 4 + 3 + 5 + 6 + 9 = 30$ cm

1 Find and label the lengths of each of the blue dotted lines below:

a)
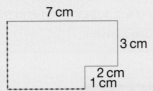
9 cm
5 cm
7 cm
8 cm

b)
7 cm
3 cm
2 cm
1 cm

c)
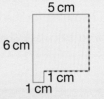
5 cm
6 cm
1 cm
1 cm

2 Now find the perimeter of each shape.

Perimeter = _____ cm   Perimeter = _____ cm   Perimeter = _____ cm

To find the area, split the shape into rectangles and find the area of each first before adding them all together to find the total area.

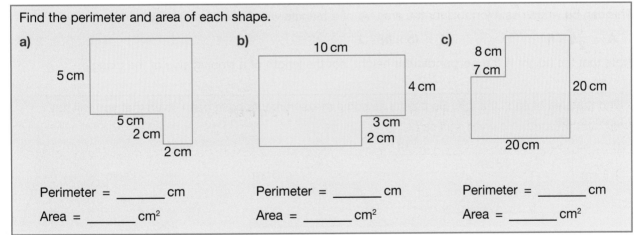

5 cm
3 cm
4 cm
3 cm

5 cm
3 cm
4 cm
3 cm
6 cm
9 cm

5 cm
4 cm
30 cm² 6 cm
3 cm 12 cm²

The area of the shape is 12 cm² + 30 cm² = 42 cm²

Practice

1 Find the perimeter and area of each shape.

a)
5 cm
5 cm
2 cm
2 cm

Perimeter = _____ cm

Area = _____ cm²

b)
10 cm
4 cm
3 cm
2 cm

Perimeter = _____ cm

Area = _____ cm²

c)
8 cm
7 cm
20 cm
20 cm

Perimeter = _____ cm

Area = _____ cm²

How did I do?

I know the formulae for the perimeter and area of a rectangle.

I can find the lengths of unmarked sides.

I can calculate the area and perimeter of shapes made from rectangles.

✔

54: Area

In this unit you will revise:
- the formulae for the area of a triangle, parallelogram and trapezium
- how to calculate areas of compound shapes.

What you should know

Area is the amount of surface that a shape covers. In a 2-D shape (flat shape) it is the space inside the lines or within a boundary. In a 3-D shape (solid shape) it is the total amount of surface of all the faces. Area is measured in square units like square centimetres (cm^2) or square metres (m^2).

For 3-D shapes this is often called **surface area**.

Here is the formula for the area, A, of a rectangle with length (*l*) and width (*w*):   **A = *l* × *w***

Get started

The diagrams below show that the area of a triangle is half the area of a rectangle.

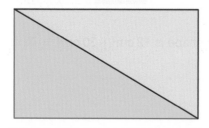 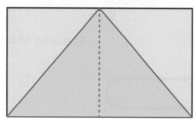 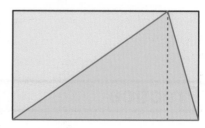

This can be written as a formula for the area, A, of a triangle with base (*b*) and height (*h*):

$$A = \frac{1}{2}b \times h \qquad \text{or} \qquad A = (b \times h) \div 2$$

Note that the height is the **perpendicular** height, not the length of a sloping side of the triangle.

1 Find the area of each triangle. Be careful as some measurements have been given that you will not need to use.

a)

5 cm   13 cm
12 cm

Area = _____ cm²

b)

3 cm
5 cm
8 cm

Area = _____ cm²

c)

13 cm   5 cm
14 cm

Area = _____ cm²

d)

5 cm   3 cm
4 cm

Area = _____ cm²

e)

8 cm   4 cm   8 cm
14 cm

Area = _____ cm²

f)

3 cm   10 cm
6 cm

Area = _____ cm²

These are the formulae for the area of a parallelogram and a trapezium:

Parallelogram

Area = base × perpendicular height

$A = b \times h$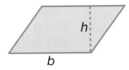

Trapezium

Area = $\frac{1}{2}$(sum of parallel sides) × perpendicular height

$A = \frac{1}{2}(a + b) \times h$

2 Find the area of each shape. Be careful as some shapes have been rotated.

a)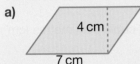

Area = _____ cm²

b)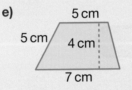

Area = _____ cm²

c)

Area = _____ cm²

d)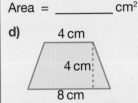

Area = _____ cm²

e)

Area = _____ cm²

f)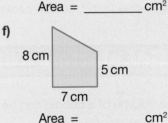

Area = _____ cm²

When finding the area of something made from more than one shape, split it into parts and find the area of each part first before adding them all together to find the total area. You may also need to work out the lengths of unmarked sides.

Practice

1 Find the area of each shape by splitting it into parts.

a)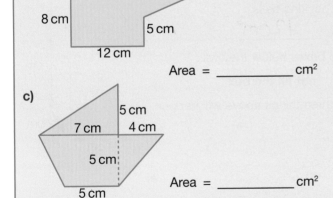

Area = _____ cm²

b)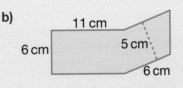

Area = _____ cm²

c)

Area = _____ cm²

d)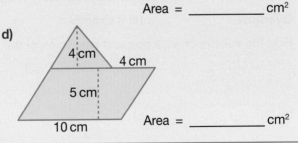

Area = _____ cm²

55: Volume and surface area (1)

In this unit you will revise:
- the formula for the volume of a cuboid
- how to deduce and calculate the volume of shapes made from cuboids
- how to use a formula to find the surface area of cuboids.

In an exam it is very important that you follow instructions carefully. Listen to the teacher giving the instructions and ask if there is anything you don't understand.

What you should know

Volume is the space inside a 3-D shape. It is measured in cubic millimetres (mm³), cubic centimetres (cm³) and cubic metres (m³).

The **surface area** of a 3-D shape is the total amount of surface of all the faces. It is measured in square millimetres (mm²), square centimetres (cm²) and square metres (m²).

Get started

The volume of a cuboid can be found by:

- counting the cubes in one layer   **8 cubes**
- counting how many layers there are   **2 layers**
- multiplying the number in one layer by the number of layers

$$\textbf{Volume} = \textbf{8} \times \textbf{2} = \textbf{16 cm}^3$$

A quicker way of finding the volume of a cuboid is to use the formula:

V = **lbh** where *l* is length, *b* is breadth and *h* is height.

$$\textbf{Volume} = \textbf{4} \times \textbf{2} \times \textbf{2} = \textbf{16 cm}^3$$

1

This box is filled to the brim with small polystyrene packing balls.

a) What is the volume of this box?   _72cm³_

If the balls are tipped from this box into each of the boxes below they will:

Overflow   **fill it exactly**   or   **not fill the box**

Find the volume of each box and say which of the three things above will happen.

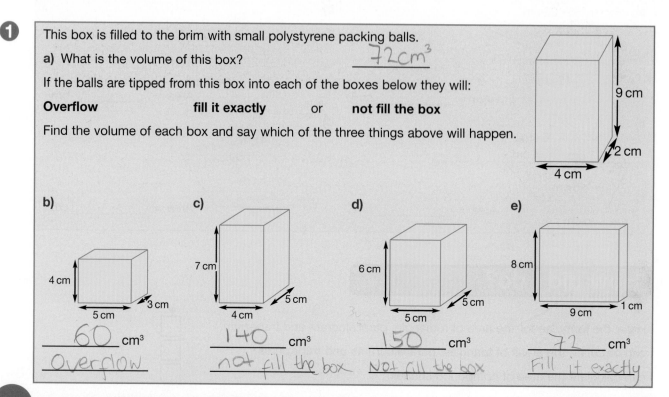

b)
4 cm, 5 cm, 3 cm
_60_ cm³
Overflow

c)
7 cm, 4 cm, 5 cm
_140_ cm³
not fill the box

d)
6 cm, 5 cm, 5 cm
_150_ cm³
Not fill the box

e)
8 cm, 9 cm, 1 cm
_72_ cm³
Fill it exactly

To find the **volume** of shapes made from cuboids joined together, split the shape into cuboids and find the volume of each first before adding them all together to find the total volume.

$5 \times 8 \times 6 = 240$ $3 \times 6 \times 7 = 126$

Volume $= 240 \, cm^3 + 126 \, cm^3 = \textbf{366 cm}^3$

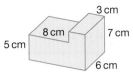

② Find the volume of these prisms:

$3 \times 2 \times 8 = 48$
$8 \times 10 \times 2 = 160$
$5 \times 3 \times 8 = 120$

a)

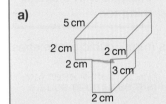

Volume $= 5 \times 2 \times 2 + 2 \times 2 \times 3$

_____32_____ cm³ $= 20 + 12$

b)

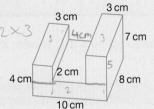

Volume $= 328$

____328____ cm³

The **surface area** of a cuboid can be found by adding up the areas of each section of the net of the shape.

Surface area $= 12 + 12 + 18 + 18 + 6 + 6 = \textbf{72 cm}^2$

A quicker way of finding the surface area of a cuboid is to use the formula:

$$S = 2bl + 2hl + 2hb$$

where l is length, b is breadth and h is height.

Surface area $= 2(2 \times 6) + 2(3 \times 6) + 2(2 \times 3)$

$= 2(12) + 2(18) + 2(6) = 24 + 36 + 12 = \textbf{72 cm}^2$

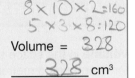
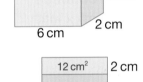

Practice

① Use the formula to find the surface area of each of the five cuboids in question 1 on page 38.

a) _____ cm²   b) _____ cm²   c) _____ cm²

d) _____ cm²   e) _____ cm²

② Complete this table:

Box	Dimensions			Volume	Surface Area
	l	*b*	*h*	*V = lbh*	*S = 2bl + 2lh + 2hb*
A	6 cm	5 cm	2 cm	60	
B	5 cm	4 cm	3 cm		
C	9 cm	2 cm	2 cm		
D	4 cm	3 cm	10 cm		
E	6 cm	1 cm	5 cm		
F	7 cm	4 cm	4 cm		

How did I do?

I know the formula for the volume of a cuboid.

I can deduce and calculate the volume of shapes made from cuboids.

I can use the formula to find the surface area of cuboids.

✔

In this unit you will revise:

▶ how to calculate the volume of prisms
▶ how to calculate the surface area of prisms.

> Don't be afraid to ask questions at school. Maths is a subject that builds on what you understand. If you don't understand something you'll struggle with the next thing too.

What you should know

Volume is the space taken up by a 3-D shape. It is measured in cubic millimetres (mm³), cubic centimetres (cm³) and cubic metres (m³).

The **surface area** of a 3-D shape is the total amount of surface of all the faces. It is measured in square millimetres (mm²), square centimetres (cm²) and square metres (m²).

Here are some area formulae you should know.

Area of rectangle

Area = length × width

$$A = lw$$

Area of triangle

Area = half the base × **perpendicular** height

$$A = \frac{1}{2}b \times h \quad \text{or} \quad A = (b \times h) \div 2$$

Area of parallelogram

Area = base × perpendicular height

$$A = b \times h$$

Area of trapezium

Area = ½(sum of the **parallel** sides) × perpendicular height

$$A = \frac{1}{2}(a + b) \times h$$

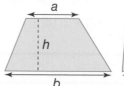
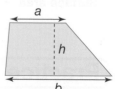

Get started

A prism is a 3-D shape that has the same cross-section all the way along its length.

To find the volume of a prism, first find the **area of the end face**, then **multiply by the length** of the prism.

1 Calculate the volume of each prism.

a) 3 cm, 5 cm, 5 cm

_____ cm³

b) 4 cm, 8 cm, 4.5 cm

_____ cm³

c) 5 cm, 4 cm, 10 cm, 3 cm

_____ cm³

d) 5 cm, 6 cm, 11 cm

_____ cm³

e) 5 cm, 6 cm, 8 cm

_____ cm³

f) 3 cm, 10 cm, 9 cm

_____ cm³

g) 3 cm, 4 cm, 9 cm, 7 cm

_____ cm³

h) 3 cm, 8 cm, 6 cm, 8 cm

_____ cm³

The **surface area** of a prism can be found by adding up the areas of each section of the net of the shape.

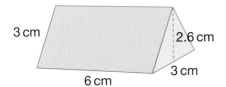

3 cm

2.6 cm

3 cm

6 cm

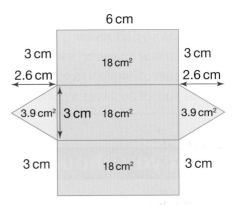

6 cm

3 cm   18 cm²   3 cm

2.6 cm   2.6 cm

3.9 cm² 3 cm 18 cm² 3.9 cm²

3 cm   18 cm²   3 cm

Surface area = 18 + 18 + 18 + 3.9 + 3.9 = **61.8 cm²**

2 Sketch the net for each prism and label the dimensions. Use your sketches to help you find the surface area of each prism. The first net has been drawn for you.

a)

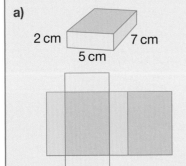

2 cm   7 cm
      5 cm

_____ cm²

b)

6 cm   10 cm
              20 cm
      8 cm

_____ cm²

c)

5 cm   13 cm   10 cm
          12 cm

_____ cm²

Practice

1 Find the surface area of each of the first three prisms in question 1 of the Get started section.

a) _____ cm²   b) _____ cm²   c) _____ cm²

2 Find the volume of each prism in question 2 of the Get started section.

a) _____ cm³   b) _____ cm³   c) _____ cm³

3 Find the volume of the prisms below.

a)

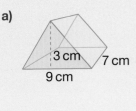

3 cm 7 cm
9 cm

_____ cm³

b)

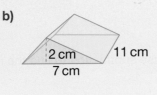

2 cm   11 cm
7 cm

_____ cm³

c)

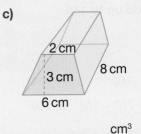

2 cm
                8 cm
3 cm
6 cm

_____ cm³

d)

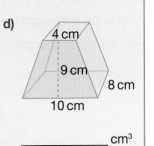

4 cm
          9 cm
              8 cm
10 cm

_____ cm³

How did I do?

✔

I can calculate the volume of prisms. ☐

I can calculate the surface area of prisms. ☐

57: Angles (1)

In this unit you will revise:
- the sum of angles on a straight line
- the sum of angles in a triangle
- the sum of angles at a point.

What you should know

An angle is an amount of turn measured in degrees (°). There are 360° in a full turn.

There are different types of angles you should know:

a An angle less than 90° is called an **acute** angle.

b An angle of 90° is called a **right** angle.

c An angle between 90° and 180° is called an **obtuse** angle.

d An angle of 180° is called a **straight** angle.

e An angle between 180° and 360° is called a **reflex** angle.

Get started

There are many types of angle questions where you are expected to calculate, rather than measure, the size of missing angles. Here are some facts to learn:

Angles on a straight line add up to 180°.

Find the missing angle:

76° + ? = 180°, so use subtraction to find the missing angle

180° − 76° = **104°**

Check: 76° + 104° = 180°

---

1 Calculate the size of each of the marked angles:

a)

_____ °

b)

115°

_____ °

c)

36°

_____ °

Angles inside a triangle add up to 180°.

This can be shown by tearing a triangle into three pieces, with a corner in each. Join the corners together to make a straight line. Because there are 180° on a straight line there must be 180° in a triangle.

Find the missing angle:

$$55° + 65° = 120°$$

$$180° - 120° = \mathbf{60°}$$

Check: $55° + 65° + 60° = 180°$

2 Calculate the size of each of the marked angles:

a)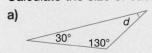

_____ °

b)

_____ °

c)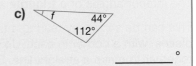

_____ °

Angles around a point add up to 360°.

Find the missing reflex angle:

$$55° + ? = 360°.$$

$$360° - 55° = \mathbf{305°}$$

Check: $305° + 55° = 360°$

3 Calculate the size of each of the marked angles:

a)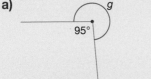

_____ °

b)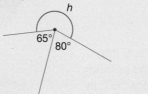

_____ °

c)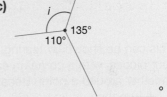

_____ °

Practice

1 Fill in the missing angles: *a, b* and *c.*

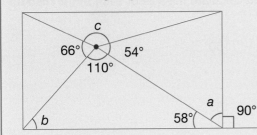

a = _____ °

b = _____ °

c = _____ °

How did I do?

✔

I know the sum of angles on a straight line. ☐

I know the sum of angles in a triangle. ☐

I know the sum of angles at a point. ☐

In this unit you will revise:

▶ the sum of angles in a triangle and in a quadrilateral
▶ alternate and corresponding angles.

Start each revision session by trying to remember what you revised during your last one. If you have forgotten anything, go back and look at the topic again before starting a new topic.

What you should know

An **angle** is an amount of turn measured in degrees (°).

Make sure you know this fact about the interior angles of a triangle.

The interior angles of a **triangle** add up to **180°**.

This can be shown by tearing a triangle into three pieces, with a corner in each. Join the corners together to make a straight line. Because there are 180° on a straight line there must be 180° in a triangle.

Get started

The interior angles of a **quadrilateral** add up to **360°**.

This can be shown by tearing a quadrilateral into four pieces, with a corner in each. Join the corners together around a point. Because there are 360° in a full turn there must be 360° in a quadrilateral.

Also, because a quadrilateral can be split into two triangles it can be seen that 2 lots of 180° is 360°.

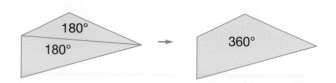

1 Use the sum of the interior angles of a quadrilateral to help you calculate the size of each of the marked angles:

a)

130° 100°
40° a

b)
150°
b
35°
165°

c)
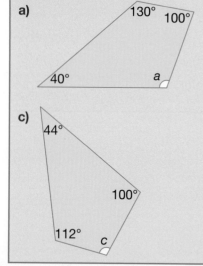
44°
100°
112° c

a) _____ °

b) _____ °

c) _____ °

When a straight line crosses two parallel lines, some equal angles are formed.

The angles in an 'F' shape are **equal**. These are called **corresponding angles**.

• = •

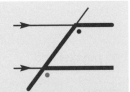

The angles in a 'Z' shape are **equal**. These are called **alternate angles**.

• = •

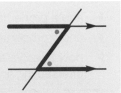

When you look at the angles in 'F' or 'Z' shapes notice that the angles can be acute (less than 90°) or obtuse (between 90° and 180°). Also twist the paper around as the 'F' or 'Z' shapes can be in a rotated or reflected position.

2 Write statements to show four corresponding angles and two alternate angles.
One has been done for you.

l = *p* (corresponding angles)

_____   _____

_____   _____

_____

Practice

1 This diagram shows a line going through three parallel lines.

Write the size of each angle from *a* to *h*:

a) *a* = _____°   b) *b* = _____°   c) *c* = _____°   d) *d* = _____°

e) *e* = _____°   f) *f* = _____°   g) *g* = _____°   h) *h* = _____°

2 Use what you know about interior angles of triangles and quadrilaterals and alternate and corresponding angles to find the size of each angle from *o* to *s*.

a) *o* = _____°   b) *p* = _____°

c) *q* = _____°   d) *r* = _____°

e) *s* = _____°

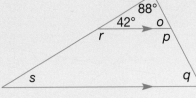

How did I do?

I know the sum of angles in a triangle and in a quadrilateral.

I can recognise and use alternate and corresponding angles to solve problems.

✔

59: Angles (3)

In this unit you will revise:

▶ angle properties of parallel and intersecting lines
▶ angle properties of triangles and quadrilaterals
▶ how to solve angle problems involving polygons and parallel and intersecting lines.

What you should know

The interior angles of a **triangle** add up to **180°**.

The angles **on a straight line** add up to **180°**.

The interior angles of a **quadrilateral** add up to **360°**.

The angles **about a point** add up to **360°**.

Get started

When two lines cross to form an 'X' shape the opposite angles are equal.

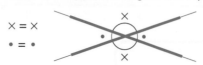

When a straight line crosses two parallel lines, some equal angles are formed.

The angles in an 'F' shape are **equal** and are called **corresponding angles.** • = •

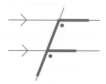

The angles in a 'Z' shape are **equal**. These are called **alternate angles.** • = •

The angles in 'F', 'Z' or 'X' shapes can be acute (less than 90°) or obtuse (between 90° and 180°). They can be in a rotated or reflected position.

❶ In each diagram write the size of every angle. Remember that there are 180° on a straight line.

a)

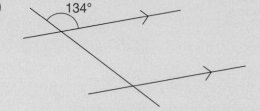

b)

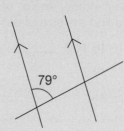

c)

d)

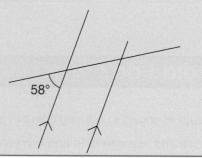

Sometimes questions involve parallel lines and other polygons, such as triangles and quadrilaterals.

To find the angles *a*, *b* and *c*:

● use the fact that angles **on a straight line** add up to **180°** to find *a*

● then use corresponding angles to find *b*

● then use the fact that interior angles of a **quadrilateral** add up to **360°** to find *c*.

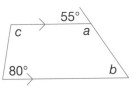

a = 180 − 55 = 125°   *b* = 55°   *c* = 360 − 80 − 55 − 125 = 100°

❷ Find the value of the angles marked by each letter.

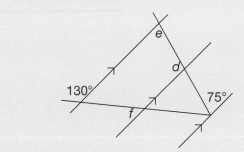 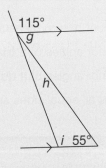

d = _____   *e* = _____   *f* = _____   *g* = _____   *h* = _____   *i* = _____

Practice

❶ In each diagram write the size of every angle.

a)

b)

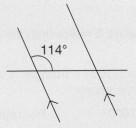

c)

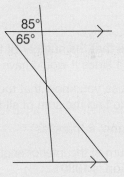

❷ If you know the size of the angles that are marked with stars, which of the other angles in this diagram can be found by calculating? Mark with a cross any angles that you think cannot be found.

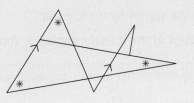

How did I do?

I know angle properties of parallel and intersecting lines.

I know angle properties of triangles and quadrilaterals.

I can solve angle problems involving polygons and parallel and intersecting lines.

✔
☐
☐
☐

60: Angles (4)

When a test or exam is getting closer, don't worry about it. Use the checklist at the back of this book. It will help you to realise how much you already know and can point you towards topics that you need to revise a little more.

In this unit you will revise:

▶ how to calculate and use interior angles of polygons
▶ how to calculate and use exterior angles of polygons
▶ the sum of exterior angles of any polygon.

What you should know

An **angle** is an amount of turn measured in degrees (°).

The sum of the interior angles of a **triangle** is **180°**.

The sum of the interior angles of a **quadrilateral** is **360°**.

A **regular** shape has all equal sides and all equal angles.

Get started

To find the sum of the interior angles of other polygons, imagine splitting the shape into triangles from just one corner.

An octagon, 8 sides, can be split into 6 triangles.   A pentagon, 5 sides, can be split into 3 triangles.

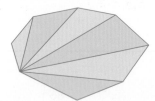   

Notice that the number of triangles is always **2 fewer** than the number of sides of the shape, so if a shape has 24 sides it would have 22 triangles.

Because you know that the sum of the angles of a **triangle** is 180°, multiply the number of triangles by 180° to find the sum of all the angles in the shape.

Octagon: 6 triangles $6 \times 180° = \textbf{1080°}$ **Pentagon**: 3 triangles $3 \times 180° = \textbf{540°}$

The sum of the interior angles of an **octagon** is **1080°**.

The sum of the interior angles of a **pentagon** is **540°**.

This can be shown by the formula:

The sum of the interior angles = (number of sides − 2) × 180°

Find the sum of the interior angles of each polygon. You can use a calculator.

a) Hexagon (6 sides)   b) Decagon (10 sides)

   Sum of interior angles = _____°   Sum of interior angles = _____°

c) Dodecagon (12 sides)   d) Nonagon (9 sides)

   Sum of interior angles = _____°   Sum of interior angles = _____°

e) Heptagon (7 sides)   f) Icosagon (20 sides)

   Sum of interior angles = _____°   Sum of interior angles = _____°

For regular shapes, once the sum of the interior angles is known, each angle can be found.

Divide the sum of the interior angles by the number of sides.

A regular pentagon has interior angles with the sum 540°.

540 divided by 5 (the number of sides) is 108°.

Each angle is 108°.

105°

❷ Find the size of each angle in the regular polygons below. You can use a calculator. Give your answers to the nearest degree.

a) Regular dodecagon (12 sides)   b) Regular heptagon (7 sides)   c) Regular hexagon (6 sides)

   angle = _____°   angle = _____°   angle = _____°

d) Regular decagon (10 sides)   e) Regular nonagon (9 sides)   f) Regular icosagon (20 sides)

   angle = _____°   angle = _____°   angle = _____°

An exterior angle is the angle made by extending the sides of a shape.
An interior and its related exterior angle will always add up to 180°.

If the marked interior angle of this irregular hexagon is 100° then the exterior angle marked is 80°.

Remember also that the **sum of the exterior angles** of any polygon always add up to **360°**.

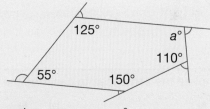

Exterior angle

Practice

❶ Label each of the exterior angles of this irregular polygon and find the missing interior angle, *a*.

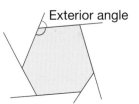

125°   *a*°
        110°
55°   150°

❷ A regular shape has 24 sides. Find the size of one of its interior angles. _____°

❸ A regular shape has equal exterior angles. Each is 24°. How many sides has the shape? _____

❹ An irregular shape has interior angles with the sum of 2520°. How many sides has the shape? _____

❺ An irregular hexagon has interior angles of 24°, 45°, 170°, 140°, 100° and *x*°.

Find the value of *x*. _____°

❻ An irregular polygon has exterior angles of 34°, 36°, 72°, 44°, 19°, 26°, 33°, 63° and *y*°.

Find the value of *y*. _____°

How did I do?

✔

I can calculate and use interior angles of polygons.   ☐

I can calculate and use exterior angles of polygons.   ☐

I know that the sum of exterior angles of any polygon is 360°.   ☐

61: Bearings (1)

In this unit you will revise:
▸ the meaning of the term bearing
▸ how bearings can be used to specify direction.

What you should know

A **bearing** is an angle that describes a direction in relation to a turn in a **clockwise** direction from **North**. A bearing should always contain three figures, so for angles up to 100° a zero is used as the first digit, 053°, 079°, 030°, 006°.

Get started

A girl faces due North. She turns through an angle of 45° in a clockwise direction. She now faces North East.

After turning, she now walks a short distance in the direction she is facing (NE) and then stops.

If point A is where she started and point B where she stopped, it is said that:

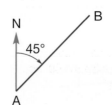

the bearing of B from A is 045°

① Complete the sentences to describe the bearing shown in each diagram.

a)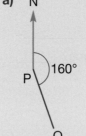

The bearing of Q

from P is _____°

b)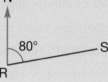

The bearing of S

from R is _____°

c)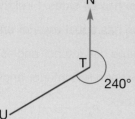

The bearing of U

from T is _____°

Two sets of bearings can be described if two points are marked, such as **the bearing of A from B** and **the bearing of B from A**. These are very different.

When describing bearings always look to see which letter follows the word **'from'**, such as 'from B'. This tells you to look at the clockwise angle at point B.

Notice that two North lines are drawn, one at each point.

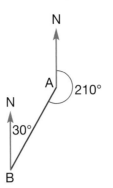

The bearing of B from A = **210°**

The bearing of A from B = **030°**

2 Answer these questions:

a)

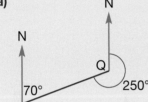

b)

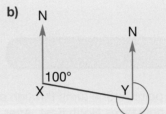

What is the bearing of P from Q? _____°

What is the bearing of X from Y? _____°

What is the bearing of Q from P? _____°

What is the bearing of Y from X? _____°

c) Find the difference between the bearings in each pair. What do you notice?

_____

_____

A bearing of A from B is called the back bearing to the bearing of B from A and vice versa. You may have noticed that back bearings have a difference of 180°. If the bearing is greater than 180°, subtract 180° to find the back bearing. If the bearing is less than 180°, add 180° to find the back bearing.

If the bearing of A from B is 270°, the bearing of B from A will be 270 – 180 = 090°.

If the bearing of C from D is 020°, the bearing of D from C will be 020 + 180 = 200°.

(**Practice**)

1 Give the missing back bearings.

a) The bearing of F from E is 140°. The bearing of E from F is _____°

b) The bearing of G from H is 010°. The bearing of H from G is _____°

c) The bearing of J from K is 260°. The bearing of K from J is _____°

d) The bearing of L from M is 075°. The bearing of M from L is _____°

(**How did I do?**)

I know the meaning of the term bearing.

I know how bearings can be used to specify direction.

62: Bearings (2)

When making your own revision notes, use different colours to show different things.

In this unit you will revise:

▶ how bearings can be used to specify direction
▶ how to find back bearings and solve problems.

What you should know

A **bearing** is an angle that describes a direction in relation to a turn in a **clockwise** direction from North. A bearing should always contain three figures, so for angles up to 100° a zero is used as the first digit, as in 053°, 079°, 030° and 006°.

Get started

A girl faces due North at point A. She turns through an angle of 45° in a clockwise direction. She now faces North East. After turning, she now walks a short distance in the direction she is facing (NE) and then stops at point B. It is said that:

the bearing of B from A is 045°

If two points are marked, two sets of bearings can be described, such as **the bearing of A from B** and **the bearing of B from A**. These are very different.

When describing bearings always look to see which letter follows the word '*from*', such as 'from B'. This tells you to look at the clockwise angle at point B. Notice that two North lines are drawn, one at each point.

The bearing of B **from A** = **045°**

The bearing of A **from B** = **225°**

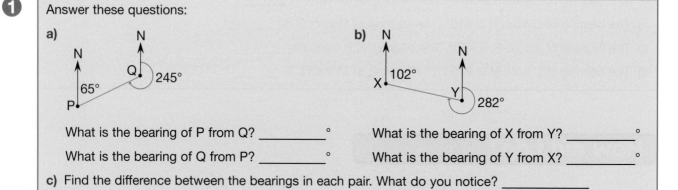

1   Answer these questions:

a) What is the bearing of P from Q? _____°

What is the bearing of Q from P? _____°

b) What is the bearing of X from Y? _____°

What is the bearing of Y from X? _____°

c) Find the difference between the bearings in each pair. What do you notice? _____

A bearing of A from B is called the back bearing to the bearing of B from A and vice versa. You may have noticed that bearings and back bearings have a difference of 180°. If the bearing is greater than 180°, subtract 180° to find the back bearing. If the bearing is less than 180°, add 180° to find the back bearing.

If the bearing of A from B is 272°, the bearing of B from A will be 272 − 180 = 092°

If the bearing of C from D is 025°, the bearing of D from C will be 025 + 180 = 205°

❷ Give the missing back bearings:

a) The bearing of F from E is 145°. The bearing of E from F is _____°

b) The bearing of G from H is 017°. The bearing of H from G is _____°

c) The bearing of J from K is 275°. The bearing of K from J is _____°

d) The bearing of L from M is 320°. The bearing of M from L is _____°

Practice

❶ Sketch diagrams to match these bearings.

a)

b)

The bearing of P from Q is 330°

The bearing of Q from P is 150°

The bearing of X from Y is 210°

The bearing of Y from X is 030°

❷ Answer these bearing questions:

a) A ship travels on a bearing of 023° from a port. It must return to the port. On what bearing must it travel now?

_____°

b) A lifeboat travels on a bearing of 270° from the lifeboat station. In which compass direction is it travelling?

_____

c) A helicopter flies 20 miles on a bearing of 116° from its pad. What is its back bearing?

_____°

How did I do?

I know how bearings can be used to specify direction. ☐

I can find back bearings and solve problems. ☐

63: Construction

What you should know

These pages are about construction: drawing shapes and lines accurately. You will need a pair of compasses (that aren't too loose), a sharp pencil and a ruler.

Perpendicular means 'at right angles to'. Lines that are perpendicular are at 90° to each other. The perpendicular height of a triangle is the height, at right angles to the base, shown here as a dotted line:

To **bisect** means to cut exactly in half. If you bisect an angle, you split it exactly in half down the middle.

Get started

To 'construct the perpendicular bisector of a line' means to draw another line at right angles to it exactly in the middle. To do this, follow these instructions:

- ● **Start with the line AB.**

- ● Make sure the compasses are wider than half the length of the line. Put the point on A and draw two arc lines, one above and one below the line AB.

- ● Keeping the compasses set at the same width, lift the point and place it on B. Draw two arc lines that cross the previous ones.

- ● Finally use the ruler to draw a straight line exactly through the points where the arc lines cross.

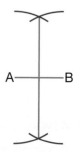

---

1 Construct the **perpendicular bisector** of each of these lines:

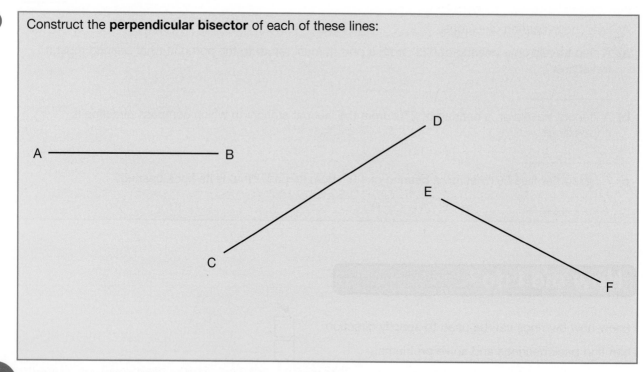

To construct the bisector of an angle means to split the angle exactly in half. To do this, follow these instructions:

- **Start with the angle**.

- Put the point of the compasses on the corner of the angle and draw a large arc that crosses both lines of the angle.

- Lift the point and place it on the point where the large arc crosses one of the lines. Draw a small arc line.

- Keeping the compasses set at the same width, lift the point and place it where the arc crosses the other line. Draw a small arc line to cross the other one.

- Finally use the ruler to draw a straight line from the corner of the angle to where the arc lines cross.

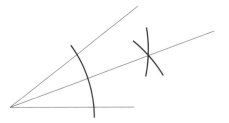

2 Construct the **bisector** of each of these angles.

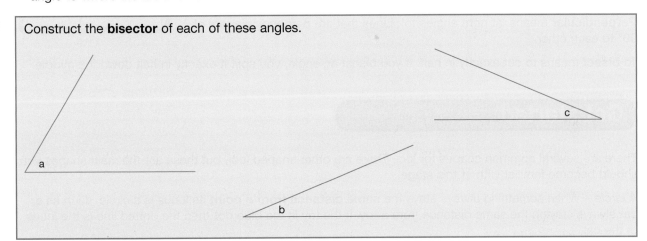

Practice

1 On paper, draw four lines at different orientations on the page.

a) On each, draw the perpendicular bisector.

b) Then join the ends of the original line to the places where the arcs cross to make a **rhombus**, like this:

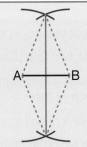

2 On paper, draw angles in different orientations on the page.

a) On each, draw the bisector of the angle.

b) Then join the points where the large arc crosses the lines of the angle to the places where the small arcs cross to make a **rhombus**, like this:

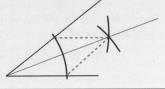

How did I do?

I can construct the perpendicular bisector of a line. ☐

I can construct a bisector of an angle. ☐

In this unit you will revise:

▶ what a locus is and the different types of loci

▶ how to draw the locus of a point that moves according to a simple rule.

Make sure your pencil case has all the right equipment. Make sure that you have a good pair of compasses, a sharp pencil and a ruler.

What you should know

A moving object creates a path of points called a locus. The plural of locus is loci: one locus, two loci. This **blue** line shows the locus of the tip of a car windscreen wiper. It shows all the possible points that the tip could be.

Perpendicular means 'at right angles to'. Lines that are perpendicular are at 90° to each other.

To **bisect** means to cut exactly in half. If you bisect an angle, you split it exactly in half down the middle.

Get started

There are several common shapes for loci. There are other shaped loci, but these are the main shapes you should become familiar with at this stage.

A circle – When something always stays the **same distance from a point** its locus is a circle, such as a cat always staying the same distance from a toy. If the toy is the blue dot then the dotted line is the locus of the cat.

1 Tick which of these you think are **circular** loci:

a) A goat is tied to a post. It walks around the post with the rope pulled tight. ☐

b) A man is in a field with two bulls. He walks between them keeping the same distance from each of them. ☐

c) The tip of a pencil in a set of compasses draws a shape on a piece of paper. ☐

d) A pea is sitting at the edge of the rotating plate in a microwave oven. ☐

e) A boat travels on a journey, keeping exactly 1 km from a buoy, until it returns to its starting point. ☐

f) A girl stands next to a long thin bench in a gymnasium. She walks around it, keeping exactly 1 m from it at all times. ☐

A straight line – When something always stays the **same distance between two points** its locus is a straight line – the perpendicular bisector.

If a fire station is to be built at exactly the same distance from a police station (P) and a hospital (H) it can be built anywhere along the perpendicular bisector of the line PH. In this diagram the red line shows where the fire station could be built.

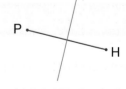

(The line could be continued further in either direction.)

A straight line – When something always stays the **same distance between two lines** its locus is a straight line – the bisector of the angle.

If a tree is to be planted the same distance from two walls that meet at a point, it can be planted anywhere along the bisector of the angle (the blue dotted line).

② Sketch these loci:

a) A car is driving, keeping the same distance from building F as building G.

Sketch the locus of the car.

b) A moving robot keeps an equal distance from two lines, AB and AC. Sketch the locus of the robot.

c) A horse is tethered to post P on a 3 metre rope. Sketch the locus of the maximum distance the horse can be from the post as a locus.

.G

F.

C

A

B

P.

Straight lines with semicircles – When something always stays the **same distance from a line** its locus is made from straight lines with semicircles at each end.

A girl stands next to a long thin bench in a gymnasium.
She walks around it, keeping exactly 1 m from it at all times.

Practice

① Construct an <u>accurate</u> scale diagram of each situation. You will need a pair of compasses and a ruler.

A wall is 8 m long. A dog is tied halfway along the wall on a 3.5 m length of rope. Shade the area where the dog can reach. Use the scale 1 cm to 1 m.

A police station (P) and a hospital (H) are 8 km apart. A fire station is to be built at exactly the same distance from each building. It must also not be more than 5 km from the hospital. Draw all the positions that the fire station could be built. Use the scale 1 cm to 2 km.

How did I do?

✔

I know what a locus is.

I can draw different types of loci.

65: Co-ordinates (1)

In this unit you will revise:
- co-ordinates in all four quadrants
- how to find the co-ordinates of corners of rectangles.

Don't be afraid to ask questions at school. Maths is a subject that builds on what you understand. If you don't understand something you'll struggle with the next thing too.

What you should know

Co-ordinates are written as pairs of numbers inside brackets, like (**3**, **2**). The first number tells you how many across from zero to move and the second number tells you how many up or down to move.

The first number is called the **x co-ordinate** and the second number is called the **y co-ordinate**, (**x**, **y**).

It is useful to remember the phrase 'Along the corridor and up or down the stairs' to remind you to move across first.

The **origin** is the point (0, 0) on a co-ordinate grid.

Get started

When you first learn about co-ordinates you use only positive numbers, like (3, 4) and (2, 1) and use a co-ordinate grid that looks like this:

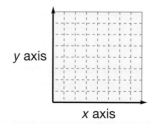

If a pair of co-ordinates includes a negative number, the axes must be extended through the origin to create four sections on a grid. These sections are known as **quadrants.**

A negative x co-ordinate means you move to the left from the origin.

A negative y co-ordinate means you move down from the origin.

(4, –3) means start at the origin and move **4** to the **right** and **3 down**.

(–4, –3) means start at the origin and move **4** to the **left** and **3 down**.

(–4, 3) means start at the origin and move **4** to the **left** and **3 up**.

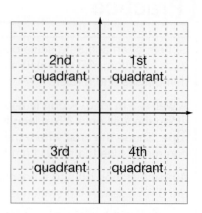

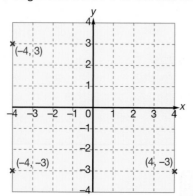

1 On the grid above plot and label these points:

a) (–1, 4)   b) (0, –1)   c) (–2, –1)   d) (3, 0)   e) (2, –2)

If you know some of the co-ordinates of the vertices (corners) of a rectangle, you can say what the other co-ordinates will be. Look at this:

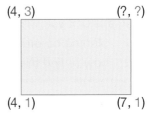

A rectangle has vertices at these three co-ordinates: (4, 3), (4, 1) and (7, 1). What are the co-ordinates of the fourth vertex?

Notice that the <u>x co-ordinates</u> of points above or below one another are the same!

4 and 4 are on the same vertical line.

7 and ? are on the same vertical line.

Notice that the <u>y co-ordinates</u> of points along the same horizontal line are the same!

1 and 1 are along the same horizontal line.

3 and ? are along the same horizontal line.

So the missing co-ordinates are **(7, 3).**

> The x co-ordinates of points above or below each other are the same.
>
> The y co-ordinates of points along the same horizontal line are the same.

❷ Fill in the missing co-ordinates.

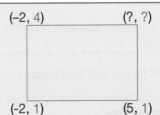

(___)

Practice

❶ Write the co-ordinates of the points marked A, B and C.

A = (___)

B = (___)

C = (___)

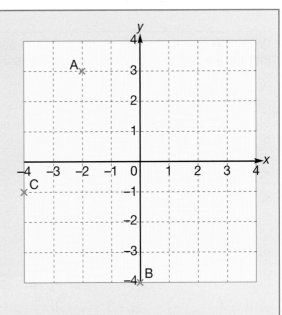

❷ A rectangle has vertices at these three co-ordinates: (0, 4), (5, 4) and (0, –3). What are the co-ordinates of the fourth vertex?

(___)

❸ A rectangle has vertices at these three co-ordinates: (–3, 6), (–3, –2) and (–1, –2). What are the co-ordinates of the fourth vertex?

(___)

How did I do?

I can use co-ordinates in all four quadrants. ☐

I can find the co-ordinates of corners of rectangles. ☐

66: Co-ordinates (2)

In this unit you will revise:

▶ plotting co-ordinates in all four quadrants
▶ how to find the co-ordinates of a mid-point along a line.

What you should know

The **origin** is the point (0, 0) on a co-ordinate grid.

Co-ordinates are written as pairs of numbers inside brackets, like (**3**, **2**). The first number, the **x co-ordinate,** tells you how many across from the origin to move and the second number, the **y co-ordinate**, tells you how many up or down to move.

Positive and negative co-ordinates are shown in four **quadrants.**

(**4, –3**) means start at the origin and move **4** to the **right** and **3 down**.

(**–4, –3**) means start at the origin and move **4** to the **left** and **3 down**.

(**–4, 3**) means start at the origin and move **4** to the **left** and **3 up**.

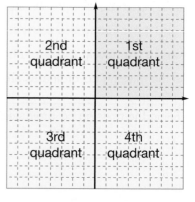

Get started

The mid-point of a line is the point exactly in the middle of it. The co-ordinates of the mid-point of a line can be found. On the grid below is the line AB. The mid-point is the point exactly half-way between A and B.

1 Write the co-ordinates of the letters in each pair. Join the two points on the grid with a line. Mark the mid-point of the line and give its co-ordinates. One has been done for you.

a) A = (**–1, 4**)   B = (**5, 4**)

   mid-point of AB = (**2, 4**)

b) C = (__,__)   D = (__,__)

   mid-point of CD = (__,__)

c) E = (__,__)   F = (__,__)

   mid-point of EF = (__,__)

d) C = (__,__)   E = (__,__)

   mid-point of CE = (__,__)

e) B = (__,__)   H = (__,__)

   mid-point of BH = (__,__)

f) F = (__,__)   G = (__,__)

   mid-point of FG = (__,__)

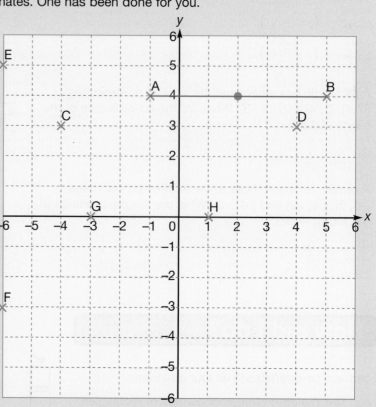

There is a formula for finding the co-ordinates of the mid-point of a line. If the end-points of the line have the co-ordinates (x_1, y_1) and (x_2, y_2) then:

- the x co-ordinate of the mid-point is $\frac{1}{2}(x_1 + x_2)$
- the y co-ordinate of the mid-point is $\frac{1}{2}(y_1 + y_2)$.

Or put in another way:

- To find the x co-ordinate of the mid-point: add the x co-ordinates and halve the answer.
- To find the y co-ordinate of the mid-point: add the y co-ordinates and halve the answer.

So for a line with the end-points (2, 3) and (−4, −3)

The x co-ordinate of the mid-point is:

$\frac{1}{2}(2 + -4) = \frac{1}{2}(-2) = -1$

The y co-ordinate of the mid-point is:

$\frac{1}{2}(3 + -3) = \frac{1}{2}(0) = 0$

So the mid-point has co-ordinates (−1, 0).

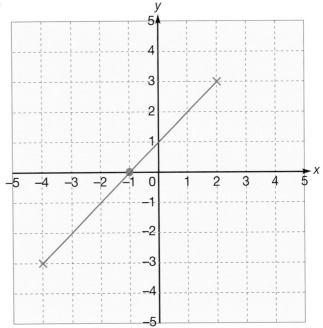

2 Find the co-ordinates of the mid-point (M) of the line PQ if the co-ordinates of P and Q are as follows:

a) P (−2, 3) Q (4, −1) M = (___,___)

b) P (−3, −2) Q (1, −4) M = (___,___)

c) P (−3, 0) Q (3, −4) M = (___,___)

d) P (−1, −3) Q (−5, 5) M = (___,___)

3 Check your answers by plotting each of the pairs of points P and Q and finding their mid-point on the grid above.

Practice

1 Find the co-ordinates of the mid-point (M) of the line PQ if the co-ordinates of P and Q are as follows:

a) P (5, −9) Q (−3, 5) M = (___,___)

b) P (−3, −7) Q (5, 7) M = (___,___)

c) P (−6, 4) Q (8, −8) M = (___,___)

d) P (−8, −3) Q (0, 5) M = (___,___)

e) P (−8, −6) Q (4, 4) M = (___,___)

f) P (−2, 7) Q (8, −3) M = (___,___)

g) P (−1, −4) Q (9, −6) M = (___,___)

h) P (−5, −2) Q (7, −8) M = (___,___)

i) P (−6, 2) Q (5, −4) M = (___,___)

j) P (−5, 0) Q (4, −6) M = (___,___)

How did I do?

I can plot and read co-ordinates in all four quadrants. ☐

I can find the co-ordinates of a mid-point along a line. ☐

In this unit you will revise:

▶ reflection, rotation and translation and combinations of these
▶ scale factors of enlargement.

What you should know

Transformations are ways of changing or moving shapes. There are several transformations you should know about: **reflection**, **rotation** and **translation**. As a shape is changed, the new shape is called the **image**.

To **reflect** a shape you need a mirror line. Mirror lines can be horizontal, vertical or diagonal.

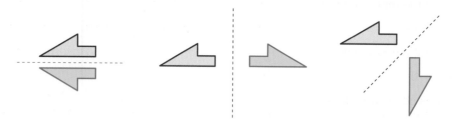

Translation just means move or slide without turning. A **translation** can be vertical, horizontal or diagonal.

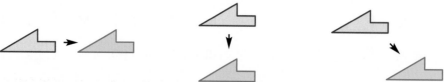

A translation of $\begin{pmatrix} 0 \\ -3 \end{pmatrix}$ means 0 squares across and 3 squares down.

A translation of $\begin{pmatrix} -1 \\ 4 \end{pmatrix}$ means 1 square to the left and 4 squares up.

A **rotation** means a turn. To **rotate** a shape you need a **centre of rotation**. The **centre of rotation** can be inside a shape, on one of its edges or even outside the shape. You also need to know through what angle you are rotating the shape.

The rotation or new shape is called the **image**.

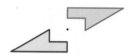

Get started

It is possible to describe some movements as a single transformation, such as a reflection. Some movements, however, can be described as several transformations, such as a reflection followed by a rotation or a translation followed by a reflection. In the grid below, it can be said that to map shape A onto shape D involves a reflection in the **y axis**, followed by a translation of (0, −9).

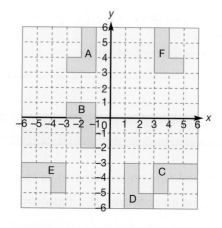

❶ Describe, in detail, the single transformation that will map:

a) C onto D _____

_____

b) A onto B _____

_____

c) F onto D _____

_____

❷ Describe, in detail, two transformations that will map:

a) C onto F _____

_____

b) D onto E _____

_____

An **enlargement** of a shape changes the size of it. An enlargement of scale factor 2 makes every side of the shape twice as long. An enlargement of scale factor 3 makes every side of the shape three times as long and so on. To find the scale factor of an enlargement, measure the lengths of the sides of the object. Then measure the corresponding sides of the image and divide each by the original lengths.

Practice

❶ In each case, find the scale factor of enlargement that maps the blue shape onto the grey shape.

a)   **b)**   **c)**   **d)**

Scale factor ____   Scale factor ____   Scale factor ____   Scale factor ____

❷ For each object and image above, draw straight lines with a ruler to join corresponding vertices (corners). For each pair of shapes, extend the lines so that they meet at a point and label it P. These are called the centres of enlargement.

How did I do?

I know the meaning of the words reflection, rotation and translation.

I can recognise transformations and combinations of them.

I can find scale factors of enlargement.

✔
☐
☐
☐

68: Transformations (2)

In this unit you will revise:

- the transformations of rotation, reflection and translation
- how to enlarge shapes, given a centre of enlargement and scale factor.

What you should know

Transformations are ways of changing or moving shapes. There are several transformations you should know about: **reflection**, **rotation**, **translation** and **enlargement.** As a shape is changed, the new shape is called the **image**.

To **reflect** a shape you need a mirror line. Mirror lines can be horizontal, vertical or diagonal.

Translation just means move or slide without turning. A **translation** can be vertical, horizontal or diagonal.

A translation of $\begin{pmatrix} 0 \\ -3 \end{pmatrix}$ means 0 squares across and 3 squares down.

A translation of $\begin{pmatrix} -1 \\ 4 \end{pmatrix}$ means 1 square to the left and 4 squares up.

A **rotation** means a turn. To **rotate** a shape you need a **centre of rotation**. The **centre of rotation** can be inside a shape, on one of its edges or even outside the shape. You also need to know through what angle you are rotating the shape.

An **enlargement** of a shape changes the size of it. An enlargement of scale factor 2 makes every side of the shape twice as long. An enlargement of scale factor 3 makes every side of the shape three times as long and so on.

Get started

Follow these rules to enlarge a shape when given a centre of enlargement and positive scale factor:

- Draw lines from the **centre of enlargement** to each vertex and **extend the lines**.
- Measure the distance from the centre of enlargement to a vertex.
- Multiply this distance by the scale factor to get a new distance.
- Mark this new distance along the extended line from the centre of enlargement to make a vertex of the image.
- Repeat for each vertex and join up the new vertices to create a larger image.

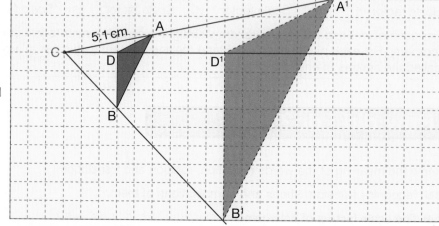

Scale factor 3

From C to A = 2.5 cm
2.5 × **3** = 7.5
So C to A¹ = 7.5 cm

1 Enlarge the blue kite in different ways as described below and label each image.

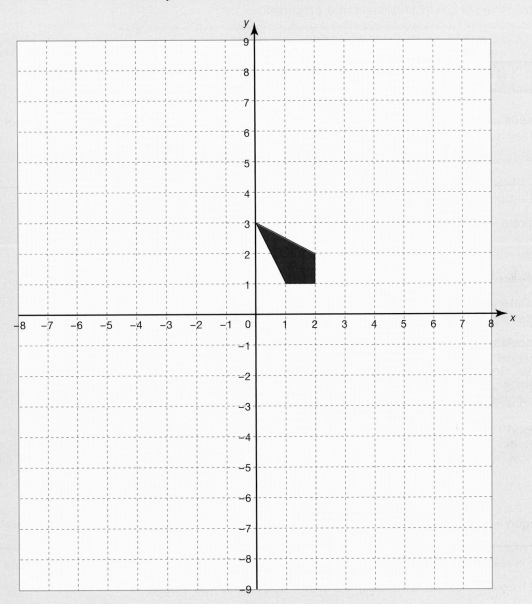

a) By scale factor 3 with centre of enlargement at (0, 0) to make image A.

b) By scale factor 2 with centre of enlargement at (–3, 5) to make image B.

c) By scale factor 5 with centre of enlargement at (2, 3) to make image C.

d) By scale factor 2 with centre of enlargement at (4, –1) to make image D.

e) Measure the corresponding sides of the images to check your answers.

How did I do?

I know the transformations of reflection, rotation and translation.

I can enlarge shapes, given a centre of enlargement and scale factor.

In this unit you will revise:

▶ the names of triangles and other 2-D shapes
▶ parallel and perpendicular lines
▶ the names of quadrilaterals and their properties.

What you should know

2-D shapes are flat shapes. They are called **2-D** because they have **2 D**imensions, length (or height) and width. They have no depth.

Here are some 2-D shapes you need to know, with their properties:

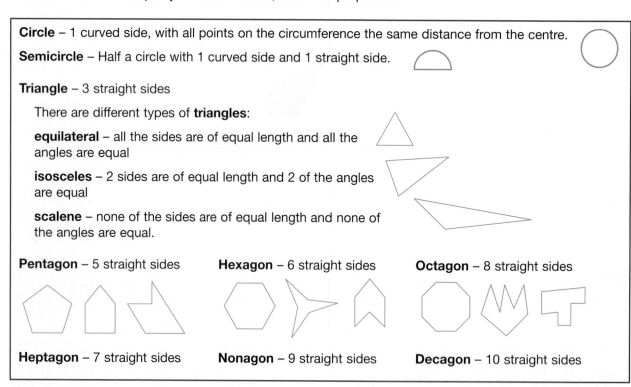

Circle – 1 curved side, with all points on the circumference the same distance from the centre.

Semicircle – Half a circle with 1 curved side and 1 straight side.

Triangle – 3 straight sides

There are different types of **triangles**:

equilateral – all the sides are of equal length and all the angles are equal

isosceles – 2 sides are of equal length and 2 of the angles are equal

scalene – none of the sides are of equal length and none of the angles are equal.

Pentagon – 5 straight sides   **Hexagon** – 6 straight sides   **Octagon** – 8 straight sides

Heptagon – 7 straight sides   **Nonagon** – 9 straight sides   **Decagon** – 10 straight sides

A shape is said to be **regular** when all its sides are the same length <u>and</u> all its angles are the same size.

Parallel lines are lines that are the same distance apart along their length.

Perpendicular lines are at right angles to each other.

Get started

A 2-D shape with <u>4 straight sides</u> is called a **quadrilateral**. Here are different types of **quadrilaterals:**

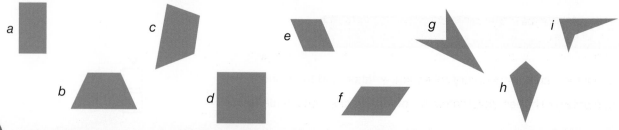

A **parallelogram** has 2 sets of parallel lines. (Shapes *a*, *d*, *e* and *f*)

A **rectangle** has 4 right angles. It is a type of parallelogram. (Shape *a*)

A **square** has 4 right angles and 4 sides of equal length. It is a type of rectangle. (Shape *d*)

A **rhombus** has 2 sets of parallel lines and 4 sides of equal length. It is a type of parallelogram. (Shapes *e* and *d*, Shape *d* is a special rhombus – a square)

A **trapezium** has 1 set of parallel lines (one of the parallel lines is longer than the other). (Shapes *b* and *c*)

A **kite** has 2 short sides adjacent and of equal length and 2 longer ones adjacent and of equal length. (Shapes *g* and *h*. Shape *g* can also be called an **arrowhead**.)

(Shape *i* is not any of the shapes above, so is just called a quadrilateral.)

Practice

1 Name these shapes:

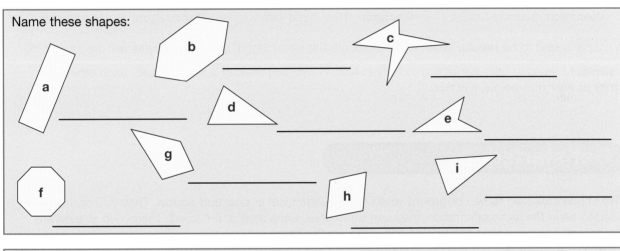

2 Write the name of each shape being described.

a) This quadrilateral has 2 sets of parallel lines and 4 sides of equal length. _____

b) This triangle has 3 sides of equal length and 3 lines of symmetry. _____

c) This quadrilateral has 2 short sides adjacent and of equal length and 2 longer ones adjacent and of equal length. _____

d) This shape has 5 equal sides and 5 equal angles. _____

e) This quadrilateral has 1 set of parallel lines. _____

3 Are these statements true?

a) A parallelogram is always a quadrilateral. _____

b) A quadrilateral is always a parallelogram. _____

c) A rectangle is a type of a parallelogram. _____

How did I do?

✔

I know the names of 2-D shapes including the different triangles. ☐

I can recognise parallel and perpendicular lines. ☐

I know the names of quadrilaterals and their properties. ☐

70: 2-D shape (2)

In this unit you will revise:

▶ what congruent means
▶ how to recognise congruent shapes
▶ the names and properties of 2-D shapes.

What you should know

Here are some 2-D shapes (polygons) you should know:

Triangle: 3 straight sides	**Quadrilateral**: 4 straight sides	**Pentagon**: 5 straight sides
Hexagon: 6 straight sides	**Heptagon**: 7 straight sides	**Octagon**: 8 straight sides
Nonagon: 9 straight sides	**Decagon**: 10 straight sides	**Dodecagon**: 12 straight sides

A shape is said to be **regular** when all its sides are the same length <u>and</u> all its angles are the same size.

To **bisect** means to split something exactly in half. When diagonals of a shape bisect each other they cross at their mid-points, like this:

Get started

Two shapes are said to be **congruent** when they are identical in **size and shape**. They do not, however, need to be in the same orientation, they can be rotated, translated or reflected. These two shapes are congruent. The corresponding angles and sides are the same.

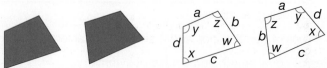

1 Tick the shapes in each row that are congruent to the blue shape:

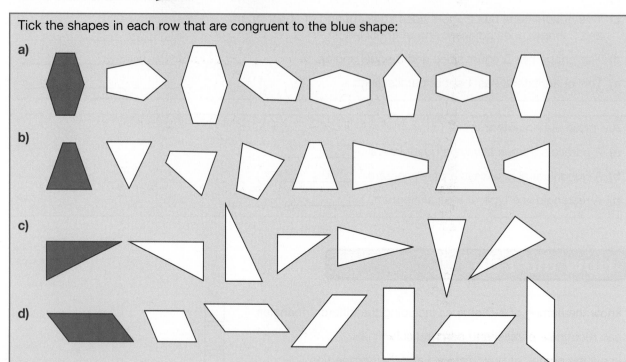

a)

b)

c)

d)

A **parallelogram** is a type of **quadrilateral**.
   Its opposite sides are equal and parallel.
   Its diagonals **bisect** each other.

A **rhombus** is a parallelogram with four equal sides.
   Its diagonals **bisect** at right angles.
   Both diagonals are lines of symmetry.
   It has a rotational symmetry of order 2.

2 Tick whether each sentence is true or false when describing the properties of a kite.

A **kite** is a quadrilateral that has two pairs
of adjacent sides that are equal   True ☐   False ☐

Its diagonals **bisect** each other.   True ☐   False ☐

Its diagonals cross at right angles.   True ☐   False ☐

Its diagonals are the same length.   True ☐   False ☐

One diagonal is a line of symmetry.   True ☐   False ☐

It has two lines of symmetry.   True ☐   False ☐

It has a rotational symmetry of order 2.   True ☐   False ☐

3 Tick whether each sentence is true or false when describing the properties of an isosceles trapezium:

An **isosceles trapezium** is a trapezium in which the
two opposite non-parallel sides are the same length.   True ☐   False ☐

Its diagonals **bisect** each other.   True ☐   False ☐

Its diagonals cross at right angles.   True ☐   False ☐

Its diagonals are the same length.   True ☐   False ☐

It has one line of symmetry.   True ☐   False ☐

It has a rotational symmetry of order 2.   True ☐   False ☐

Practice

1 Each of these shapes is made from two polygons. Draw lines to show the join. One has been done
for you.

a) Isosceles trapezium
   and rhombus

b) Square and kite

c) Trapezium and kite

d) Trapezium and parallelogram

e) Trapezium and triangle

f) Rhombus and an
   arrowhead

g) Irregular quadrilateral and
   parallelogram

h) Rectangle and hexagon

i) Trapezium and trapezium

How did I do?

I know what congruent means.   ☐

I can recognise congruent shapes.   ☐

I can recognise and describe properties of 2-D shapes.   ☐

71: Circles

In this unit you will revise:
- ▶ the definition of a circle and the names of its parts
- ▶ the formula for the circumference of a circle
- ▶ the formula for the area of a circle.

What you should know

A circle is a set of points all the same distance from its centre.

Get started

Each circle diagram has a part that is shaded or in bold. The diagrams show the circle words that you should know.

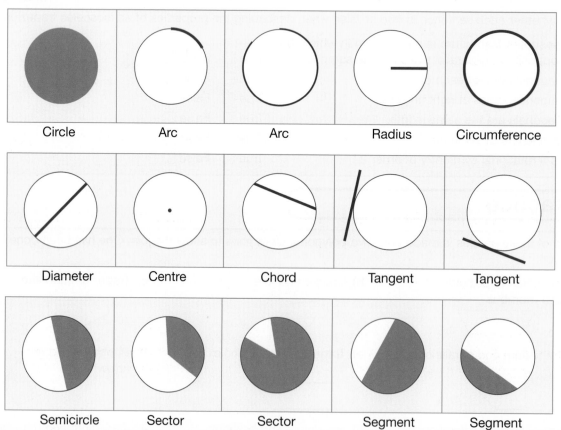

| Circle | Arc | Arc | Radius | Circumference |

| Diameter | Centre | Chord | Tangent | Tangent |

| Semicircle | Sector | Sector | Segment | Segment |

1 Write the circle words to complete the sentences:

a) The length from the centre of a circle to its circumference is called is the _____. It is half the length of the _____.

b) A chord that goes through the centre of a circle is called is the _____. It splits the circle into two equal _____.

c) Part of the circumference is called is an _____. The area surrounded by this and two radii is called a _____.

d) A straight line that goes through part of a circle, but not through its centre, is called is a _____. It splits the circle into two _____.

There is a relationship between the circumference and diameter of any circle. The circumference is always just over 3 times larger. It is *pi* times larger. Pi, shown by the π symbol, stands for the number 3.141 592 65... and is usually described as 3.14.

The **circumference** of a circle is found by multiplying the diameter by pi, π.

Circumference = $\pi \times d$ or Circumference = $\pi \times r \times 2$

❷ Find the circumference of each using the π key on your calculator.
Round your answers to 2 decimal places.

a)
6 cm

b)
10 cm

c)
4 cm

d)
2.5 cm

C = _____ cm   C = _____ cm   C = _____ cm   C = _____ cm

The **area** of a circle is found by squaring the radius and multiplying by π. This can be written as:

Area of circle = $\pi \times r \times r$ or Area of circle = πr^2

Practice

❶ Find the area of each circle using the x^2 and π keys on your calculator.
Round your answers to 2 decimal places.

a)
4 cm

b)
6 cm

c)
4.9 cm

d)
3.7 cm

A = _____ cm²   A = _____ cm²   A = _____ cm²   A = _____ cm²

e)
5.4 cm

f)
7.3 cm

g)
8.5 cm

h)
10.2 cm

A = _____ cm²   A = _____ cm²   A = _____ cm²   A = _____ cm²

❷ Find the area of each circle using the x^2 and π keys on your calculator. Round your answers to 2 decimal places. Notice that the diameter of each circle is given, not the radius.

a)
6.5 cm

b)
7.9 cm

c)
8.8 cm

d)
10.7 cm

A = _____ cm²   A = _____ cm²   A = _____ cm²   A = _____ cm²

How did I do?

I know the names of parts of a circle.   ☐

I know and can use the formula for circumference of a circle.   ☐

I know and can use the formula for the area of a circle.   ☐

In this unit you will revise:
- ▶ the names of 3-D shapes
- ▶ plans and elevations of 3-D shapes.

What you should know

3-D shapes have **3 D**imensions: length (or height), width and depth.

These are the names of the 3-D shapes you should know:

Cube

Cuboid *(rectangular prism)*

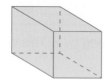

Prism

A prism has the same cross-section along its length. This cross-section can be any of the 2-D shapes. Think of a prism as a 2-D shape that has been stretched to make a 3-D shape.

Triangular prism   Hexagonal prism   Octagonal prism

Pyramid (*Square-based pyramid, pentagonal-based pyramid*)

A pyramid has a 2-D base, like a square, triangle or pentagon. The other **faces** are triangles and join together at a point or **vertex.**

A 3-D shape with only flat faces is called a **polyhedron.** The shapes above are all **polyhedra.** The shapes below are not polyhedra as they have curved faces.

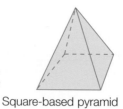

Square-based pyramid   Pentagonal-based pyramid

Cylinder *(circular prism)*   **Sphere**   **Hemisphere**   **Cone**

Remember that even a coin is a 3-D shape and so is called a cylinder.

Get started

A 3-D shape can be viewed from four elevations, from a plan view and from below. A plan view is what you see when you look down on a shape from above. The elevations of a 3-D shape are the four views you get when you look at it from the front, the back and the two sides.

This model has been made with four different-coloured interlocking cubes.

Front   Right   Back   Left
elevation elevation elevation elevation Plan

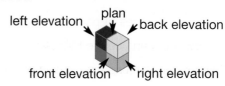

left elevation   plan   back elevation

front elevation   right elevation

1 Sketch the four elevations and plan for each of these shapes

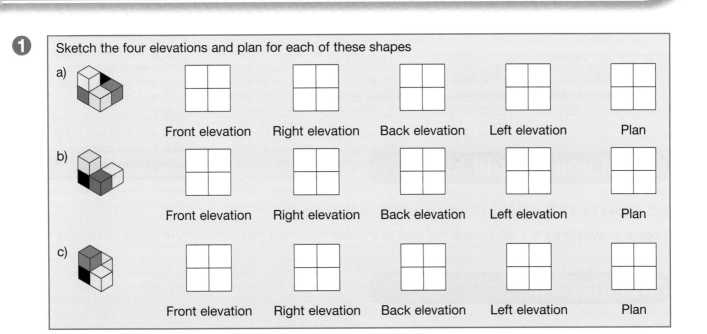

a)

Front elevation Right elevation Back elevation Left elevation Plan

b)

Front elevation Right elevation Back elevation Left elevation Plan

c)

Front elevation Right elevation Back elevation Left elevation Plan

Practice

1 For each of these 3-D shapes sketch a **plan** view:

a)

b)

c)

d)

2 In every square of each of your plan views in the question above, write how many cubes are on top of one another.

How did I do?

I know the names of 3-D shapes.

I can draw plans and elevations of 3-D shapes.

149

In this unit you will revise:

▶ planes of symmetry in 3-D shapes
▶ how to find the number of planes of symmetry of prisms.

When revising, take regular breaks. If you can, get some fresh air outside. It will help to clear your head and you will come back to your revision feeling more alert.

What you should know

3-D shapes have **3 D**imensions: length (or height), width and depth.

A **plane of symmetry** is a flat surface that acts as a mirror, splitting a 3-D shape into two reflected halves.

Get started

These cuboids are made from linking 12 cubes together.

Each cuboid is then broken in half along a plane of symmetry.

These show vertical and horizontal planes of symmetry.

Planes of symmetry can be vertical, horizontal or sloping.

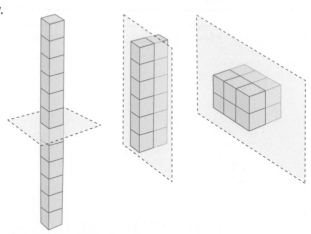

❶ Tick which of these show planes of symmetry.

Check that the shapes on each side of the plane of symmetry are reflections of each other.

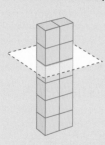 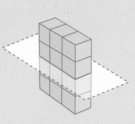 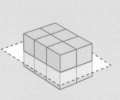 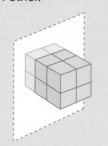

❷ Tick which of these show planes of symmetry.

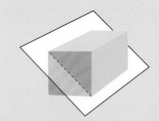 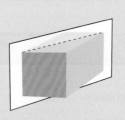 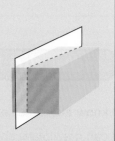

A prism is a 3-D shape that has the same cross-section all the way along its length. A plane of symmetry splits any prism half way along its length. In addition to this one plane of symmetry, it can also have other planes of symmetry. The number of these depends upon the number of lines of symmetry of the end face.

A triangular prism with an **equilateral triangle** as its end face will have 4 planes of symmetry. One plane is half way along its length and 3 slice along its length from end to end.

4 planes of symmetry

Unless all the faces of the prism are squares, the number of planes of symmetry will always be one more than the number of lines of symmetry of the end face. A cylinder has an infinite number of planes of symmetry as a circle has an infinite number of lines of symmetry.

Practice

1 State the number of planes of symmetry of each of these prisms:

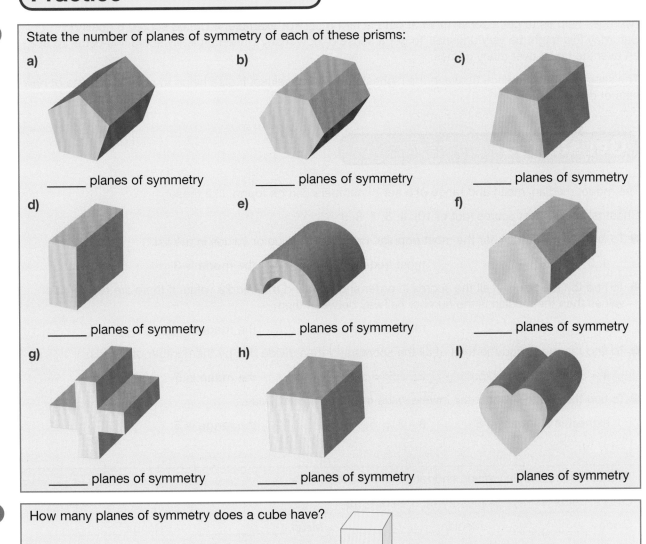

a)

_____ planes of symmetry

b)

_____ planes of symmetry

c)

_____ planes of symmetry

d)

_____ planes of symmetry

e)

_____ planes of symmetry

f)

_____ planes of symmetry

g)

_____ planes of symmetry

h)

_____ planes of symmetry

I)

_____ planes of symmetry

2 How many planes of symmetry does a cube have?

_____

How did I do?

✔

I know about planes of symmetry.

☐

I can find the number of planes of symmetry of prisms.

☐

74: Statistics (1)

In this unit you will revise:

- how to find the mode, median and range of a set of data
- how to calculate the mean, including from a simple frequency table.

What you should know

Statistics means collecting, organising and analysing data. One way of analysing data is to find averages.

Averages are used to represent a middle or typical value in a set of numbers. There are three types of average: **mean, median** and **mode**.

Averages help us to get a sense of what data is telling us. For example, if United scored 6 goals on Saturday this might be very unusual. To get a sense of how many United typically score it is better to use an average taken over many games.

The **range** is the difference between the highest and lowest values. It also helps to give us a sense of how sets of data differ.

Get started

The mode, median, mean and range of a set of numbers can be found, like these:

Christos's Maths test scores (out of 10): 4, 3, 7, 8, 3

- To find the **mode** look for the most popular, or frequent, value or values in the list.

    4, 3, 7, 8, 3   most frequent value   the **mode** is **3**

- To find the **median** put all the scores in order and then find the middle value. If there are two middle values then the median is the number halfway between them.

    3, 3, 4, 7, 8   middle value   the **median** is **4**

- To find the **mean** find the total of all the scores and then divide this by the number of scores.

    $4 + 3 + 7 + 8 + 3 = 25$ $25 \div 5 = 5$ the **mean** is **5**

- To find the **range** subtract the lowest value from the highest value.

    highest is 8, lowest is 3 $8 - 3 = 5$ the **range** is **5**

1   Find the mode, median, mean and range of this set of data:

Luba's Maths test scores (out of 10): 8, 9, 5, 8, 10

Mode _____   Median _____   Mean _____   Range _____

Sometimes data is presented in a frequency table, which can make it more difficult to find averages.

The same set of scores is shown here in two ways:

4 7 7 5 5 6 6 7 7

Score (s)	Frequency (f)
4	1
5	2
6	2
7	4

To find the mode and mean when the data is in a table follow these steps:

- To find the **mode** look for the score with the highest frequency.

  the score 7 has the frequency 4   the **mode** is **7**

- To find the **mean** multiply each score by the frequency and add these values. Then divide by the total frequency. It can help to draw an extra column and row in the table.

Score (s)	Frequency (f)	s × f
4	1	4
5	2	10
6	2	12
7	4	28
Totals	9	54

$54 \div 9 = 6$ the **mean** is **6**

Practice

1 These diagrams show the number of pupils in each class in different schools.

Find the mode, median, mean and range of each set of data:

a)

32	37	29	17	23
27	23	32	28	32

mode = _____   median = _____

mean = _____   range = _____

b)

35	23	28	29
31	35	19	32

mode = _____   median = _____

mean = _____   range = _____

c)

28	32	25
19	27	18
28	33	15

mode = _____   median = _____

mean = _____   range = _____

d)

25	24	32	30
36	31	29	24
20	29	26	24

mode = _____   median = _____

mean = _____   range = _____

2 Find the mean of this set of data, by completing the table:

a)

Score (s)	Frequency (f)	s × f
2	1	
3	6	
4	0	
5	2	
6	3	
Totals		

mean = _____

b) Write the mode of the data.

mode = _____

c) Find the range of the data.

range = _____

How did I do?

✔

I can find the mean, median, mode and range of data in a list.   ☐

I can calculate the mean from a simple frequency table.   ☐

75: Statistics (2)

In this unit you will revise:

▶ the mode, median, mean and range

▶ how to find the mean of a set of data in a table

▶ how to calculate the mean using an assumed mean.

> When you are reorganising a set of data, always cross off the numbers as you count them and always check that you have the correct total at the end.

What you should know

Statistics means collecting, organising and analysing data. One way of analysing data is to find averages. **Averages** are used to represent a middle or typical value in a set of numbers. There are three types of average: **mean**, **median** and **mode**. The mode, median and mean of a set of numbers can be found, like this:

Rob's Maths test scores (out of 10):   4   3   7   8   3

● to find the **mode** look for the most popular, or frequent, value or values in the list.

4, 3, 7, 8, 3   most frequent value   the **mode** is **3**

● to find the **median** put all the scores in order and then find the middle value. If there are two middle values then the median is the number half-way between them.

3, 3, 4, 7, 8   middle value   the **median** is **4**

● to find the **mean** find the total of all the scores and then divide this by the number of scores.

4 + 3 + 7 + 8 + 3 = 25   25 ÷ 5 = 5   the **mean** is **5**

The **range** is the difference between the highest and lowest values. It also helps to give us a sense of how sets of data differ. The range here is 5, which is found by subtracting 3 from 8.

Get started

Sometimes data is presented in a **frequency** table, which can make it more difficult to find averages.

The same set of scores is shown here in two ways:

4 7 7 5 5 6 6 7 7

Scores (s)	Frequency (f)
4	1
5	2
6	2
7	4

To find the **mean**, when the data is in a table, multiply each score by its frequency and add these values. Then divide by the total frequency. It can help to draw an extra column and row in the table.

Scores (s)	Frequency (f)	s × f
4	1	4
5	2	10
6	2	12
7	4	28
Totals	9	54

54 ÷ 9 = 6   the **mean** is **6**

154

1 Find the mean of this set of data, by completing the table:

Scores (s)	Frequency (f)	s × f
2	1	
3	2	
4	7	
5	6	
6	4	
Totals		

Mean = _____

To find the mean using a mental method, use an **assumed mean** as explained below.

Find the mean of these numbers: 48.6,   51.2,   52.1,   49.9,   50.2

1. Look at the values and choose an easy number that lies somewhere in the middle. Call this the 'assumed mean':

    50.0

2. Find the differences between each number and the assumed mean, saying whether they are more or less using the positive or negative signs.

    −1.4,   +1.2,   +2.1,   −0.1,   +0.2

3. Find the total of all these differences (watch out, this might be negative).   +2.0

4. Then divide this number by the number of values.   2.0 ÷ 5 = 0.4

5. Finally add this total to your assumed mean. This is the actual mean.   50.4

Practice

1 Use an assumed mean to find the mean of each set of numbers:

a) 10.2, 9.9, 10.4, 9.9   mean = _____   b) 10.2, 9.7, 10.1, 9.6   mean = _____

c) 11.9, 12.2, 11.7, 11.4   mean = _____   d) 8.1, 8.3, 8.5, 7.9, 7.7   mean = _____

e) 15.7, 16.3, 16.3, 16.8, 15.9   mean = _____   f) 63.2, 63.8, 63.4, 62.8, 63.8   mean = _____

g) 37.6, 38.5, 38.2, 38.4, 37.3   mean = _____   h) 24.6, 24.3, 25.1, 25.3, 24.7   mean = _____

2 The mean of four numbers is 9.8.

These are three of the numbers: 10.1,   10.2,   9.5,   ...

Find the fourth number.

How did I do?

I know how to find the mean, median, mode and range of data in a list.   ✔ ☐

I can calculate the mean of a set of data in a table.   ☐

I can calculate the mean using an assumed mean.   ☐

76: Collecting data (1)

In this unit you will revise:

▶ different ways in which data can be obtained, such as a survey, an experiment or using secondary sources

▶ how to design a questionnaire to use in a simple survey

▶ important things to consider when conducting a survey.

What you should know

When people want to find out some information about something, data can be collected in various ways:

● A survey can be conducted, by asking people questions.

● An experiment can be conducted, such as measuring or timing something.

● Data can be found from books, magazines or the internet. This is called **secondary** data, as someone else has already collected it for you. The data collected in the first two ways is known as **primary** data, as you are collecting it yourself.

Get started

If you are conducting a survey, usually you must design your own questionnaire. When doing this always make the questions as simple as possible and make sure that the person can answer them quickly. You don't want them to give you too much information that is not relevant to your survey. Never ask leading questions that encourage the person to give a particular response. Also think about whether a question is too personal, like asking someone their age. You can ask this more generally like this:

In which age group are you?   0–19   20–39   40–59   60+

1 Give at least three reasons why questionnaire 2 is better than questionnaire 1 below:

Questionnaire 1

Do you watch TV?   For how long do you watch it?
How often do you watch it?   What is your favourite type of programme?

Questionnaire 2

1. Do you watch TV?   Yes ☐   No ☐   (If no, stop the survey now.)

2. How often do you watch TV?
             Every day ☐   Most days ☐   Once or twice a week ☐
   Less than once a week ☐   Other ....

3. For about how many hours do you watch TV in a day?
   Less than 1 hour a day ☐   About 1–2 hours a day ☐
   About 2–4 hours a day ☐   More than 4 hours a day ☐

4. What are your favourite types of programmes?
   Comedy Soaps ☐   News ☐   Documentary ☐   Children's ☐
        Reality TV ☐   Wildlife ☐   Films ☐
         Cartoons ☐   Dramas ☐   Other ....

_____

_____

David is deciding how best to conduct a survey. He must consider how many people to survey. The information will be more reliable if a large number of people are asked. It is important that he thinks carefully about whom he will survey. The data might be unreliable unless a wide range of people is asked, of different ages, in different places and so on.

He is choosing between these two ways:

1 by giving a questionnaire sheet to lots of people to fill in themselves

2 by a person (or several people) asking the questions directly and filling in a data collection sheet.

There are advantages and disadvantages of each method.

Some advantages of the first method:

- A large number of people could be given sheets to fill in.
- People could fill them in, in their own time and wouldn't need to be stopped in the street.
- Lots of responses could be collected very quickly.

Some disadvantages of the first method:

- Photocopying costs might be expensive.
- People might not fill them in and give or send them back.
- People might not understand the questions and there would be no one to ask.

❷ Write two advantages and two disadvantages of the second method above:

Two advantages of the second method:

- _____
- _____

Two disadvantages of the second method:

- _____
- _____

Practice

❶ Jo wants to find out about the people who use the leisure centre. Her questions below would not make a very good questionnaire. Design some better questions for her questionnaire that will give clearer information and will be easier to fill in. This will need to be completed in a separate work book.

- What sport are you here to play?
- For how long do you play?
- How old are you?
- How often do you play it?
- What other sports do you play here?

_____

_____

How did I do?

✔

I know different ways that data can be obtained. ☐

I can design a questionnaire to use in a simple survey. ☐

I know some of the important things to consider when conducting a survey. ☐

77: Collecting data (2)

In this unit you will revise:
- ▶ how to use two-way tables
- ▶ how to construct tables for large sets of raw data, choosing suitable class intervals.

! When you are reorganising a set of data, always cross off the numbers as you count them and always check that you have the correct total at the end.

What you should know

When people want to find out some information about something, data can be collected in various ways:

- ● A survey can be conducted, by asking people questions.
- ● An experiment can be conducted, such as measuring or timing something.
- ● Data can be found from books, magazines or the internet. This is called **secondary** data, as someone else has already collected it for you. The data collected in the first two ways is known as **primary** data, as you are collecting it yourself.

Get started

When collecting data to help you answer a question, it is sometimes appropriate to use a two-way table. A two-way table lets you see the relationship between two things.

Here 600 people of different age groups were asked to say how frequently they spoke to their neighbours. This information was gathered to see whether older people could be said to be friendlier than younger people.

Indicators of neighbourliness: by age

	Age groups					
	16–29	30–39	40–49	50–59	60–69	70+
Frequency of speaking to neighbours (%)						
Daily	18	24	21	27	39	44
3–6 days per week	20	23	26	24	24	22
1–2 days per week	32	32	36	33	26	22
Less than once a week	30	21	17	16	11	12

Use the data shown in the two-way table above to help you answer these questions:

1 How many adults in their forties spoke to their neighbours:

a) every day? _____   b) less than once a week? _____

2 How many adults aged 70 or above spoke to their neighbours:

a) every day? _____   b) less than once a week? _____

3 How many people aged 16 to 29 spoke to their neighbours:

a) every day? _____   b) less than once a week? _____

4 Write one statement about the figures for different age ranges.

_____

5 Does the information suggest that 'In this survey, older people are friendlier than younger people'?

_____

Large sets of data can be organised into tables, by grouping the data into equal class intervals. If the data is **continuous data** (where intermediate values make sense), data must be grouped using the ≤ and < signs, like this:

Equal class intervals (E)	Tally	Frequency
$0 \leq E < 10$		
$10 \leq E < 20$		
$20 \leq E < 30$		

Notice that a value of 20 would be shown in the bottom row, not in the row above it.

To choose equal class intervals, follow these steps:

- First look for the highest and lowest values in the list and subtract the lowest from the highest to find the **range**. Round this to a suitable value.
- Decide on the number of equal class intervals to have and divide the rounded range by this number.
- Use the ≤ and < signs to record the equal class intervals and use tallying to group the data.

Practice

1 The birth weights of 100 babies are shown in the list below.

Birth weights of 100 babies (in ounces)

138, 111, 87, 143, 122, 128, 129, 110, 143, 146, 124, 124, 145, 106, 104, 97, 137, 103, 142, 130, 156, 133, 120, 155, 110, 122, 145, 115, 108, 102, 120, 113, 128, 123, 108, 136, 138, 132, 120, 143, 140, 144, 141, 110, 114, 115, 92, 115, 144, 125, 114, 122, 93, 119, 105, 115, 137, 122, 131, 103, 146, 114, 130, 119, 113, 134, 107, 134, 75, 107, 124, 122, 101, 128, 91, 127, 153, 121, 120, 99, 125, 114, 128, 134, 114, 92, 85, 135, 87, 125, 128, 105, 149, 129, 139, 114, 138, 129, 138, 131.

a) Find the highest and lowest values and give the range _____ – _____ = _____

b) Complete the frequency table by grouping the data into 5 equal class intervals.

Birth weights of babies (B) in ounces	Tally	Frequency

c) Check that your frequencies add up to 100.

2 Use the information in your table to find the modal class (the group with the highest **frequency**).

_____

How did I do?

I can use two-way tables. ☐

I can construct tables for large sets of raw data, choosing suitable class intervals. ☐

In this unit you will revise:

▶ how to construct a frequency table where the data is grouped
▶ how to draw a bar chart/frequency diagram where the data is grouped.

When looking at graphs, always read the numbers on the scale carefully. When finding the height of a bar on a bar chart it can help to draw extra lines across the graph with a ruler.

What you should know

A **frequency table** shows us how often something happens or how many things you have. To record data tallying can be used, where data is grouped in fives, like this:

卅 = 5

We then write the frequency (or total) in the next column. These tables are also known as tally charts.

A frequency table showing how many birds visited the bird table in 1 hour

Type	Tally	Frequency
Robin	卅	5
Blackbird	‖	2
Sparrow	卅 ‖	7
Chaffinch	‖‖	4
Greenfinch	卅 卅 ‖	11

Get started

Sometimes, when collecting data, it is best to group the information.

A group of 20 teenagers did a sponsored fun-run in aid of charity. This list shows the amount of money (in pounds) each of them raised.

£34, £17, £26, £28, £21, £16, £12, £22, £17, £19, £28, £24, £11, £16, £23, £25, £15, £30, £20, £21

We can put this information into a frequency table, but, to ensure that there are not too many rows in the table, it is best to group the data, as shown on the right:

Notice that each group in the table is of equal size. They can be called 'equal class intervals'.

Number of pounds (£)	Frequency
10–14	2
15–19	6
20–24	6
25–29	4
30–34	2

1

a) Finish writing the equal class intervals in the frequency table on the right.

b) Now group this data into the table. Cross each value off as you count it and check that your frequency total is 20 when you have finished.

£34, £11, £26, £13, £55, £35, £40, £10, £31, £44, £57, £26, £18, £41, £36, £32, £22, £17, £49, £48

Number of pounds (£)	Frequency
10–19	
20–29	
30–	

Once data is grouped it can be shown in a bar chart or frequency diagram:

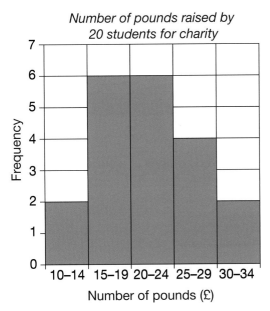

Number of pounds raised by 20 students for charity

Practice

1 This data shows the number of hours of TV watched by 24 pupils during one week:

16, 4, 8, 17, 22, 37, 36, 25, 24, 9, 37, 44, 48, 35, 25, 27, 11, 23, 27, 36, 41, 39, 36, 20

a) Complete the frequency table for the data shown.

b) Show this data in a bar chart/frequency diagram.

Number of hours	Frequency
0–9	
10–	

Frequency

Number of hours

How did I do?

I can construct a frequency table where the data is grouped. □

I can draw a bar chart/frequency diagram where the data is grouped. □

In this unit you will revise:
- ▶ how to calculate the angle of each sector in a pie chart
- ▶ how to construct a pie chart using a protractor or angle measurer.

What you should know

A **pie chart** shows information as different-sized portions of a circle. It can help you to compare proportions.

Get started

When asked to draw a pie chart of some data you will need a pair of compasses to draw a circle, a protractor or angle measurer and a calculator.

Look at how the data in this table can be represented in a pie chart.

This data shows the activities or items that 100 twelve-year-old boys spend the largest part of their pocket money on.

When constructing a pie chart the angle of each sector must be calculated.

To do this, find the fraction of the whole (of 360°) that each section represents. It is helpful to add extra columns to the table. The total number of boys is **100**, so this is the denominator of each fraction. The fraction is multiplied by 360° to find the angle of the sector. The angles are rounded to the nearest degree.

Activity or item	Number of boys
Sports and hobbies	45
Going out	10
CDs, videos, DVDs	18
Clothes	9
Computer games	11
Other	7

Activity or item	Number of boys	Calculation (fraction × 360)	Angle of sector
Sports and hobbies	45	$\frac{45}{100} \times 360$	162°
Going out	10	$\frac{10}{100} \times 360$	36°
CDs, videos, DVDs	18	$\frac{18}{100} \times 360$	64.8 → 65°
Clothes	9	$\frac{9}{100} \times 360$	32.4 → 32°
Computer games	11	$\frac{11}{100} \times 360$	39.6 → 40°
Other	7	$\frac{7}{100} \times 360$	25.2 → 25°

Then use the protractor to draw each angle about the centre of a circle.

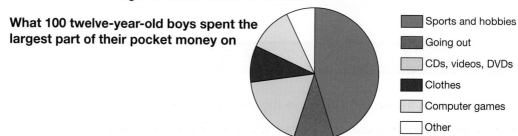

What 100 twelve-year-old boys spent the largest part of their pocket money on

- Sports and hobbies
- Going out
- CDs, videos, DVDs
- Clothes
- Computer games
- Other

Practice

1 Complete both tables and use them to help you draw two pie charts.

Table 1: What 120 twelve-year-old girls spent the largest part of their pocket money on.

Activity or item	Number of girls	Calculation (fraction × 360)	Angle of sector
Sports and hobbies	27	$\frac{27}{120} \times 360$	81°
Going out	26		
CDs, videos, DVDs	25		
Clothes	23		
Toiletries	12		
Other	7		

Table 2: What 100 fourteen-year-old girls spent the largest part of their pocket money on.

Activity or item	Number of girls	Calculation (fraction × 360)	Angle of sector
Sports and hobbies	3	$\frac{3}{100} \times 360$	10.8° → 11°
Going out	29		
CDs, videos, DVDs	22		
Clothes	24		
Toiletries	19		
Other	3		

When completing the pie charts, use the same colours for the sectors in both pie charts to help you to compare them. Give each pie chart a title and label or provide a key for each sector.

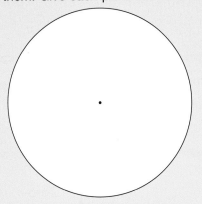 

2 Compare the two pie charts and write three statements about differences between the spending habits of 12- and 14-year-old girls.

How did I do?

I know how to calculate the angle of each sector in a pie chart. ☐

I know how to construct a pie chart using a protractor or angle measurer. ☐

163

In this unit you will revise:

▶ how to interpret scatter graphs

▶ ideas of correlation.

> When looking at graphs, always read the numbers on the scale carefully. When finding the height of a bar on a bar chart it can help to draw extra lines across the graph with a ruler.

What you should know

A **pie chart** shows information as different sized portions of a circle. It can help you to compare proportions.

A **bar chart** shows information as vertical or horizontal bars. Often bar charts are used to show frequency and also might show data that is grouped.

A **bar-line graph** shows information as lines. It is similar to a bar chart and often shows frequency.

A **line graph** shows points joined together. It is used commonly for time graphs and for information that has been measured.

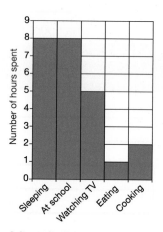

A pie chart

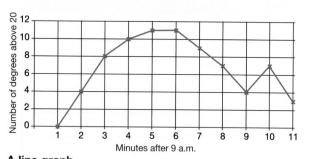

A line graph

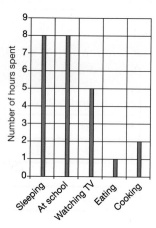

A bar chart   **A bar-line graph**

Get started

Scatter graphs show whether there is a connection between two sets of values. A connection could show:

● that one value increases as the other increases (a positive correlation)

● that one value increases as the other decreases (negative correlation)

● no connection at all (zero correlation).

The arrangement of the dots on the graph show whether the correlation is positive, negative or zero.

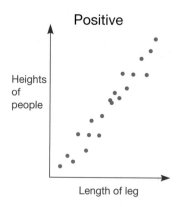

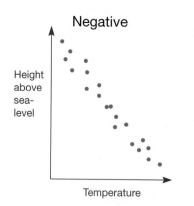

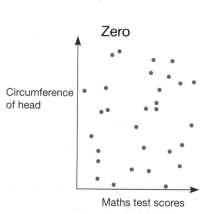

1 Do these scatter graphs show a positive, a negative or a zero correlation?

a)

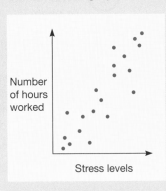

Number of hours worked

Stress levels

b)

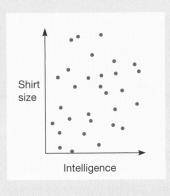

Shirt size

Intelligence

c)

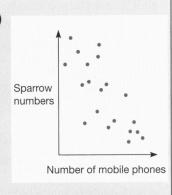

Sparrow numbers

Number of mobile phones

_____   _____   _____

If there is a correlation between two things a **line of best fit** can be drawn. This is a line that best represents the data on the graph. When drawing a line of best fit, use a ruler. Try to have as many points above the line as below the line. The line does not have to go through all the points or through the **origin**.

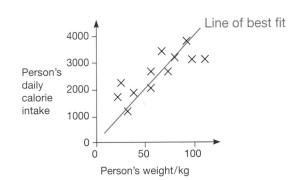

The line of best fit can be used to help predict or estimate other information. It can be seen from the graph that a person of about 50 kg would have a daily intake of about 2000 calories.

2 Estimate the daily calorie intake for a person weighing:

a) 75 kg _____   b) 100 kg _____

Practice

1 Explain the type of correlation in each of these newspaper headlines:

a) The more one eats, the more one weighs. The less one eats, the less one weighs.

_____

b) A study claims that the more mobile phones there are, the greater the fall in sparrow numbers.

_____

c) According to a new study, the more violence teenagers watch on television, the more likely they are to grow into violent adults. _____

d) The more hours you work, the more likely you are to suffer from stress. _____

e) Mathematicians tend to make good jugglers. _____

f) The greater the number of walkers crossing a bird's territory, the less the bird sings.

_____

How did I do?

I know how to interpret scatter graphs. ☐

I understand ideas of correlation. ☐

81: Probability (1)

When a test or exam is getting closer, don't worry about it. Use the checklist at the back of this book. It will help you to realise how much you already know and can point you towards topics that you need to revise a little more.

In this unit you will revise:

▶ the meaning of the term mutually exclusive

▶ that if the probability of an event is p, then the probability of it not occurring is $1 - p$

▶ how to find experimental probabilities.

What you should know

The probability of something happening can be measured in several ways:

1 Seeing how often it has happened before

2 By doing an experiment

3 Using equally likely outcomes

A probability based on **equally likely outcomes** is known as **theoretical probability.**

This formula can be used:

$$\text{Theoretical probability (P)} = \frac{\text{the number of things you want}}{\text{the number of equally likely outcomes}}$$

Get started

The probability of an event happening is related to the probability of the event NOT happening.

They are related because every single possible **outcome** will fall into either group. Either the event will happen or it will NOT. There are no other possibilities. These two probabilities are said to be **mutually exclusive**.

The probabilities of mutually exclusive events have a total of 1.

A bag contains 12 balls, seven of which are blue. One ball is picked at random.

The probability of picking a blue ball is $\frac{7}{12}$.

What is the probability of NOT picking a blue ball?

This can be calculated by subtracting $\frac{7}{12}$ from 1.

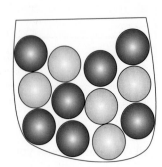

$$1 - \frac{7}{12} =$$

$$\frac{12}{12} - \frac{7}{12} = \frac{5}{12}$$

The probability of NOT picking a blue ball is $\frac{5}{12}$.

1 Answer these probability questions:

a) If the probability that a dice rolls an even number is $\frac{1}{2}$, what is the probability that it will not be even? _____

b) If the probability that it will rain today is $\frac{2}{7}$, what is the probability that it will NOT rain today? _____

c) If the probability that a card picked from a pack is a spade is $\frac{1}{4}$, what is the probability that it will NOT be a spade? _____

Experimental probability can be found by conducting an experiment many times and recording the results. Using the results, probabilities can be calculated using this formula:

$$\text{Experimental probability} = \frac{\text{number of times the event has happened}}{\text{total number of results}}$$

If a dice was rolled 100 times and the number 4 was rolled 20 times the experimental probability of rolling a 4 would be $\frac{20}{100}$.

This can be written as a fraction in its simplest form.

$$P(4) = \frac{20}{100} = \frac{1}{5}$$

The more times an experiment is carried out, the more likely that the **experimental** probability will be closer to the **theoretical** probability.

Practice

1 Write the experimental probabilities of the events given as fractions in their simplest form:

a) One playing card was randomly picked from a full pack. This was repeated 100 times. A heart was picked 22 times.

Experimental probability of picking a heart = _____

b) One playing card was randomly picked from a full pack. This was repeated 500 times. A spade was picked 124 times.

Experimental probability of picking a spade = _____

c) One playing card was randomly picked from a full pack. This was repeated 1000 times. A diamond was picked 249 times.

Experimental probability of picking a diamond = _____

2 Write the experimental probabilities of the events in question 1 as decimals. Use a calculator.

a) _____   b) _____   c) _____

3 The theoretical probability of picking each suit is $\frac{1}{4}$. Which of these decimals is closest to $\frac{1}{4}$? _____

How did I do?

I know the meaning of the term mutually exclusive. ☐

I know that if the probability of an event is p, then the probability of it not occurring is $1 - p$. ☐

I can find experimental probabilities. ☐

82: Probability (2)

Use the checklist at the back of this book to help you decide which topics to work on. Go back and read through any notes you have made and look at the sections of this book again. Try the tests on pages 20, 34 and 54.

In this unit you will revise:
- ▶ how to estimate probabilities from experimental data
- ▶ how to compare experimental and theoretical probabilities.

What you should know

A probability based on **equally likely outcomes** is known as **theoretical probability**.

This formula can be used:

$$\text{Theoretical probability (P)} = \frac{\text{the number of things you want}}{\text{the number of equally likely } \textbf{outcomes}}$$

Outcomes are said to be **mutually exclusive** when every single possible outcome is distinct and there are no other possible outcomes.

The probabilities of mutually exclusive events have a **total of 1**.

Get started

A bag contains 7 red, 8 blue and 5 green balls. One ball is picked at random and replaced. This is done 100 times. Here are the results:

Red	Blue	Green
33	41	26

The experimental probability can be written as a fraction or decimal. This is found by dividing the result by the total number of times the experiment is conducted.

$P(\text{red}) = \dfrac{33}{100}$ or 0.33 $P(\text{blue}) = \dfrac{41}{100}$ or 0.41 $P(\text{green}) = \dfrac{26}{100}$ or 0.26

1 The experiment was repeated three times. Write the experimental probability for each set of results as a fraction and as a decimal.

a)

Red	Blue	Green
36	38	26

P(red) = _____

P(blue) = _____

P(green) = _____

b)

Red	Blue	Green
34	41	25

P(red) = _____

P(blue) = _____

P(green) = _____

c)

Red	Blue	Green
36	40	24

P(red) = _____

P(blue) = _____

P(green) = _____

2 **a)** Use the results from the four experiments put together to complete this table for the 400 results:

Red	Blue	Green

b) Write the experimental probability for each set of results as a fraction and a decimal.

P(red) = _____   P(red) = _____   P(red) = _____

To find the **theoretical probability** of each colour being picked, use the number of different-coloured balls in the bag. The bag contains 7 red, 8 blue and 5 green balls so the theoretical probabilities are as follows:

P(red) = $\frac{7}{20}$ or 0.35   P(blue) = $\frac{8}{20}$ or 0.4   P(green) = $\frac{5}{20}$ = 0.25

The more times an experiment is carried out the more likely it is that the **experimental** probability will be close to the **theoretical** probability.

The theoretical probabilities of picking different-coloured balls from a **different** bag are shown in this table as decimals.

Red	Blue	Green
0.1	0.7	0.2

If the total number of balls in the bag is known, you can find out how many of each colour there are by multiplying the probability by the total number.

If there are 40 balls in the bag: 0.1 × 40 = 4 red, 0.7 × 40 = 28 blue and 0.2 × 40 = 8 green

Practice

1 Each table shows the theoretical probabilities (as decimals) of picking colours from a bag.

Write the number of balls of each colour in the bags.

a)

Red	Blue	Green
0.1	0.7	0.2

Total number of balls = 60

_____ red   _____ blue   _____ green

b)

Red	Blue	Green
0.5	0.2	0.3

Total number of balls = 50

_____ red   _____ blue   _____ green

c)

Red	Blue	Green
0.05	0.65	0.3

Total number of balls = 20

_____ red   _____ blue   _____ green

d)

Red	Blue	Green
0.45	0.15	0.4

Total number of balls = 40

_____ red   _____ blue   _____ green

How did I do?

I know how to estimate probabilities from experimental data. ☐

I know how to compare experimental and theoretical probabilities. ☐

83: Test (5)

1 Sketch these loci:

a) A car is driving, keeping the same distance from building A as building B.

Sketch the locus of the car.

A.

.B

b) A moving robot keeps an equal distance from two lines, CD and CE. Sketch the locus of the robot.

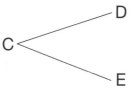

c) A goat is tied to post F on a 1 metre rope. Sketch the locus of the maximum distance the goat can reach from the post.

F.

2 Find the area and circumference of each circle using the x^2 and π keys on your calculator.

Round your answers to 2 decimal places.

a)

3 cm

Circumference = _____ cm

Area = _____ cm²

b)

7 cm

Circumference = _____ cm

Area = _____ cm²

c)

4.6 cm

Circumference = _____ cm

Area = _____ cm²

d)

5.7 cm

Circumference = _____ cm

Area = _____ cm²

3 In each diagram write the size of every angle.

a)

72°

b)

121°

c)

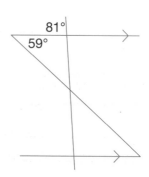
81°
59°

4 Find the mean of this set of data, by completing the table:

Number of children (c)	Frequency (f)	c × f
0	5	
1	12	
2	35	
3	19	
4	18	
5	11	
Totals		

mean = _____

5 Use an assumed mean to find the mean of each set of numbers:

a) 89, 92, 87, 84   mean = _____

b) 151, 153, 155, 149, 147   mean = _____

c) 92, 87, 91, 86, 89, 92, 93   mean = _____

d) 107, 113, 113, 118, 109, 108, 112, 115, 105, 110   mean = _____

6 For each of these scatter graphs state whether the correlation is positive, negative or zero.

a)
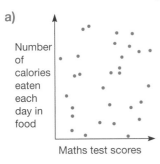

Number of calories eaten each day in food

Maths test scores

_____ correlation

b)
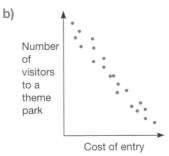

Number of visitors to a theme park

Cost of entry

_____ correlation

c)
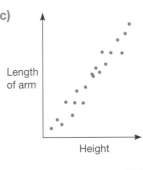

Length of arm

Height

_____ correlation

7 These two spinners are spun together and the **total** is found. List the possible outcomes in the table:

What is the probability of:

a) spinning a total of 0? _____

b) spinning a total of 3? _____

c) spinning a negative total? _____

d) spinning a total of 0 or 1? _____

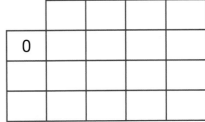

e) spinning a total greater than 0? _____   f) spinning a total less than 2? _____

8 A bag contains some number cards showing the numbers 1 to 6. The probabilities of picking the numbers 1 to 5 are:

P(1) = 0.15   P(2) = 0.25   P(3) = 0.05   P(4) = 0.05   P(5) = 0.35

a) What is the probability of picking the number 6? P(6) = _____

b) What is the probability of picking an odd number?   P(odd) = _____

1 Find the volume and surface area of each prism.

a)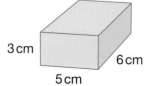

3 cm
6 cm
5 cm

b)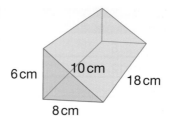

6 cm
10 cm
18 cm
8 cm

c)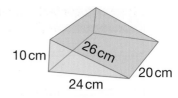

10 cm
26 cm
24 cm
20 cm

Volume = _____ cm³   _____ cm³   _____ cm³

Surface area = _____ cm²   _____ cm²   _____ cm²

2 These measurements include lengths, areas and volumes. Convert these measurements to the units shown.

a) 18 cm = _____ mm
b) 26 mm = _____ cm
c) 9000 mm² = _____ cm²
d) 180 m³ = _____ cm³
e) 6 m² = _____ cm²
f) 8 000 000 mm³ = _____ cm³
g) 5 m = _____ cm
h) 14 000 cm² = _____ m²
i) 69 million cm³ = _____ m³
j) 7 m³ = _____ cm³
k) 2500 cm = _____ m
l) 6 million mm³ = _____ cm³

3 Find the sum of the interior angles of each polygon. You can use a calculator.

a) Pentagon (5 sides)
   sum of interior angles = _____ °

b) Heptagon (7 sides)
   sum of interior angles = _____ °

c) Octagon (8 sides)
   sum of interior angles = _____ °

4 Find the size of each angle in the regular polygons below. You can use a calculator.

a) Regular decagon (10 sides)   b) Regular hexagon (6 sides)   c) Regular dodecagon (12 sides)
   angle = _____ °   angle = _____ °   angle = _____ °

5 Label each of the exterior angles of this irregular polygon and find the missing interior angle, a.

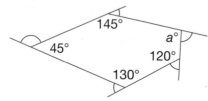

145°
45°
a°
120°
130°

6 A regular shape has 18 sides. Find the size of one of its interior angles. _____ °

7 An irregular shape has interior angles with the sum of 4140°. How many sides has the shape?

_____

8 An irregular hexagon has interior angles of 26°, 40°, 168°, 145°, 90° and x°. Find the value of x.

_____ °

9 A ship travels on a bearing of 037° from a port. It must return to the port. On what bearing must it travel now?

_____ °

10 Enlarge the blue shape in different ways as described below and label each image.

a) By the scale factor 3 with centre of enlargement at (0, 0) to make image A.

b) By the scale factor 2 with centre of enlargement at (–3, 5) to make image B.

c) By the scale factor 5 with centre of enlargement at (2, 3) to make image C.

d) By the scale factor 2 with centre of enlargement at (4, –1) to make image D.

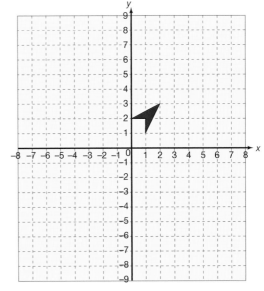

11 State the number of planes of symmetry of each of these prisms.

a)

b)

c)

_____ planes of symmetry   _____ planes of symmetry   _____ planes of symmetry

12 Complete the table and use it to help you draw a pie chart of the information.

What 120 twelve-year-old girls spent the largest part of their pocket money on.

Activity or item	Number of girls	Calculation (fraction × 360)	Angle of sector
Going out	30	$\frac{30}{120}$ × 360	90°
Sports and hobbies	11		
CDs, videos, DVDs	25		
Clothes & toiletries	48		
Other	6		

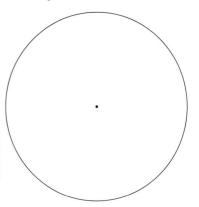

13 Each table shows the theoretical probabilities (as decimals) of picking colours from a bag.

Write the number of balls of each colour in the bags.

a)

Red	Blue	Green
0.4	0.5	0.1

Total number of balls = 60

_____ red   _____ blue   _____ green

b)

Red	Blue	Green
0.7	0.2	0.1

Total number of balls = 50

_____ red   _____ blue   _____ green

Answers

Unit 1: Pages 6–7

Get started

1. a) 150   b) 700
   c) 4000   d) 270
   e) 4400   f) 17 000
2. a) 0.5   b) 3.6
   c) 3   d) 10

Practice

1.
Number	To the nearest 10	To the nearest 100	To the nearest 1000
5541	5540	5500	6000
2943	2940	2900	3000
8467	8470	8500	8000
12 489	12 490	12 500	12 000
31 555	31 560	31 600	32 000
6004	6000	6000	6000
2985	2990	3000	3000

2.

3.
   a) 30.6   b) 58.2
   c) 17   d) 22

Unit 2: Pages 8–9

Get started

1. One tenth, 0.1, $\frac{1}{10}$, $\frac{1}{10^1}$, 10^{-1}

   One hundredth, 0.01, $\frac{1}{100}$, $\frac{1}{10^2}$, 10^{-2}

   One thousandth, 0.001, $\frac{1}{1000}$, $\frac{1}{10^3}$, 10^{-3}

2. a) 6240   b) 4250
   c) 27 500   d) 0.9
   e) 0.076   f) 0.0032
   g) 0.427   h) 1.26
   i) 653.2   j) 200
   k) 2640   l) 9200

Practice

1. a) 10^3 b) 10^{-2}
   c) 10^2 d) 10^7
   e) 10^{-3} f) 10^6
   g) 10^{-1} h) 10^5
   i) 10^0 j) 10^{-2}
   k) 10^1 l) 10^{-1}
2. a) 838.6   b) 4903
   c) 9200   d) 0.475
   e) 0.008 34   f) 0.1942
   g) 8.386   h) 0.197
   i) 0.9545   j) 60
   k) 700   l) 15 000

3. a) True   b) False
   c) True   d) True
   e) False   f) True

Unit 3: Pages 10–11

Get started

1.
Number	To the nearest whole number	To 1 d.p.	To 2 d.p.	To 3 d.p.
32.1522	32	32.2	32.15	32.152
86.8379	87	86.8	86.84	86.838
39.6045	40	39.6	39.60	39.605
9.9891	10	10.0	9.99	9.989
7.4993	7	7.5	7.50	7.499

2. Other approximations could be acceptable:
   a) $3000 \times 50 = 150\,000$
   b) $480 \div 8 = 60$
   c) $6 \times (3.5 - 0.5) = 18$
   d) $6 \times (3 + 3) = 36$
   e) $(6000 \div 2000) \times 200 = 600$
   f) $\sqrt{(8 \times 2)} + 16 = 20$
   g) $(0.03 \times 20)^2 = 0.6^2 = \pm0.36$

Practice

1. a) 3.4   b) 1.333
   c) 0.64   d) 1.1
   e) 1.5   f) 5.82
   g) 2.167   h) 66.667
2. Other approximations could be acceptable:
   a) $(5 \div 2.5) \times 10 = 20$
   b) $(18 \div 3) + 17 = 23$
   c) $8 \times (5 \times 4) = 160$
   d) $(6 \times 4) \div \sqrt{\frac{1}{4}} = 48$
   e) $0.4 \times 0.5 \div 0.01 = 0.2 \div 0.01 = 20$

Unit 4: Pages 12–13

Get started

1. Or equivalent fractions:
   a) $\frac{16}{24}\checkmark$, $\frac{15}{24}$
   b) $\frac{12}{20}$, $\frac{15}{20}\checkmark$
   c) $\frac{20}{24}$, $\frac{21}{24}\checkmark$ or $\frac{40}{48}$, $\frac{42}{48}\checkmark$
   d) $\frac{70}{90}$, $\frac{72}{90}\checkmark$
   e) $\frac{20}{35}$, $\frac{21}{35}\checkmark$
2. $\frac{10}{24}$, $\frac{15}{24}$, $\frac{16}{24}$, $\frac{18}{24}$, $\frac{20}{24}$
3. a) 0.222…, 0.25, 0.3, 0.6, 0.625
   b) 0.4, 0.444…, 0.667, 0.833, 0.875

Practice

1. a) $\frac{5}{20}$, $\frac{6}{20}$, $\frac{7}{20}$, $\frac{8}{20}$
   b) $\frac{14}{24}$, $\frac{15}{24}$, $\frac{16}{24}$, $\frac{18}{24}$, $\frac{20}{24}$
   c) $\frac{16}{36}$, $\frac{20}{36}$, $\frac{22}{36}$, $\frac{27}{36}$, $\frac{30}{36}$

2 **a)** 0.6, 0.625, 0.7, 0.75, 0.85
   b) 0.48, 0.53, 0.6, 0.67, 0.7
   c) 0.1666, 0.25, 0.333, 0.375, 0.417
3 **a)** 0.2
   b) 0.875
   c) 0.556

Unit 5: Pages 14–15

Get started

1 **a)** 45
   b) 16
   c) $\frac{40}{7}$
   d) $\frac{55}{9}$
   e) 18 kg
   f) $\frac{27}{10}$ or 2.7 km
   g) 30 m
   h) $\frac{80}{9}$ cm
   i) 27
   j) $\frac{14}{8}$ or $\frac{7}{4}$
   k) $\frac{63}{10}$ or 6.3
   l) $\frac{63}{11}$
2 **a)** $\frac{5}{7}$ **b)** $\frac{8}{11}$
   c) 1   **d)** $\frac{16}{20} = \frac{4}{5}$
   e) $\frac{4}{9}$ **f)** $\frac{2}{12} = \frac{1}{6}$
   g) $\frac{1}{6}$ **h)** $\frac{8}{24} = \frac{1}{3}$
3 **a)** $\frac{29}{30}$ **b)** $\frac{13}{24}$
   c) $\frac{45}{56}$ **d)** $\frac{14}{15}$
   e) $\frac{1}{24}$ **f)** $\frac{13}{20}$
   g) $\frac{13}{40}$ **h)** $\frac{13}{35}$

Practice

1 **a)** $\frac{66}{10}$ or 6.6   **b)** $\frac{45}{8}$
   c) $\frac{35}{12}$ **d)** $\frac{16}{6}$ or $\frac{8}{3}$
   e) $\frac{60}{7}$ **f)** $\frac{63}{10}$ or 6.3
   g) $\frac{33}{5}$ **h)** $\frac{12}{7}$
2 **a)** $\frac{13}{40}$ **b)** $\frac{12}{35}$
   c) $\frac{23}{20}$ or $1\frac{3}{20}$ **d)** $\frac{21}{20}$ or $1\frac{1}{20}$
   e) $\frac{16}{45}$ **f)** $\frac{7}{30}$
   g) $\frac{9}{12}$ or $\frac{3}{4}$ **h)** $\frac{11}{20}$

Unit 6: Pages 16–17

Get started

1 **a)** $\frac{43}{30}$ or $1\frac{13}{30}$ **b)** $\frac{13}{8}$ or $1\frac{5}{8}$
   c) $\frac{113}{60}$ or $1\frac{53}{60}$ **d)** $\frac{55}{36}$ or $1\frac{19}{36}$
   e) $\frac{3}{8}$ **f)** $\frac{8}{45}$
   g) $\frac{13}{72}$ **h)** $\frac{40}{63}$

Practice

1 **a)** $\frac{15}{28}$ **b)** $\frac{5}{22}$
   c) $\frac{7}{40}$ **d)** $\frac{2}{11}$

   e) $\frac{1}{4}$ **f)** $\frac{1}{8}$
2 a, b and d ticked
3 **a)** $\frac{9}{8}$ or $1\frac{1}{8}$ **b)** $\frac{1}{5}$
   c) $\frac{7}{45}$ **d)** $\frac{3}{16}$
   e) $\frac{5}{22}$ **f)** $\frac{3}{10}$

Unit 7: Pages 18–19

Get started

1 **a)** £12.10   **b)** 7.2 m
   c) £21   **d)** 63 g
   e) 107.1 cm   **f)** 20.8 m
   g) 30.4 cm   **h)** 114 kg
2 **a)** 65%   **b)** 32%
   c) 80%   **d)** 60%
   e) 28%   **f)** 45%
   g) 72%   **h)** 90%

Practice

1 Clockwise from £122.40: £2.40, £26.40, £36,
   £228, £84, £98.40, £62.40
2 Andy = 80%, Mandy = 84%✓,
   Sandy = 70%
3 80%
4 68.4%

Unit 8: Pages 20–21

Get started

1 **a)** £15.20   **b)** £9.90
   c) £47.56   **d)** 5.46 kg
   e) 2.34 kg   **f)** 80.64 kg
   g) 10.07 ml   **h)** 108.75 ml
   i) 301.95 ml
2 **a)** £99.20   **b)** £41
   c) £87.36   **d)** £105.09
   e) £196.98   **f)** £394.44
3 **a)** £60.80   **b)** £9
   c) £8.64   **d)** £80.91
   e) £71.02   **f)** £61.56

Practice

1 **a)** £146.70
   b) £89.78
   c) £51.36
   d) £92.07
   e) £100.01
   f) £1.80
2 **a)** 69 m.p.h.
   b) 65.52 kg
   c) £13.50

Unit 9: Pages 22–23

Get started

1 **a)** £60.76   **b)** £122 840
   c) £28.62   **d)** £25.38
   e) £6432   **f)** £43.05 (to 2 d.p.)

2

	Original price	Percentage change	New price	New price as percentage of original price
	£37	17% increase	£43.29	100% + 17% = 117%
	£85	8% decrease	£78.20	100% − 8% = 92%
	£143	63% increase	£233.09	100% + 63% = 163%
	£12 400	36% decrease	£7936	100% − 36% = 64%

Practice

1 a) £42.40   b) £35
   c) £12.75   d) 45 m.p.h.
   e) 68.5 kg

Unit 10: Pages 24–25

Get started

1 a) D = 0.1, P = 10%
      D = 0.75, P = 75%
      D = 0.27, P = 27%
   b) P = 1%, F = $\frac{1}{100}$
      P = 40%, F = $\frac{2}{5}$
      P = 81%, F = $\frac{81}{100}$
   c) F = $\frac{27}{100}$, D = 0.27
      F = $\frac{1}{20}$, D = 0.05
      F = $\frac{1}{5}$, D = 0.2

Practice

1 a) $\frac{39}{100}$ b) 8%
   c) $\frac{16}{25}$ d) 31%
2 a) $\frac{7}{8}$, 0.875, 87.5%   b) $\frac{11}{14}$, 0.786, 78.6%
   c) $\frac{2}{3}$, 0.667, 66.7%
3 0.83, 83%, $\frac{83}{100}$

Unit 11: Pages 26–27

Get started

1 a) D = 0.429, P = 42.9%
      D = 0.556, P = 55.6%
      D = 0.157, P = 15.7%
   b) P = 24%, F = $\frac{6}{25}$
      P = 63.5%, F = $\frac{127}{200}$
      P = 80.5%, F = $\frac{161}{200}$
   c) F = $\frac{9}{100}$, D = 0.09
      F = $\frac{41}{100}$, D = 0.41
      F = $\frac{7}{40}$, D = 0.175
2 1%, 12%, 83%, so Bangladesh

Practice

1 6%, 5.5%, 5%, so 1 cent
2 94%, 94.5%, 95%, so 5 cent
3 5%, 10.1%, 9.65%, so €1

Unit 12: Pages 28–29

Get started

1 a and c should be ticked
2 a) £35   b) £35
   c) £30   d) £16

Practice

1 a and c should be ticked
2 a) £6   b) £21
   c) £15   d) £35
   e) £6   f) £9
3 a) 36   b) 18
   c) 60
4 82 g flour   2 eggs
   60 ml water   78 g spinach

Unit 13: Pages 30–31

Get started

1 Approximate answers:
   a) 2.5   b) 5
   c) 10.2   d) 3.8
   e) 14   f) 15.4
   g) 2   h) 5.5
   i) 2.5   j) 1.6
   k) 4.7   l) 2.75 or 2.8
2 a) 4217.74 yen   b) £38.50

Practice

1 a) £6.90
   b) $55.48
   c) 11.2 km
2 314 g flour   229 g margarine
   143 g sugar   57 g cocoa

Unit 14: Pages 32–33

Get started

1 a) 30   b) 6
2 a) 9   b) 36
3 a) Ali £28, Baz £16
   b) Craig £60, Deepa £90

Practice

1 a) 28   b) 3
   c) 800 ml
2 a) 21 males, 3 females
   b) 35 males, 21 females
   c) Ella £18, Fi £45

Unit 15: Pages 34–35

Get started

1 a) 5 : 4   b) 1 : 6
   c) 7 : 1   d) 1 : 2
   e) 6 : 5   f) 3 : 4
   g) 8 : 1   h) 3 : 4
2 a) 1 : 3.5   b) 1 : 2.25
   c) 1 : 3.4   d) 1 : 1.375
   e) 1 : 1.5625   f) 1 : 0.7
   g) 1 : 0.65   h) 1 : 3

Practice

1 a) 1 : 2.5　　　　b) 1 : 1.2
   c) 1 : 0.667　　　d) 1 : 1.75
   T shirt 1

2 a) 8 : 5　　　　　1 : 0.625
   　　5 : 14　　　　 1 : 2.8
   　　2 : 7　　　　　1 : 3.5
   　　5 : 9　　　　　1 : 1.8
   　　8 : 7　　　　　1 : 0.875
   b) Art　　　　　　c) Geology

Unit 16: Pages 36–37

Get started

1 a) Males: 56, Females: 8
   b) Ali: £63 Baz: £36
   c) Pete: £32, Christine: £56, Louis: £8
   d) 280°, 60°, 20°
   e) 240 g flour, 160 g sugar, 320 g butter

2 a) 1 km　　　　　b) 5.5 km
   c) 12 km

3 a) 12 cm　　　　 b) 32 cm
   c) 16.8 cm

Practice

1 a) 60°, 20°, 100°
   b) 246 g flour, 164 g sugar, 410 g butter

2 a) 1 km　　　　　b) 1.75 km
   c) 2.1 km

3 a) 4 cm　　　　　b) 10 cm
   c) 24 cm

4 a) 4 km　　　　　b) 5.125 km
   c) 1.875 km

5 a) 2.4 cm　　　　b) 6.4 cm
   c) 33.6 cm

Unit 17: Pages 38–39

Get started

1 a) 6　　　　　　　b) 5
   c) −4　　　　　　 d) −3
   e) 11　　　　　　 f) −17
   g) −10　　　　　 h) −19
   i) −11　　　　　 j) −18

2 a) 15 + 5 = 20
   b) −17 + 14 = −3
   c) −19 − 1 = −20
   d) 20 − 32 = −12
   e) 8 + 15 = 23
   f) −16 − 4 = −20

Practice

1 a) −18　　　　　 b) 11
   c) −19　　　　　 d) 11
   e) 17　　　　　　f) 22
   g) −20　　　　　 h) 19

2 a) 72　　　　　　b) −99
   c) −7　　　　　　d) 7
   e) −32　　　　　 f) 48
   g) 7　　　　　　 h) −8
   i) 54　　　　　　j) −35

k) 8　　　　　　　 l) −6

3 a) ±6　　　　　　b) ±8
   c) ±9　　　　　　d) ±10
   e) ±3　　　　　　f) ±7
   g) ±5　　　　　　h) ±12

Unit 18: Pages 40–41

Get started

1 a) [12: 1, 2, 3, 4, 6, 12; 24: 1, 2, 3, 4, 6, 8, 12, 24] CF: 1, 2, 3, 4, 6, 12
   b) [45: 1, 3, 5, 9, 15, 45; 27: 1, 3, 9, 27] CF: 1, 3, 9
   c) [28: 1, 2, 4, 7, 14, 28; 32: 1, 2, 4, 8, 16, 32] CF: 1, 2, 4
   d) [18: 1, 2, 3, 6, 9, 18; 30: 1, 2, 3, 5, 6, 10, 15, 30] CF: 1, 2, 3, 6
   e) [24: 1, 2, 3, 4, 6, 8, 12, 24; 40: 1, 2, 4, 5, 8, 10, 20, 40] CF: 1, 2, 4, 8
   f) [30: 1, 2, 3, 5, 6, 10, 15, 30; 36: 1, 2, 3, 4, 6, 9, 12, 18, 36] CF: 1, 2, 3, 6

2 a) 12　　　　　　b) 9
   c) 4　　　　　　 d) 6
   e) 8　　　　　　 f) 6

3 a) 15, 30, 45　　b) 12, 24, 36
   c) 28, 56, 84　　d) 9, 18, 27
   e) 35, 70, 105　 f) 24, 48, 72

4 a) 15　　　　　　b) 12
   c) 28　　　　　　d) 9
   e) 35　　　　　　f) 24

Practice

1 a) 72, 80　　　　　　　b) 72, 42 or 54, 42
   c) 42, 35　　　　　　　d) 80, 35
   e) 80, 42 or 54, 80　　f) 72, 54

2 a) 66　　　　　　b) 40
   c) 12　　　　　　d) 60
   e) 60

Unit 19: Pages 42–43

Get started

1 a) 51 is **not** prime as 1, 3, 17 and 51 are factors
   b) 79 is prime as 1 and 79 only are factors
   c) 91 is **not** prime as 1, 7, 13 and 91 are factors

2 a) $42 = 2 \times 3 \times 7$
   b) $45 = 3 \times 3 \times 5$
   c) $36 = 2 \times 2 \times 3 \times 3$
   d) $60 = 2 \times 2 \times 3 \times 5$

Practice

1 53, 59, 61, 67, 73

2 a) 2×3^2　　　　　b) $2^2 \times 5^2$
   c) $2^2 \times 7$　　　　　d) $2^5 \times 3$

3 a) $2^2 \times 5 \times 7$　　b) $2^2 \times 3 \times 7$
   c) $2^3 \times 11$　　　　 d) $2^3 \times 3^2$
   e) 2×3^3　　　　　f) $2^3 \times 3 \times 5$

Unit 20: Pages 44–45

Get started

1. a) $2 \times 5 \times 7$
   b) $3^2 \times 7$
   c) $2 \times 3 \times 5^2$
   d) $2^2 \times 3^2 \times 5$

Practice

1. a) $2^3 \times 3 \times 5$ b) 2^6
   c) $2^4 \times 3$ d) $3^3 \times 5$
   e) 2×7^2 f) $2 \times 3 \times 5 \times 7$
2. a) 15 b) 900
3. a) 24 b) 240
   c) 15 d) 1890

Unit 21: Pages 46–47

Get started

1. a) 49 b) ±5
   c) 81 d) ±7
   e) 100 f) 25
   g) ±2 h) 36
   i) ±3 j) 144
2. a) 125 b) 4
   c) 2 d) 1000
   e) 1

Practice

1. a) 1024 b) ±54
   c) 2304 d) ±92
   e) 169 f) 343
   g) 8 h) 6
   i) 729 j) 1331
2. a) ±18 b) 2025
   c) Correct d) 262 144
   e) 0.01 f) ±268
   g) Correct h) Correct
   i) Correct
3. a) 49 b) ±4
   c) 0 d) n^2
   e) 6.9

Unit 22: Pages 48–49

Get started

1. a) 4^5
   b) 3^{12}
   c) 2^5
   d) 10^{11}
   e) f^9
   f) g^5
   g) d^{11}
   h) n^6
2. a) 7^4
   b) $4^0 = 1$
   c) 2^6
   d) a^3
   e) 9^6
   f) $y^1 = y$
3. a) $7^{-4} = \frac{1}{7^4}$

b) $4^{-2} = \frac{1}{4^2}$

c) $2^{-1} = \frac{1}{2}$

d) $a^{-4} = \frac{1}{a^4}$

e) $9^{-7} = \frac{1}{9^7}$

f) $y^{-4} = \frac{1}{y^4}$

Practice

1. a) 8^5
   b) 4^{10}
   c) a^5
   d) 6^3
   e) $y^{-3} = \frac{1}{y^3}$
   f) $2^{-1} = \frac{1}{2}$
   g) $3^{-4} = \frac{1}{3^4}$
   h) $m^0 = 1$
   i) $y^1 = y$
2. a) $3^2 \times 3^5 = 3^7$
   b) $7^3 \times 7^5 = 7^8$
   c) $2^3 \times 2^3 = 2^6$
   d) $4^2 \div 4^5 = 4^{-3} = \frac{1}{4^3}$
   e) $y^1 \times y^7 = y^8$
   f) $a^6 \div a^6 = a^0 = 1$
   g) $4^2 \div 4^3 = 4^{-1} = \frac{1}{4}$
   h) $m^3 \div m^5 = m^{-2} = \frac{1}{m^2}$
   i) $n^2 \div n^3 = n^{-1} = \frac{1}{n}$

Unit 23: Pages 50–51

Test 1

1. a) 3810 b) 1860
   c) 264 000 d) 0.712
   e) 0.005 37 f) 0.2348
   g) 0.512 h) 1.34
   i) 284.6 j) 80
   k) 400 l) 16 000
2. a) 10^2 b) 10^{-3}
   c) 10^3 d) 10^4
   e) 10^{-2} f) 10^7
   g) 10^{-1} h) 10^1
   i) 10^0 j) 10^{-3}
   k) 10^5 l) 10^{-1}
3. a) $\frac{61}{40}$ or $1\frac{21}{40}$ b) $\frac{103}{56}$ or $1\frac{47}{56}$
   c) $\frac{125}{88}$ or $1\frac{37}{88}$ d) $\frac{9}{10}$
   e) $\frac{25}{56}$ f) $\frac{3}{40}$
   g) $\frac{1}{10}$ h) $\frac{13}{35}$
4. a) $\frac{5}{42}$ b) $\frac{7}{30}$
   c) $\frac{3}{35}$ d) $\frac{3}{16}$
5. a) £1710.10 b) £45 500
   c) £6976 d) £20.30
   e) £95.76 f) £9696.15
6. a) D = 0.143, P = 14.3%
      D = 0.889, P = 88.9%
      D = 0.111, P = 11.1%

b) P = 42%, F = $\frac{21}{50}$

    P = 58.6%, F = $\frac{293}{500}$

    P = 90.4%, F = $\frac{113}{125}$

c) F = $\frac{7}{100}$, D = 0.07

    F = $\frac{9}{25}$, D = 0.36

    F = $\frac{3}{8}$, D = 0.375

7 a) 3 : 2   1 : 0.667
      4 : 17   1 : 4.25
      3 : 10   1 : 3.333
      1 : 6   1 : 6
      16 : 21   1 : 1.3125
  b) Yoga   **c)** French

8 a) −15   **b)** 3
  c) −13   **d)** 12
  e) 19   **f)** 26
  g) −18   **h)** −8
  i) 56   **j)** −54
  k) −6   **l)** 9
  m) −40   **n)** 64
  o) 6   **p)** −7

9 a) ±7   **b)** ±9
  c) ±11   **d)** ±12

10 a) 6^{14} **b)** 4^8
   c) 7^7 **d)** $a^1 = a$
   e) b^4 **f)** n^2
   g) a^3 **h)** 9^5
   i) c^3

Unit 24: Pages 52–53

Test 2

1 a) 2.1   **b)** 2.143
  c) 1.09   **d)** 0.9
  e) 1.524   **f)** 4.64

2 Other approximations could be acceptable.
  a) (5 ÷ 2.5) × 11 = 22
  b) (20 ÷ 4) + 6 = 11
  c) 7 + (4 × 9) = 43
  d) √(6 × 6) ÷ 0.5 = 6 × 2 = 12

3 a) $\frac{5}{12}$ **b)** $\frac{5}{22}$
  c) $\frac{1}{24}$ **d)** $\frac{3}{22}$

4 a) tick   **b)** tick
  c) no tick   **d)** tick

5 a) $\frac{21}{20}$ or $1\frac{1}{20}$ **b)** $\frac{1}{5}$
  c) $\frac{1}{5}$ **d)** $\frac{3}{32}$

6 a) £22.40
  b) £30.51
  c) £18.27

7 229 g flour
    86 g margarine
    257 g sugar
    114 g cocoa

8 a) £22.50, £37.50, £60   c = 2.5n
  b) £6.45, £15.05, £43   c = 2.15n
  c) £18.90, £23.10, £210   c = 2.1n

9 a) 80°, 40°, 60°
  b) 192 g flour, 128 g sugar, 320 g butter

10 a) 2 km   **b)** 2.75 km
   c) 3.1 km

11 a) 8 cm   **b)** 14 cm
   c) 30 cm

12 a) 8^7 **b)** 3^{10}
   c) a^8 **d)** 6^4
   e) y^{-6} **f)** $2^1 = 2$
   g) 4^{-2} **h)** $m^0 = 1$
   i) y^2

13 a) $2^5 \times 3$ **b)** $2^2 \times 3^2$
   c) 2^6 **d)** $2 \times 5 \times 11$

14 a) 12   **b)** 192
   c) 2

Unit 25: Pages 54–55

Get started

1 a) 20   **b)** 30
  c) 7   **d)** 10

2 a) −9   **b)** 9
  c) −98   **d)** 0
  e) −36   **f)** −4
  g) 4   **h)** −4
  i) 4

Practice

1 a) 2   **b)** 1
  c) 28   **d)** 18

2 a) 3   **b)** −15
  c) 27

3 a) first = −5, second correct
  b) first correct, second = 28
  c) first correct, second = 13
  d) first correct, second = −35

Unit 26: Pages 56–57

Get started

1 a) 108   **b)** 13.9
  c) 656   **d)** 12
  e) 1.6   **f)** 1109
  g) 2700   **h)** 832
  i) 4200

2 a) 57.6   **b)** 35
  c) 40.7   **d)** 63
  e) 11.04   **f)** 6.08

Practice

1 a) 43.8   **b)** 19.9
  c) 95.6   **d)** 1.1
  e) 1389   **f)** 13.49

2 a) 7.2   **b)** 6600
  c) 240   **d)** 360
  e) 2.8   **f)** 48
  g) 660   **h)** 81
  i) 56

3 a) 67.2   **b)** 48
  c) 1.36   **d)** 6.63

Unit 27: Pages 58–59

Get started

1. a) 104.2   b) 11.67
   c) 4.376   d) 10.663
   e) 18.3   f) 12.79
   g) 6.394   h) 11.79
2. a) 42.24   b) 114.24
   c) 8.48   d) 37.434
   e) 2.13   f) 2.07
   g) 6.16   h) 3.65
3. a) 27.09 m   b) 19.71 kg

Practice

1. a) 102.3   b) 7.8
   c) 5.548   d) 11.426
   e) 18   f) 40.59
   g) 5.694   h) 12.39
   i) 77.52   j) 138
   k) 11.715   l) 251.43
   m) 4.13   n) 5.07
   o) 8.16   p) 4.65
2. a) 6.14 m   b) 1.86 m

Unit 28: Pages 60–61

Get started

1. a) $2416 \div 4 \approx 600$
   b) $32\,360 \div 8 \approx 4000$
   c) $630 \div 15 \approx 40$
   d) $6078 \div 6 \approx 1000$
   e) $42\,630 \div 7 \approx 6000$
   f) $4.29 \div 39 \approx 0.1$

Practice

1. a) $3852 \div 4 \approx 1000$, 963
   b) $29\,757 \div 7 \approx 4000$, 4251
   c) $377 \div 13 \approx 30$, 29
   d) $7.434 \div 42 \approx 0.2$, 0.177
2. a) 604   b) 4045
   c) 42   d) 1013
   e) 6090   f) 0.11

Unit 29: Pages 62–63

Get started

1. a) 216   b) 625
   c) 2 097 152   d) 1245
   e) 32   f) 78.54
   g) −1176   h) 570
   i) −1512   j) 30 176
   k) 6480   l) −1917
2. a) $\frac{1}{35}$ b) $\frac{5}{8}$
   c) $\frac{4}{9}$
3. a) 0.8125   b) 0.625
   c) 0.53125
4. a) $\frac{87}{250}$ b) $9\frac{1}{16}$
   c) $3\frac{3}{8}$

Practice

1. a) 28 568   b) −1005.31
   c) $1\frac{1}{48}$ or $\frac{49}{48}$ d) $1\frac{1}{8}$ or $\frac{9}{8}$
   e) $\frac{95}{164}$ f) $\frac{7}{9}$
   g) 0.6875   h) 0.444 444 4

Unit 30: Pages 64–65

Get started

1. a) $4g + 3h$ b) $6m + n$
   c) $x + 3y$ d) $5e + f$
   e) $3c + 2d$ f) $5j + 2k$
   g) q h) $4s - t$
   i) $a - b$

Practice

1. a) $a - b + 4c$ b) $2p + 3q + 3r$
   c) $4g - h + 5$ d) $3m + 4n - 3$
   e) $c + 2$ f) $3s + t - 3$
   g) $w + 6v + 3$ h) $10x - 2y + 4$
   i) $7a - 2b - c + 9$
2. $9n + 10m + 11$
   $5n + 7m + 1$ $4n + 3m + 10$
   $3n + 5m - 4$ $2n + 2m + 5$ $m + 2n + 5$
3. a) $7a + 6$
   b) $3e + 1$
   c) $15g + 23$

Unit 31: Pages 66–67

Get started

1. a) $10a - 20$ b) $14m + 21$
   c) $6p + 30$ d) $27y - 9$
   e) $22 - 11n$ f) $70 - 20f$
2. a) True   b) False
   c) False   d) True
   e) True   f) True

Practice

1. a) $13y + 17$ b) $8a - 4$
   c) $2n + 24$ d) $2m + 13$
   e) $2p + 36$ f) $3e - 12$
   g) $30g + 19$ h) $7y - 2$
2. a) $7a + 2$ b) $3e + 1$
   c) $15g + 28$

Unit 32: Pages 68–69

Get started

1. a) $10ab - 20bc$ b) $14kp + 21k$
   c) $6p^2 + 30pq$ d) $6y^2 - 2y$
   e) $20n - 10n^2$ f) $-2x^2y - 6xy^2$
   g) $-42ef + 18e^2$ h) $-20x^2 + 4x$
2. a) $3(a + 2)$ b) $4(a + 2)$
   c) $5(d + 3e)$ d) $3(3c + 2d)$
   e) $2(x + 4y)$ f) $10(p + q)$
   g) $4(a - 3b)$ h) $x(x - 1)$
   i) $2(5s - 4t)$ j) $5x(3 - x)$
   k) $6(t - 1)$ l) $2g(4 - 9g)$

Practice
1 a) 15a − 25   b) 4m − 12
  c) −5p − 55   d) 25y − 14
2 9(3n + 2)
  4(2k + 5)
  3(5g − h)
  2f(2 − 7e)
  3(8 + d)
  5(3m − 1)
  3n(5 + n)
  2xy(3 + 2y)

Unit 33: Pages 70–71

Get started
1 a) $a = 5$ b) $y = 5$
  c) $f = 4$ d) $p = 5$
  e) $d = 7$ f) $c = 8$
  g) $b = 10$ h) $e = 6$
2 a) $a = 8$ b) $y = 3$
  c) $f = 4$ d) $p = 3$
  e) $d = 10$ f) $c = 8$
  g) $b = 8$ h) $e = 4$

Practice
1 a) $2n + 7 = 19$ $n = 6$
  b) $5n + 10 = 25$ $n = 3$
  c) $3n − 5 = 16$ $n = 7$
  d) $4n − 8 = 20$ $n = 7$

Unit 34: Pages 72–73

Get started
1 a) $m = −18$ b) $y = −17.5$
  c) $f = 5.75$ d) $r = −6$
  e) $p = −4.5$ f) $q = −0.5$
  g) $n = −5$ h) $e = −0.5$
  i) $p = −1.125$
2 a) $h = −0.5$ b) $k = −4.6$
  c) $c = 2$ d) $g = 7.4$
  e) $x = 4.125$ f) $p = 5.75$

Practice
1 a) $y = −4$ b) $f = 0.5$
  c) $g = 0.75$ d) $b = −6.875$
  e) $y = −1$ f) $e = 2.5$
  g) $m = 15.667$ h) $n = 2.625$
  i) $p = 5.389$ j) $h = 0$
  k) $j = 4$ l) $k = 4.778$
2 a) $n = −1.075$ b) $m = 7$
  c) $p = 1.2$ d) $q = −4.25$

Unit 35: Pages 74–75

Get started
1 a) 40 cm^2 b) 54 cm^2
  c) 56 cm^2
2 a) 26 cm   b) 30 cm
  c) 36 cm

Practice
1 a) 14   b) 40
  c) 89   d) 68
  e) 19   f) 38
2 30
3 a) 80 miles per hour
  b) 97 miles per hour

Unit 36: Pages 76–77

Get started
1 a) 40   b) 2
  c) 1   d) 100
  e) 64   f) 46
  g) 30   h) 14
  i) 2
2 a) $E = 12$ b) $E = 9$
  c) $E = 8$ d) $E = 18$
  e) $E = 6$ f) $E = 10$

Practice
1 a)

19	51	−8
38	−32	24
5	11	14

  b)

5	51	−15
24	−32	45
12	18	7

  c)

57	156	−24
111	−102	72
21	27	33

2 a) 280 cm
  b) 118 cm
  c) 142 cm
  d) 528 cm

Unit 37: Pages 78–79

Get started
1 a) 41   b) 59
  c) 68   d) 90
  e) 14   f) −22
  g) 63   h) 73
  i) −18   j) 99
  k) −8   l) −11
2 a) 10   b) 35
  c) 40   d) −5
  e) −15   f) −25
  g) 0   h) 8
  i) 12   j) 24
  k) −29   l) −31

Practice
1 a) 50.24   b) 125
  c) 26   d) 72
  e) 5   f) 5
  g) 62
2

49	51	2
28	0	30
5	3	1.5

Unit 38: Pages 80–81

Get started

1 **a)** 8 and 9   **b)** 7 and 8
   c) 9 and 10   **d)** 6 and 7
2 **a)** 2 and 3   **b)** 3 and 4
   c) 1 and 2   **d)** 3 and 4

Practice

1 2.29
2 4.23

Unit 39: Pages 82–83

Get started

1 **a)** $x \to 3(x + 2)$ **b)** $x \to 4x - 2$
   c) $x \to 2x + 5$
   d) $x \to (x - 1) \times 4$ or $x \to 4(x - 1)$
   e) $x \to (x + 5) \times 2$ or $x \to 2(x + 5)$
   f) $x \to 4x \div 2$ or $x \to \frac{4x}{2}$ or $x \to 2x$

2
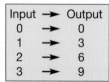

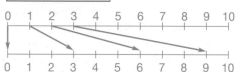

Practice

1 **a)**
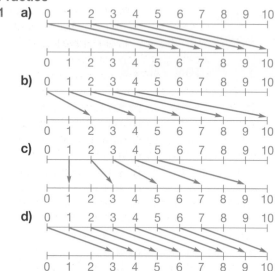

   b)

   c)

   d)

2 a and d should be ticked
3 $x \to x - 5$ and $x \to x + 4$ should be ticked

Unit 40: Pages 84–85

Get started

1 **a)**
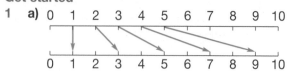

b)
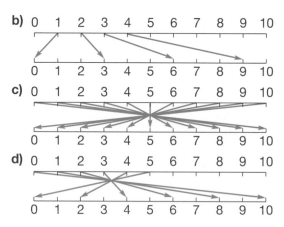

c)

d)

Practice

1 **a)**
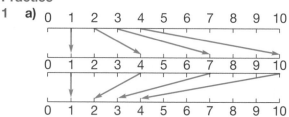

   Yes, the functions are inverses

   b)
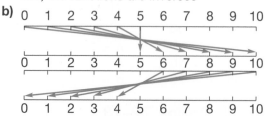

   Yes, the functions are inverses
   c) Yes, the function is a self-inverse function

Unit 41: Pages 86–87

Get started

1 **a)** 7, 9, 11, 13, 15, 17, 19, 21
   b) 84, 79, 74, 69, 64, 59, 54, 49
   c) 1, 2, 4, 8, 16, 32, 64, 128
   d) 512, 256, 128, 64, 32, 16, 8, 4
2 **a)** The first term is 4. Each term increases by 3.
   b) The first term is 7. Each term increases by 5.
   c) The first term is 100. Each term decreases by 25.
   d) The first term is 8. Each term decreases by 2.
3 **a)** 5, 7, 9, 11, 13   **b)** 1, 6, 11, 16, 21
   c) 8, 6, 4, 2, 0

Practice

1 **a)** 7, 18, 29, 40, 51, 62
   b) 100, 85, 70, 55, 40, 25
   c) 4, 8, 16, 32, 64, 128
   d) 0, −2, −4, −6, −8, −10
2 **a)** 4, 8, 12, 16, 20
   b) The first term is 4. Each term increases by 4.
   c) Multiply the position number by 4.

Unit 42: Pages 88–89

Get started

1 a) $3n + 1$ b) $5n - 1$
   c) $4n - 3$ d) $5n + 2$

Practice

1 a) $2n + 1$ b) $2n + 3$
   c) $3n + 1$ d) $4n + 1$

Unit 43: Pages 90–91

Get started

1 a) (5, 13)   b) (1, 1)
   c) (4, 10)   d) (2, 4)
2 Check graph.

Practice

1 a) (2, 1) (3, 3), (4, 5) (5, 7), (6, 9)
   b) Check graph.
2 (10, 51) and (2, 6) are incorrect.

Unit 44: Pages 92–93

Get started

1 a) $y = -2$ b) $x = 4$
   c) $x = -5$ d) $y = 3$
   e) $y = 5$ f) $x = -1$

Practice

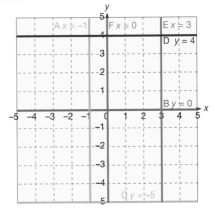

Unit 45: Pages 94–95

Get started

1 a) $y = 4x + 6$ b) $y = -2x + 7$
   c) $y = -9x - 5$ d) $y = x - 5$
   e) $y = 5x + 1$ f) $y = -x + 2$
2 a) gradient = -4, intercept = 1
   b) gradient = 3, intercept = -7
   c) gradient = 7, intercept = 0
   d) gradient = 1, intercept = 5

Practice

1 a) $y = 3x - 4$, gradient = 3, intercept = -4
   b) $y = x + 2$, gradient = 1, intercept = 2
   c) $y = -6x + 5$, gradient = -6, intercept = 5
   d) $y = -x$, gradient = -1, intercept = 0

Unit 46: Pages 96–97

Get started

1 a) At 7:10 the man leaves the starting location and travels at 12 km per hour (possibly running or cycling). He pauses for 5 minutes before travelling 1 km in about 2 minutes (possibly running/cycling very fast or being given a lift in a car). After about 13 minutes staying at the same location, another 1 km is travelled (back in the direction towards the starting location) in about 2 minutes. The final return journey is travelled at a similar speed as previously (about 12 km per hour). The man returns at about 7:55.

   b) At 7:00 the man leaves the starting location and travels at 12 km per hour for 10 minutes. He increases his speed and travels a further $1\frac{1}{2}$ km away from the starting location in about 3 minutes. He remains in the same location for about 24 minutes before going back to a position 2 km from the starting location, reaching there at 7:40 and remaining there until after 8:00.

   c) The man travels 4 km at 24 km per hour. This takes 10 minutes. He then immediately travels $1\frac{1}{2}$ km back in the direction of the starting position. He pauses for about 5 minutes and then travels back away from the starting position for 1 km. From about 7:22 he stays still for about 15 minutes and then returns for 1 km. After pausing for about 8 minutes he makes his slower return journey, taking about 15 minutes and travelling to his starting location at 9 km per hour.

   d) The man leaves the starting location at 7:10 and walks at about 4 km per hour for 20 minutes. He then speeds up and moves a further 1 km from home in about 2 minutes. After a 10-minute rest he moves as quickly for 1 km back in the direction of the starting location, before his final walk back which takes about 15 minutes, and is slightly quicker than in the first part of his journey.

   e) At 7:00, the man travels 1 km in 10 minutes, before remaining still for 15 minutes. He moves 1 km further away from the starting location over the next 12 minutes or so. Moving at a very fast speed he travels a further $1\frac{1}{2}$ km away, reaching his furthest distance from the starting location at 7:40. At about 7:47 he travels $1\frac{1}{2}$ km in the direction of his starting location in 3 minutes (about 30 km per hour). Finally, moving more slowly (about 12 km per hour) he returns to the starting location at 8:00.

f) The man leaves home at 7:20, moving at a speed of 9 km per hour. Moving at a very quick speed he travels a further $\frac{1}{2}$ km away from home, before resting for about 15 minutes. At about 7:45 he travels in the direction of home for about 2 minutes, travelling $\frac{1}{2}$ km (about 15 km per hour). After a short rest of about 5 minutes he returns home, travelling at about 9 km per hour.

10

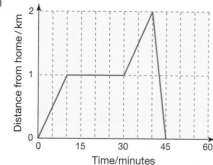

Practice

1

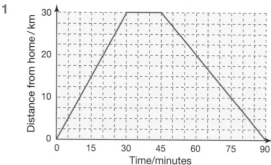

2 **a)** 10
   b) 10
3 **a)** 20 minutes and 60 minutes
   b) 15 minutes and 67.5 minutes
   c) 25 minutes and 52.5 minutes
   d) 5 minutes and 82.5 minutes
4 60 km h⁻¹ and 40 km h⁻¹

11 a) $\frac{3}{4}$ km   **b)** 1 km
12 a) 35 and 41   **b)** 5 and 44

Unit 48: Pages 100–101

Test 4
1 **a)** 33.8   **b)** 17.2
   c) 32.9   **d)** 0.87
   e) 959   **f)** 15.92
2 **a)** 4.2   **b)** 5200
   c) 120   **d)** 240
   e) 3.8   **f)** 36
   g) 330   **h)** 63
   i) 56
3 **a)** $(7 \times 12) + (0.2 \times 12) = 86.4$
   b) $(32 \times 1) + (32 \times 0.2) = 38.4$
   c) $(0.6 \times 1) + (0.6 \times 0.7) = 1.02$
   d) $(3 \times 1) + (3 \times 0.3) + (0.7 \times 1) + (0.7 \times 0.3) = 4.81$
4 **a)** $1362 \div 4 = 340.5$
   b) $8404 \div 4 = 2101$
   c) $832 \div 32 = 26$
   d) $201.6 \div 36 = 5.6$
5 **a)** 6568
   b) 424 115.01
   c) $\frac{11}{16}$
   d) $1\frac{71}{504}$ or $\frac{575}{504}$
   e) $\frac{73}{104}$
   f) $\frac{9}{17}$
   g) 0.625
   h) 0.635
6 **a)** $12ab - 6bc$
   b) $10mk + 30k$
   c) $5p^2 + 30pq$
   d) $12y^2 - 6y$
7 **a)** $12a - 20$ **b)** $-2m + 6$
   c) $-7p - 65$ **d)** $18y - 10$
8 $9(3n + 2)$
   $5(2k + 3)$
   $3(4g - h)$
   $6f(1 - 3e)$
   $3(6 + d)$
   $5(3m - 2)$
   $3n(1 + n)$
   $4xy(2 + y)$

Unit 47: Pages 98–99

Test 3
1 **a)** 0   **b)** −36
   c) −4   **d)** 4
   e) −1   **f)** 4
   g) 12.5   **h)** 3
   i) 0   **j)** 50
2 **a)** 0   **b)** −48
   c) 48
3 **a)** 602   **b)** 4251
   c) 56   **d)** 0.92
4 **a)** $14y + 10$ **b)** $15a + 9$
   c) $-2n + 31$ **d)** $4m + 1$
5 **a)** $h = 5.25$ **b)** $k = -4.5$
   c) $c = 14$ **d)** $g = -7.875$
   e) $x = 22$ **f)** $p = 25$
6 3.81
7 33   68   3
   35   −48   19
    6   7   0.9
8 **a)** $3n + 2$ **b)** $6n - 2$
9 **a)** $y = 2x - 7$, gradient = 2, intercept = −7
   b) $y = -x + 3$, gradient = −1, intercept = 3
   c) $y = 6x + 2$, gradient = 6, intercept = 2
   d) $y = x$, gradient = 1, intercept = 0

9 a) $y = 3$ b) $f = 3$
   c) $g = 1.5$ d) $b = -0.875$
   e) $y = 10$ f) $e = 3.6$
   g) $m = 12.833333...$
   h) $n = 7.5$
   i) $p = 1.975$
   j) $h = 2$
   k) $j = 3.333333...$
   l) $k = 1.5$

10

Yes, they are inverses

Unit 49: Pages 102–103

Get started
1 1600
2 290

Practice
1 a) 244 g
   b) 190 ml
   c) 350 g
   d) 59 mm
   e) 150 ml
2 600 g

Unit 50: Pages 104–105

Get started
1 a) 480 b) 1.37
   c) 5.4 d) 12.5
   e) 1.4 f) 1.76
   g) 5.362 h) 0.467
   i) 62
2 a) 1.2 b) 1.64
   c) 4.362 d) 0.866
   e) 3500 f) 5330
   g) 1584 h) 1.647
   i) 16 670

Practice
1 a) 6.263 b) 5.7
   c) 80 d) 0.736
   e) 0.35 f) 120
2 0.45 kg
3 1700 ml
4 6

Unit 51: Pages 106–107

Get started
1 a) 12 b) 1760
   c) 14 d) 8
   e) 16 f) 3

2 a) 264 b) 1456
   c) 82.25 d) 21.016
   e) 92.4 f) 35.412
   g) 44 h) 1100
   i) 1.54 *(answers to question 2 are approximate)*

Practice
1 a) 455 b) 57.204
   c) 113.6 d) 9.9
   e) 200.2

Unit 52: Pages 108–109

Get started
1 a) 800 b) 3700
   c) 5 d) 1 250 000
   e) 140 000 f) 14

Practice
1 a) 8000 b) 37 000
   c) 50 d) 125 000 000
   e) 14 000 000 f) 2
2 a) 1600 b) 2200
   c) 0.5 d) 70 000
   e) 230 000 f) 50
3 a) 160 b) 2.2
   c) 60 d) 260 000 000
   e) 140 000 f) 2000
   g) 700 h) 2.3
   i) 14 j) 4 000 000
   k) 14 l) 8000

Unit 53: Pages 110–111

Get started
1 a) 13 cm and 16 cm
   b) 4 cm and 5 cm
   c) 4 cm and 5 cm
2 58 cm, 22 cm, 22 cm

Practice
1 a) Perimeter = 28 cm, Area = 39 cm²
   b) Perimeter = 32 cm, Area = 54 cm²
   c) Perimeter = 80 cm, Area = 344 cm²

Unit 54: Pages 112–113

Get started
1 a) 30 cm² b) 20 cm²
   c) 35 cm² d) 6 cm²
   e) 28 cm² f) 9 cm²
2 a) 28 cm² b) 45 cm²
   c) 36 cm² d) 24 cm²
   e) 24 cm² f) 45.5 cm²

Practice
1 a) 111 cm² b) 96 cm²
   c) 57.5 cm² d) 62 cm²

Unit 55: Pages 114–115

Get started

1. a) 72 cm³
   b) 60 cm³, overflow
   c) 140 cm³, not fill the box
   d) 150 cm³, not fill the box
   e) 72 cm³, fill it exactly
2. a) 90 cm³
   b) 328 cm³

Practice

1. a) 124   b) 94
   c) 166   d) 170
   e) 178
2. A 60 cm³, 104 cm² B 60 cm³, 94 cm²
   C 36 cm³, 80 cm² D 120 cm³, 164 cm²
   E 30 cm³, 82 cm² F 112 cm³, 144 cm²

Unit 56: Pages 116–117

Get started

1. a) 75 cm³   b) 144 cm³
   c) 60 cm³   d) 165 cm³
   e) 120 cm³   f) 135 cm³
   g) 180 cm³   h) 264 cm³
2. a) 118 cm²   b) 528 cm²
   c) 360 cm²

Practice

1. a) 110 cm²   b) 172 cm²
   c) 132 cm²
2. a) 70 cm³   b) 480 cm³
   c) 300 cm³
3. a) 94.5 cm³   b) 77 cm³
   c) 96 cm³   d) 504 cm³

Unit 57: Pages 118–119

Get started

1. a) $a = 135°$ b) $b = 65°$
   c) $c = 144°$
2. a) $d = 20°$ b) $e = 90°$
   c) $f = 24°$
3. a) $g = 265°$ b) $h = 215°$
   c) $i = 115°$

Practice

1. $a = 32°$ $b = 12°$
   $c = 130°$

Unit 58: Pages 120–121

Get started

1. a) 90°
   b) 10°
   c) 104°
2. $l = p$ corresponding angles
   $j = n$ corresponding angles
   $k = o$ corresponding angles
   $m = q$ corresponding angles
   $l = o$ alternate angles
   $m = n$ alternate angles

Practice

1. a) $a = 50°$ b) $b = 130°$
   c) $c = 50°$ d) $d = 50°$
   e) $e = 130°$ f) $f = 50°$
   g) $g = 130°$ h) $h = 130°$
2. a) $o = 50°$
   b) $p = 130°$
   c) $q = 50°$
   d) $r = 138°$
   e) $s = 42°$

Unit 59: Pages 122–123

Get started

1. a)

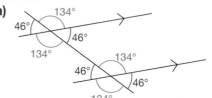

   b)

   c)

   d)

2. $d = 105°, e = 75°, f = 50°, g = 55°,$
   $h = 10°, i = 115°$

Practice

1. a)

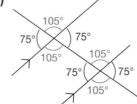

b)

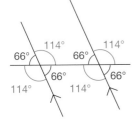

c)

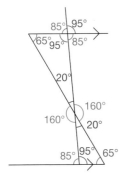

2

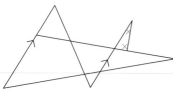

Unit 60: Pages 124–125

Get started

1 a) 720°   b) 1440°
   c) 1800°   d) 1260°
   e) 900°   f) 3240°
2 a) 150°   b) 129°
   c) 120°   d) 144°
   e) 140°   f) 162°

Practice

1 $a = 100°$,
   exterior angles (clockwise from bottom left):
   125°, 55°, 80°, 70°, 30°
2 165°
3 15
4 16
5 241°
6 33°

Unit 61: Pages 126–127

Get started

1 a) 160°
   b) 080°
   c) 240°
2 a) 250°, 070°
   b) 280°, 100°
   c) Difference of 180° for both

Practice

1 a) 320°   b) 190°
   c) 080°   d) 255°

Unit 62: Pages 128–129

Get started

1 a) 245°, 065°
   b) 282°, 102°
   c) It is 180° in each case
2 a) 325°   b) 197°
   c) 095°   d) 140°

Practice

1 a) 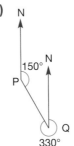   b)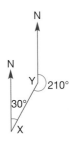

2 a) 203°
   b) West
   c) 296°

Unit 63: Pages 130–131

Get started

1 Check perpendicular bisectors are at 90° to
   original lines
2 Check two halves of original angles are equal

Practice

1 Check your constructions
2 Check your constructions

Unit 64: Pages 132–133

Get started

1 a) tick   b) no tick
   c) tick   d) tick
   e) tick   f) no tick
2 a) Perpendicular bisector of FG
   b) Bisector of angle BAC
   c) Circle, centre P, radius 3 m

Practice

1 a) 8 cm line. Semicircle radius 3.5 cm, centre
      the centre of line
   b) Line PH 4 cm. Perpendicular bisector of PH.
      Circle, centre H, radius 2.5 cm. Fire station
      can be anywhere on perpendicular bisector
      inside circle.

Unit 65: Pages 134–135

Get started

1

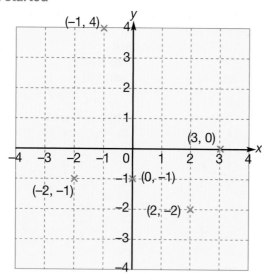

2   (5, 4)

Practice

1   A = (–2, 3), B = (0, –4), C = (–4, –1)
2   (5, –3)
3   (–1, 6)

Unit 66: Pages 136–137

Get started

1   **a)** A = (–1, 4), B = (5, 4),
        mid-point: (2, 4)
    b) C = (–4, 3), D = (4, 3),
        mid-point = (0, 3)
    c) E = (–6, 5), F = (–6, –3),
        mid-point = (–6, 1)
    d) C = (–4, 3), E = (–6, 5),
        mid-point = (–5, 4)
    e) B = (5, 4), H = (1, 0),
        mid-point = (3, 2)
    f) F = (–6, –3), G = (–3, 0),
        mid-point = (–4.5, –1.5)
2   **a)** (1, 1)   **b)** (–1, –3)
    c) (0, –2)   **d)** (–3, 1)

Practice

1   **a)** (1, –2)   **b)** (1, 0)
    c) (1, –2)   **d)** (–4, 1)
    e) (–2, –1)   **f)** (3, 2)
    g) (4, –5)   **h)** (1, –5)
    i) (–0.5, –1)   **j)** (–0.5, –3)

Unit 67: Pages 138–139

Get started

1   **a)** Rotation of 90° anticlockwise about point
        (4, –6)
    b) Reflection in the line $y = 2$
    c) Translation $\begin{pmatrix} -2 \\ -9 \end{pmatrix}$

2   There are different possible answers to the
    following, e.g.
    a) Rotation of 90° anticlockwise about point
        (3, –3) and then a translation $\begin{pmatrix} 0 \\ 6 \end{pmatrix}$
    b) Rotation of 90° clockwise about point (1, –3)
        and then a reflection in the line $x = -2.5$

Practice

1   **a)** 4   **b)** 2
    c) 3   **d)** 2
2   **a)** (0, 0)   **b)** (13, 0)
    c) (15, 2)
    d) directly in the centre of both pentagons

Unit 68: Pages 140–141

Practice

1

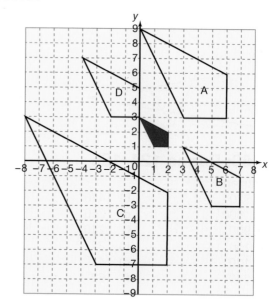

Unit 69: Pages 142–143

Practice

1   **a)** rectangle
    b) hexagon
    c) heptagon
    d) scalene triangle
    e) arrowhead kite
    f) regular octagon
    g) trapezium
    h) rhombus
    i) isosceles triangle
2   **a)** rhombus
    b) equilateral triangle
    c) kite
    d) regular pentagon
    e) trapezium
3   **a)** True
    b) False
    c) True

Unit 70: Pages 144–145

Get started

1 a) The third, fourth and seventh shapes from left to right
  b) The second, fourth and seventh shapes
  c) The first, second and sixth shapes
  d) The second, third, fifth and sixth shapes

2 True
  False
  True
  False
  True
  False
  False

3 True
  False
  False
  True
  True
  False

Practice

1 a)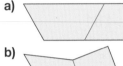

  b)

  c)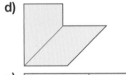

  d)

  e)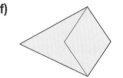

  f)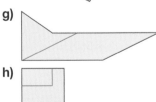

  g)

  h)

  i)

Unit 71: Pages 146–147

Get started

1 a) radius, diameter   b) diameter, semicircles
  c) arc, sector   d) chord, segments
2 a) 18.85 cm   b) 31.42 cm
  c) 25.13 cm   d) 15.71 cm

Practice

1 a) 50.27 cm²   b) 113.10 cm²
  c) 75.43 cm²   d) 43.01 cm²
  e) 91.61 cm²   f) 167.42 cm²
  g) 226.98 cm²   h) 326.85 cm²
2 a) 33.18 cm²   b) 49.02 cm²
  c) 60.82 cm²   d) 89.92 cm²

Unit 72: Pages 148–149

Get started

1 a)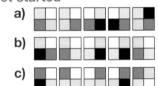

  b)

  c)

Practice

1, 2

a)   b)

c)   d)

Unit 73: Pages 150–151

Get started

1 Cross, tick, tick, cross
2 Tick, tick, cross, cross

Practice

1 a) 6   b) 7
  c) 2   d) 3
  e) 2   f) 9
  g) 5   h) 5
  i) 2
2 9

Unit 74: Pages 152–153

Get started

1 mode = 8, median = 8, mean = 8, range = 5

Practice

1 a) mode = 32, median = 28.5, mean = 28, range = 20
  b) mode = 35, median = 30, mean = 29, range = 16
  c) mode = 28, median = 27, mean = 25, range = 18
  d) mode = 24, median = 27.5, mean = 27.5, range = 16

2 a) 4
   b) 3
   c) 4

Unit 75: Pages 154–155

Get started
1   Mean = 4.5

Practice
1 **a)** 10.1   **b)** 9.9
    c) 11.8   **d)** 8.1
    e) 16.2   **f)** 63.4
    g) 38   **h)** 24.8
2   9.4

Unit 76: Pages 156–157

Get started
1   Answers such as:
   Questionnaire 2 is much quicker and easier to fill in as it has tick boxes.
   Giving different categories can help the person being surveyed to be specific.
   The question 'For how long do you watch it?' in questionnaire 1 doesn't say whether that means in a day, a week, a month or a year.
2   Advantages such as:
   If a person doesn't understand something they can ask the person conducting the survey.
   The forms are filled in by the surveyor in the same way each time.
   There are likely to be fewer mistakes.
   There are fewer photocopying costs than with the first method as there is no wastage.
   Disadvantages such as:
   It can take a long time to collect the data.
   People don't like being stopped in the street.
   People might be too busy at that time.
   If you need lots of responses you will need lots of people to conduct the survey.

Practice
1   Possible questionnaire:
   Q1 What sport are you here to play?
       Squash ☐   Badminton ☐
       Netball ☐   Gymnastics ☐
       Aerobics ☐   Netball ☐
       Swimming ☐   Other ....
   Q2 How often do you play this sport?
       Once a fortnight ☐   Once in 1–2 weeks ☐
       Once a week ☐   Twice a week ☐
       More than twice a week ☐
   Q3 For how long at one time do you play this sport?
       More than 2 hours ☐
       1–2 hours ☐   1 hour ☐
       $\frac{1}{2}$–1 hour ☐   Less than $\frac{1}{2}$ hour ☐
   Q4 What other sports do you play here?
       Squash ☐   Badminton ☐
       Netball ☐   Gymnastics ☐
       Aerobics ☐   Netball ☐
       Swimming ☐   Other ....

Q5 How old are you?
    0–9 ☐   10–19 ☐   20–39 ☐   40–59 ☐   60+ ☐

Unit 77: Pages 158–159

Get started
1 **a)** 21   **b)** 17
2 **a)** 44   **b)** 12
3 **a)** 18   **b)** 30
4   16–29 less likely to speak to neighbours
    40–49 evenly balanced as to whether they speak
    70+ very likely to speak to neighbours
5   It suggests that they talk to their neighbours more often than younger people

Practice
1 **a)** 156 – 75 = 81
   b) $70 \leq B < 90$ 4
       $90 \leq B < 110$ 18
       $110 \leq B < 130$ 44
       $130 \leq B < 150$ 31
       $150 \leq B < 170$ 3
2   $110 \leq B < 130$

Unit 78: Pages 160–161

Get started
1 **a)** 10–19   **b)** 5
      20–29   3
      30–39   5
      40–49   5
      50–59   2

Practice
1 **a)** 0–9   3
      10–19   3
      20–29   8
      30–39   7
      40–49   3
   b) Check bar chart.

Unit 79: Pages 162–163

Practice
1 **Table 1:** What 120 twelve-year-old girls spent the largest part of their pocket money on.

Activity or item	Number of girls	Calculation (fraction × 360)	Angle of sector
Sports and hobbies	27	$\frac{27}{120} \times 360$	81°
Going out	26	$\frac{26}{120} \times 360$	78°
CDs, videos, DVDs	25	$\frac{25}{120} \times 360$	75°
Clothes	23	$\frac{23}{120} \times 360$	69°
Toiletries	12	$\frac{12}{120} \times 360$	36°
Other	7	$\frac{7}{120} \times 360$	21°

Table 2: What 100 fourteen-year-old girls spent the largest part of their pocket money on.

Activity or item	Number of girls	Calculation (fraction × 360)	Angle of sector
Sports and hobbies	3	$\frac{3}{100} \times 360$	10.8 → 11°
Going out	29	$\frac{29}{100} \times 360$	104.4 → 104°
CDs, videos, DVDs	22	$\frac{22}{100} \times 360$	79.2 → 79°
Clothes	24	$\frac{24}{100} \times 360$	86.4 → 86°
Toiletries	19	$\frac{19}{100} \times 360$	68.4 → 68°
Other	3	$\frac{3}{100} \times 360$	10.8 → 11°

2   14-year-old girls far less interested in sports and hobbies, but toiletries and going out much more popular

Unit 80: Pages 164–165

Get started
1   a) positive
    b) zero
    c) negative
2   a) About 3000 calories
    b) About 4000 calories

Practice
1   a) Positive correlation
    b) Negative correlation
    c) Positive correlation
    d) Positive correlation
    e) Positive correlation
    f) Negative correlation

Unit 81: Pages 166–167

Get started
1   a) $\frac{1}{2}$
    b) $\frac{5}{7}$
    c) $\frac{3}{4}$

Practice
1   a) $\frac{22}{100} = \frac{11}{50}$
    b) $\frac{124}{500} = \frac{31}{125}$
    c) $\frac{249}{1000}$
2   a) 0.22
    b) 0.248
    c) 0.249
3   0.249

Unit 82: Pages 168–169

Get started
1   a) P(red) = $\frac{36}{100}$ or 0.36, P(blue) = $\frac{38}{100}$ or 0.38, P(green) = $\frac{26}{100}$ or 0.26
    b) P(red) = $\frac{34}{100}$ or 0.34, P(blue) = $\frac{41}{100}$ or 0.41, P(green) = $\frac{1}{4}$ or 0.25
    c) P(red) = $\frac{36}{100}$ or 0.36, P(blue) = $\frac{4}{10}$ or 0.4, P(green) = $\frac{24}{100}$ or 0.24
2   a) 139, 160, 101
    b) P(red) = $\frac{139}{400}$ or 0.3475, P(blue) = $\frac{4}{10}$ or 0.4, P(green) = $\frac{101}{400}$ or 0.2525

Practice
1   a) 6 red, 42 blue, 12 green
    b) 25 red, 10 blue, 15 green
    c) 1 red, 13 blue, 6 green
    d) 18 red, 6 blue, 16 green

Unit 83: Pages 170–171

Test 5
1   a) Perpendicular bisector of AB
    b) Bisector of angle DCE
    c) Circle, centre F, radius 1 m
2   a) C = 18.85 cm, A = 28.27 cm²
    b) C = 43.98 cm, A = 153.94 cm²
    c) C = 28.90 cm, A = 66.48 cm²
    d) C = 35.81 cm, A = 102.07 cm²
3   a)

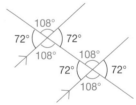

    b)

    c)

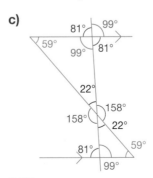

4   2.66
5   a) 88   b) 151
    c) 90   d) 111

6   Zero
    Negative
    Positive
7   a) $\frac{1}{6}$ b) $\frac{1}{12}$
    c) $\frac{1}{2}$ d) $\frac{1}{4}$
    e) $\frac{1}{3}$ f) $\frac{3}{4}$
8   a) 0.15   b) 0.55

Unit 84: Pages 172–173

Test 6
1   a) 90 cm³   126 cm²
    b) 432 cm³   480 cm²
    c) 2400 cm³   1440 cm²
2   a) 180   b) 2.6
    c) 90   d) 180 000 000
    e) 60 000   f) 8000
    g) 500   h) 1.4
    i) 69   j) 7 000 000
    k) 25   l) 6000
3   a) 540°   b) 900°
    c) 1080°
4   a) 144°   b) 120°
    c) 150°
5   $a = 100°$, exterior angles (clockwise from bottom left): 135°, 35°, 80°, 60°, 50°
6   160°
7   25
8   251°
9   217°
10

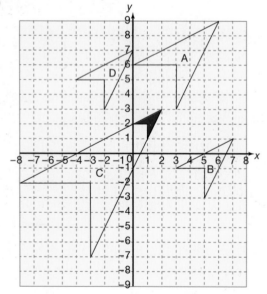

11 a) 9
    b) 3
    c) 4
12

Activity or item	Number of girls	Calculation (fraction × 360)	Angle of sector
Going out	30	$\frac{30}{120} \times 360$	90°
Sports and hobbies	11	$\frac{11}{120} \times 360$	33°
CDs, videos, DVDs	25	$\frac{25}{120} \times 360$	75°
Clothes & toiletries	48	$\frac{48}{120} \times 360$	144°
Other	6	$\frac{6}{120} \times 360$	18°

Check the angles of the pie chart
13 24 red, 30 blue, 6 green
    35 red, 10 blue, 5 green